BLACK CELEBRITY

PERFORMING CELEBRITY

Performing Celebrity publishes single-authored monographs and essay collections that explore the dynamics of fame, infamy, and technologies of image-making from the early modern period to the present day. This series of books seeks to add to exciting recent developments in the emerging field of celebrity studies by publishing outstanding works that explore mechanisms of self-fashioning, stardom, and notoriety operating across genres and media in a broad range of historical and national contexts. It focuses on interdisciplinary projects that employ current research and a wide variety of theoretical approaches to performance and celebrity in relation to literature, history, art history, media, fashion, theater, gender(s), sexuality, race, ethnicity, disability, material culture, etc.

Series Titles

Carrying All before Her: Celebrity Pregnancy and the London Stage, 1689–1800, Chelsea Phillips

Celebrity across the Channel, 1750–1850, edited by Anaïs Pédron and Clare Siviter

BLACK CELEBRITY

Contemporary Representations of Postbellum Athletes and Artists

Emily Ruth Rutter

University of Delaware Press
Newark

LCCN: 2021022261

A British Cataloging-in-Publication record for this book is available from the British Library.

∞ The paper used in this publication meets the requirements of the American National Standard for Information Sciences—Permanence of Paper for Printed Library Materials, ANSI Z39.48-1992.

udpress.udel.edu

Distributed worldwide by Rutgers University Press

Manufactured in the United States of America

CONTENTS

ACKNOWLEDGMENTS

I am grateful for the editors at the University of Delaware Press and Rutgers University Press, as well as the insightful reviewers of the manuscript. As with all of my writing and research, I could not have completed this book without the wonderfully supportive people in my life. My family, including Mike, Laura, Whitney, Dave, Ginger, Diane, Cynthia, Miles, Angie, Kitch, Bruce, Emma, Lewis, Sarah, Carolyn, and Robert, are everything to me. Thank you for your unconditional love. My students, particularly those serving on the Student Antiracism and Intersectionality Advisory Council (SAIAC) and enrolled in the African American Studies program, fill my life with collective purpose. I also want to thank my colleagues and friends for their encouragement, especially Rachel Bachenheimer, Simon Balto, Ben Bascom, Pat Collier, Allyson DeMaagd, Katy Didden, Laura Engel, Lauren Erickson, Max Felker-Kantor, Molly Ferguson, Rachel Fredericks, Maureen Gallagher, Lindsay Griffin, Marianne Holohan, Angela Jackson-Brown, Sharon Lynette Jones, Lora Klein, Sequoia Maner, E. Ethelbert Miller, Leah Milne, Rebekah Mitsein, Debbie Mix, Vanessa Rapatz, Allie Reznik, Sreyoshi Sarkar, Michele Schiavone, darlene anita scott, Jasmine and Jathan Taylor, Adriel Trott, Kiesha Warren-Gordon, and Dorica Watson.

Several writers and publishers generously granted me permission to cite passages from copyrighted works: Jeffery Allen, *Song of the Shank* (Graywolf Press); Tyehimba Jess, *Olio* (Wave Books);

Adrian Matejka, *The Big Smoke* (Penguin Random House); Caryl Phillips, *Dancing in the Dark* (Knopf); Frank X Walker, *Isaac Murphy: I Dedicate This Ride* (Old Cove Press); Kevin Young, *To Repel Ghosts* (Steerforth Press).

Finally, I thank all of the inspiring athletes, artists, and writers whom I examine in this book (and those whom I could not include). I am humbled by the opportunity to effuse about your stunning achievements.

INTRODUCTION

Portraits of Black Fame, or, The Past as Blueprint for the Present

In James Weldon Johnson's *Black Manhattan* (1930), an indispensable history of African Americans in New York, he describes the postbellum period as a time of sociocultural incubation, especially in the realm of sports and musical theater:

> I have indicated that during the fourth quarter of the last century there was a pause in the racial activities of the Negroes in the North. It would be more strictly true to say that there was a change in activities. In New York the Negro now began to function and express himself on a different plane, in a different sphere; and in a different way he effectively impressed himself upon the city and the country. Within this period, roughly speaking, the Negro in the North emerged and gained national notice in three great professional sports: horse-racing, baseball, and prize-fighting. He also made a beginning and headway on the theatrical stage.[1]

Johnson's observations are especially relevant, considering that sports and entertainment are the two arenas in which Blacks gained the strongest foothold during the twentieth century and into our own time. As he also notes, Black achievement in these fields was met with violent white resistance. For example, ruminating on the experiences of Jack Johnson, the first Black heavyweight champion, Weldon Johnson stresses not only that the boxer had "to fight [Jim] Jeffries, but that psychologically he also had to fight the majority of the thousands of spectators, many of whom were howling and praying for Jeffries to 'kill the n[*****].' "[2] In fact, the post-Reconstruction, pre–Harlem Renaissance era in which both Johnsons began their careers is often considered the nadir of the Black experience because of the racial terrorism and contraction of rights that African Americans endured during it.

Black citizens were simply driven out of some cultural spaces, as was the case in nineteenth-century baseball, the sport that was rapidly becoming the national pastime. As Weldon Johnson notes, "The Negro player could not front the forces against him in organized baseball; so he was compelled to organize for himself."[3] In musical theater—especially the ever-popular minstrel and vaudeville stages—Black performers and songwriters, including Weldon Johnson himself, persevered in the face of racial hostility, while also strategically capitulating to anti-Black stereotypes in order to attract white audiences. To this end, Bob Cole, whom Weldon Johnson calls "the most versatile theatrical man the Negro has yet produced,"[4] became nationally renowned for his "coon songs," especially his musical comedy *A Trip to Coontown* (1898)—a title that makes contemporary observers wince but aptly encapsulates the self-abnegation that was nearly a prerequisite for African American mobility within the entertainment industry from the late nineteenth through the early twentieth century.

By examining the work of a range of twenty-first-century novelists and poets, *Black Celebrity* showcases these early Black experiences in the limelight. Specifically, I argue that the decades between the end of the Civil War and the launching of the Harlem Renaissance, from 1865 to 1919, are pivotal to understanding the disjuncture between the American rhetoric of meritocracy and the realities of racial stratification, both within and beyond athletic and entertainment arenas. Sociopolitically, these decades include Reconstruction (1865–1877), the US government's first coordinated efforts toward enabling Black citizenship; the subsequent rollback of Reconstruction-era victories, perhaps most notably in the landmark 1896 *Plessy v. Ferguson* decision that deemed Jim Crow laws constitutional; the Great Migration that marked the exodus of over one million southern Blacks to northern cities in search of both gainful employment and freedom from quasi-slavery; and the 1909 founding of the NAACP, among other monumental events in the Black liberation struggle. Culturally, this period includes the precipitous rise and white-engineered fall of Isaac Burns Murphy, an African American three-time Kentucky Derby winner; the international celebrity of the pianist Thomas Greene Wiggins ("Blind Tom"); the unrivaled fame of blackface minstrel performers Bert Williams and George Walker; and the aforementioned 1910 "fight of the century," whereby Jack Johnson defeated the "Great White Hope" Jim Jeffries, only to be harassed by law enforcement as a consequence.[5] These are just a few of the many resonant milestones and setbacks that make the half century following the Civil War simultaneously the most promising and painful era in Black American history.

While historians and cultural critics have been attentive to this period, *Black Celebrity* is the first book to examine the recent literary interest in postbellum, pre–Harlem Renaissance stars. Engaging in what I term "creative recuperation," the novelists Jeffery Renard Allen and Caryl Phillips and the poets Tyehimba Jess, Kevin Young, Adrian Matejka, and Frank X Walker breathe regenerative life into figures and experiences often swept aside in the century separating the postbellum and current eras. Although Phillips's *Dancing in the Dark* (2005), Allen's *Song of the Shank* (2014), Young's *To Repel Ghosts: The Remix from the Original Masters* (2005), Walker's *Isaac Murphy: I Dedicate This Ride* (2010), Matejka's *The Big Smoke* (2013), and Jess's *Olio* (2016) render their historical representations in distinct ways, I focus on these authors' shared commitment to using innovative formal strategies in order to recover multifaceted subjectivities in the face of racialized objectification and erasure; citing historical documents while evincing archival biases and lacunae; highlighting their own modes of artistic excavation in order to remind readers of the human hands that shape all historical narratives; and drawing parallels (and distinctions) between the experiences of the first wave of Black stars and their counterparts today. As this book demonstrates, creative recuperations play a crucial interventional role in both revising understandings of Black celebrity history and making legible the through lines between the postbellum, pre–Harlem Renaissance epoch and our own time.

Given the outsized impact of Black Americans on athletic and entertainment industries, these are especially profitable arenas for examining the ways in which interconnected ideas about race, gender, and class take shape in the popular imagination. As Abby L. Ferber notes, "Athletics and entertainment are the two primary realms in which we actually see Black men presented as successful in our culture, and they are consistent with the historical stereotypes and limited opportunities available to Black men."[6] In essence, sports and music have been conduits for wealth and fame for African American men who have otherwise been denied social mobility, while these arenas also pivot on spectacle, with whites still controlling much of the means of production and consumption. As Howard Bryant notes, "Until 2017, all four major professional sports leagues combined had one black owner," even while the National Football League is 70 percent Black and the National Basketball Association is 80 percent Black.[7] Robin DiAngelo reports a similarly staggering statistic from 2017: "People who decide which music is produced: 95 percent white."[8] Exploring literary portraits of some of the first famous African American athletes and artists, this book plumbs poets' and novelists' elucidation of the paradox of racial hypervisibility and depersonalization that, even while current figures exercise more control over their own public images, continues to characterize key aspects of Black celebrity.

As is well established, famous individuals (used here interchangeably with the words "stars" or "celebrities") are "*mediated public persona*[*e*], to be differentiated from the actual, unmediated person who is almost always unknown to audiences."[9] For Black Americans, these layers of mediation are compounded by the endemic stereotypes ascribing distinct but equally devastating pathologies to men and women. As demonstrated in the chapters ahead, when African Americans enter the limelight—historically, this was often through hard-won achievement in sports or entertainment—they are subject to the heightened sense of public scrutiny and dehumanization that always already accompanies being racially othered in a white-supremacist United States. Additionally, Michele Wallace notes that Black "intellectuals, artists, and cultural workers in a wide array of fields" are rendered invisible by a culture in which fame accrues to people based on "how much controversy they can stir up."[10] Put another way, African American celebritization is often tethered to either notoriety or individualized narratives of exceptionalism, thereby distracting from systemic racial inequities. As Ken McLeod points out in regard to Black men's prominence in music and sports, "The hypervisibility of these 'exceptional' black men also serves to reinforce the racist notions that anonymous black men who disappear into the underclass, prison, or an early grave have only themselves to blame."[11] In addition to this willful denial of structural injustices, the mantle of Black exceptionalism comes with expectations of becoming a role model, a kind of paragon of respectability and leadership. As Nicole Fleetwood succinctly puts it, "*To stand apart* and *to stand for* are the jobs of the racial icon."[12] Whereas white stars would never be expected to speak for or act on behalf of their race, their African American counterparts often become responsible for collective interests and are consequently punished when they are perceived to be disturbing the status quo.

In these respects, Black celebrities' lives are relentlessly public, with the mainstream media focus rarely on their complex inner lives and almost always on their physical, sartorial, and vocal behavior. Of course, time and circumstance have meant that the manifestation of these tropes has not remained static, and current Black athletes, musicians, and entertainers of all sorts exercise a greater degree of agency than their postbellum counterparts did. Yet, as Sarah J. Jackson avers, "Black celebrities have been and continue to be subject to a unique set of public criteria for mainstream acceptance that expects them to always perform according to sanctioned scripts while sidelining their identities as members of a still oppressed group."[13] The novelists and poets examined here allow us to see with greater clarity these scripts and patterns of degradation and scapegoating that recur on US tracks, rings, fields, and stages. "The black culture industry," Ellis Cashmore notes, "is still owned by whites."[14] At the same time, Samantha Pinto reminds us that Black celebrity is a contested site indexical of "not just the well-known hegemonies but also the seams and breaks of such narratives—the idiosyncratic iterations of meaning that public circulation threatens and promises."[15] In shifting the focus inward toward deeply personal, individualized experiences,

Allen, Phillips, Jess, Young, Matejka, and Walker adumbrate these tensions and ruptures, offering another way to engage with famous African Americans that is not overdetermined by hegemonic forces.

Elucidating affective tableaux, these contemporary novelists and poets are especially adept at interpreting the inscrutability of postbellum, pre–Harlem Renaissance figures. The opera singer Sissieretta Jones and the jockey Isaac Burns Murphy, to name only two examples, occupied precarious social positions as stars dependent on white support and, therefore, left few public traces of their private thoughts about the submissiveness and subordination they were expected to embody. As Jess, Walker, Young, Matejka, Phillips, and Allen indicate, a lack of documented protest or resistance implies little about how early Black celebrities were grappling with their positions in the limelight or simply leading their lives as multifaceted individuals. As Kevin Quashie argues in *The Sovereignty of Quiet: Beyond Resistance in Black Culture* (2012), quiet "is a metaphor for the full range of one's inner life—one's desires, ambitions, hungers, vulnerabilities, fears," and through our focus on it, we can "shift attention to what is interior," thereby debunking the assumption that Blackness is always "dramatic, symbolic, never for its own vagary, always representative and engaged with how it is imagined publicly."[16] In this way, Quashie distinguishes "quiet" from W. E. B. Du Bois's notion of double consciousness—the "sense of always looking at oneself through the eyes of others, of measuring one's soul by the tape of a world that looks on in amused contempt and pity"[17]—and cautions against an emphasis on the white hegemonic gaze as the defining feature of an individual's interior life.

Congruent with Quashie's emphasis on the quiet life of the mind as "full of expression," this book's poets and novelists invite us to read between and beyond the lines of what was reported (even self-reported) about Black celebrity artists and athletes in order to probe the possibilities of what was thought but unsaid, felt but unexpressed. While their portraits certainly evince an awareness of white stereotypes, these writers are also interested in exploring emotional, creative, and intellectual lives operating independently of dominant ideologies. Further, in the centralization of the private thoughts and feelings of historical figures, the divergent poetry and prose considered here implicitly warn us against both effacing the diversity among current Black athletes and artists and reductively focusing only on "resistant expressiveness."[18] In other words, what kinds of alternative understandings of Black celebrity emerge when we reimagine the heart's mind and turn our attention away from the public spectacularity of the body? This is the live, pressing question to which Matejka, Young, Walker, Jess, Allen, and Phillips provide a rich array of possible answers.

Moreover, while these male authors revivify predominantly (but not exclusively) male experiences in the limelight, African American women poets and novelists have in key respects forged the literary pathways that Young, Matejka, Walker, Phillips, Allen, and Jess venture down. A consistent, ongoing project of Black writers, many of them women, has been reimagining whitewashed histories or probing for what the archive conceals or effaces. Particularly since the Civil Rights and Black Power movements, African American novelists have published a wide array of what have come to be called neo-slave narratives, including Margaret Walker's *Jubilee* (1966), Ernest J. Gaines's *The Autobiography of Miss Jane Pittman* (1971), Gayl Jones's *Corregidora* (1975), Ishmael Reed's *Flight to Canada* (1976), Octavia Butler's *Kindred* (1979), Sherley Anne Williams's *Dessa Rose* (1987), Toni Morrison's *Beloved* (1987), Charles Johnson's *Middle Passage* (1990), Edward P. Jones's *The Known World* (2003), James McBride's *The Good Lord Bird* (2013), and Colson Whitehead's *The Underground Railroad* (2016), among many others. In reference to Morrison's tour de force *Beloved*, she has summed up the emotional and psychological stakes of the neo-slave subgenre: "My job becomes how to rip that veil drawn over 'proceedings too terrible to relate.' The exercise is also critical for any person who is black, or who belongs to any marginalized category, for, historically, we were seldom invited to participate in the discourse even when we were its topic."[19] Distinguishing her role as a literary chronicler from that of her enslaved predecessors whose traumas were often muffled, Morrison invests in the *interior* lives of "people who didn't write it (which doesn't mean they didn't have it)."[20]

Allen's *Song of the Shank* and Phillips's *Dancing in the Dark*, as well as many other works of contemporary African American fiction, follow in Morrison's footsteps, evincing moments of "quiet" (à la Quashie) as well as double consciousness (à la Du Bois). In particular, Phillips and Allen make use of free indirect discourse—"a way of reporting a person's thoughts as if we could listen to the person talking to herself"[21]—elucidating what it may have felt like to be celebrated performers onstage while being treated as subhuman off of it. At the same time that they build on the work of Morrison and others, Phillips's and Allen's novels demonstrate an intentional confrontation with the archive, whereby press clippings, promotional materials, and other excavated fragments are self-reflexively incorporated into the landscape of the novel, suggesting both their limitations as reliable sources and the ways in which all histories, including novels, are arranged to advance particular interpretations of events.

Jess, Matejka, Walker, and Young make frequent use of persona poetry, inhabiting the first-person perspectives of various Black musicians, theatrical performers, and athletes in order to excavate the emotional and psychological experiences heretofore undocumented in written accounts. In a 2008 article, Howard Rambsy II noted, "Over the last ten years alone, persona poems have been a prevalent feature of volumes of poetry published by established and emergent poets such as Rita Dove, Cornelius Eady, Thylias Moss, Frank X Walker, and Kevin Young. Nonetheless, this mode of writing has eluded scholarly notice."[22] Four years later, Rambsy noted on his influential blog *Cultural Front*, "Persona poems by African American poets have a long history, stretching back to Robert Hayden, Gwendolyn Brooks, Langston Hughes, Paul Laurence Dunbar and beyond. The production of full-length volumes or extended series of persona poems by several poets, however, seems to represent a fairly recent phenomenon in the history of black poetry." Persona poetry represents, therefore, "one of the most important trends in contemporary black poetry."[23] Rambsy's recent monograph, *Bad Men: Creative Touchstones of Black Writers* (2020), further examines this trend by devoting a chapter to Tyehimba Jess's *leadbelly* (2005), Adrian Matejka's *The Big Smoke*, and Kevin Young's *To Repel Ghosts: The Remix from the Original Masters*. These poets, Rambsy argues, are "creatively writing and righting the wrongs of representational neglect."[24] In a recent reading of Matejka's *The Big Smoke*, Ryan Sharp similarly observes, "Persona provides a unique vehicle both for signifyin' on the Archive's historical portrayal of blackness and, in complicating how past blackness is read, a concomitant means of broadening the boundaries of contemporary black identity and the corresponding racial imaginary."[25] As Rambsy and Sharp make clear, persona poetry has become a resonant vehicle through which contemporary poets honor the underreported lives of historical figures.

Prior to the publication of *Olio*, Jess had already made a significant impact on the persona poetry landscape with his collection *leadbelly*. Therein, as I have described elsewhere,[26] Jess utilizes the first-person perspectives not only of Huddie Ledbetter (Leadbelly) but also of the figures who both propelled and endangered Leadbelly's life and career, not to mention the inanimate objects (his guitar, his gun, and the machine that recorded his music) that were a key part of the musician's life story as a prisoner-cum-famous-blues-musician. As Rambsy notes, "Jess had apparently concluded that adequately representing Leadbelly entailed involving first-person viewpoints of a large, diverse supporting cast."[27] Perhaps most daringly, Jess embodies the consciousness of the ethnomusicologist John Lomax, who serves as an especially troubling embodiment of the long, fraught history of white efforts to control and profit from Black musical production. For example, in Jess's "Ethnographer John Lomax Speaks of His Vocation," the Lomax persona claims, "This country needs a Columbus like me. / I have sighted a dark territory / to map, mount, and measure."[28] Exposing Lomax's exploitative motivations, while providing rich lyrical alternatives to racist worldviews through the personae of Leadbelly and others, *leadbelly* exemplifies the epistemological potential of persona poetry to refute, quoting the Lomax personage again, the master narratives penned "down in black on white."[29]

Women poets have also made unrivaled contributions to persona poetry by historicizing and contextualizing figures that have been rendered one-dimensional in the popular imagination, simply forgotten by the vagaries of time and circumstance and, still worse, effaced by the epistemic violence of white-supremacist approaches to US history. Just in the twenty-first century, Ai, Rita Dove, Natasha Trethewey, Patricia Smith, Thylias Moss, Evie Shockley, Vievee

Francis, Bettina Judd, Marilyn Nelson, Morgan Parker, Chet'la Sebree, and Honorée Jeffers, among others, have made salient use of the persona mode.[30] Trethewey has produced, as the critic Annette Debo has shown,[31] some of the most acclaimed and influential historical persona poetry of the past several decades in collections such as *Bellocq's Ophelia* (2002), the Pulitzer Prize–winning *Native Guard* (2006), and *Thrall* (2012). In *Bellocq's Ophelia*, Trethewey embodies the consciousness of the eponymous Ophelia, a biracial sex worker who was photographed by E. J. Bellocq in early 1900s New Orleans. In the poem "Disclosure," the Ophelia persona disentangles the objectification of Bellocq's photography from her interior life—the *quiet* of her mind, we might say—which is not controlled by his lens:

> I've learned to keep
> my face behind the camera, my lens aimed
> at a dream of my own making.[32]

Refusing the historical erasure of women like Ophelia, Trethewey gives her the agency to frame (à la the photographic medium) her own image and narrative, restoring Ophelia's subjectivity, however imagined.

Alternatively, in the Hurricane Katrina–inspired *Blood Dazzler* (2008), Patricia Smith ventriloquizes the voices of an array of victims and perpetrators, including Katrina itself, associated with the storm's travesties. Embodying, for instance, the thirty-four figures left for dead in a St. Bernard Parish nursing home, Smith bears witness to their pain and suffering: "I want somebody's hand," "I fight the rise with all the guitar left in my throat," and "Louisiana, / goddamn. / You lied to me so lush," among other haunting last words.[33] In so doing, Smith honors the humanity that federal, state, and local officials systematically disregarded in their woefully inadequate response to the needs of Louisiana residents, especially African Americans, during and after Katrina.

While the present book is concerned with creative recuperations of the first wave of Black celebrity artists and athletes, it is crucial to remember that Matejka, Young, Walker, Phillips, Allen, and Jess are not producing their literary-historical work in a vacuum but rather within the context of a community of African

American writers. In this regard, Matejka "found inspiration for a poem about [Jack] Johnson at a poetry reading where Patricia Smith was reading selections from . . . *Blood Dazzler*."[34] Young similarly credits Rita Dove's Pulitzer Prize–winning *Thomas and Beulah* (1987), a work that utilizes persona poetry in the reimagining of Dove's maternal grandparents, as an inspiration for how to develop a "concentrated poetry project" such as *To Repel Ghosts*.[35] In the essay "Memory, Research, Imagination, and the Mining of Historical Poetry" (2020), Walker calls attention to these influences in shaping his own vision of how to utilize the lyric landscape to recuperate the victims of historical erasure: "I look to both classic and contemporary forms to construct narrative houses in a collection. Studying Marilyn Nelson's *Carver* and Tyehimba Jess's *Leadbelly* helped me enter the cultural and creative space that first birthed my book *Buffalo Dance: The Journey of York*. Nelson's work demonstrated how to balance history and art, while Jess's work introduced creative new forms and ways to shape the narrative."[36] Here we see the ways in which Black poets and, by extension, novelists are generating their own discourse about the modes, methods, and stakes of historical writing.

Moreover, the writers under consideration here often invoke the same historical figures: Young and Matejka both inhabit the heavyweight champion Jack Johnson's first-person point of view, Jess and Phillips both reconstruct the personae of performers Bert Williams and George Walker, and Allen and Jess both revivify the famed pianist "Blind Tom" Wiggins. When the poet E. Ethelbert Miller asked Jess in an interview about Allen's influence on his portrait of "Blind Tom," Jess noted that he admired Allen's ability to make history "live on the page."[37] Making use of sonnet, contrapuntal, and persona forms, Jess's *Olio*, like Allen's *Song of the Shank*, provides a dynamic portal to the past, evincing the ways in which the writers I examine extend and enrich each other's literary contributions to the Black celebrity archive.

As this book demonstrates, the practice of creative recuperation —whether through persona poetry, free indirect discourse, the juxtaposition of archival fragments and imaginative interpolations, or another mode—is inherently self-reflexive. Matejka, Young, Walker, Phillips, Allen, and Jess, foregrounding the mechanisms of their imaginative excavations, are not purporting to recover "real" historical figures as much as they are offering other ways to engage with figures and experiences flattened out by dominant narratives. That is, these writers advance what the French cultural theorist Jacques Rancière conceptualizes as *heretical* history, one that questions "the procedures of meaning by which a historicity is defined" and centralizes instead "a hitherto unknown subject of speech."[38] In order to recover the people and perspectives effaced by archives and the scholars mining them, Rancière turns not to historians but rather to imaginative literature, which he argues "puts another regime of meaning to work . . . get[ting] the mute witnesses of common history to speak."[39] He explicates the work of canonical European writers—Balzac, Proust, Flaubert, Tolstoy, Mallarmé, and Brecht, among others—to exemplify literature's unique sociohistorical and political role, but his investment in both a people's history and in literature's interventional role in recuperating "the mute witnesses" accords with the work of many contemporary writers of African descent. For example, in an explication of Robin Coste Lewis's National Book Award–winning poetry collection *Voyage of the Sable Venus* (2015), John Brooks draws on Rancière both to expose the "dissidence between the past and the way it is historicized" and to argue that Lewis's poetry "read[s] existing historiography against its erasures."[40] In the chapters that follow, I too utilize Rancière's concept of heresy to examine the skepticism with which Matejka, Young, Walker, Jess, Allen, and Phillips approach master narratives of Black celebrity history as well as the documents, testimony, and artifacts enlisted to give these narratives meaning.

Additionally, Rancière's concept of *dissensus* is a profitable lens through which to read these poets' and novelists' juxtapositions of archival materials with imaginative representations of historical artists and athletes. Dissensus, as Rancière puts it, "places one world in another," denaturalizing what is conceived of as common sense and giving credence to "a possible world" in which one "hear[s] the argument that he 'normally' has no reason either to see or to hear."[41] The artistic sphere is a particularly potent arena for juxtaposing dominant and subversive cultural memories, elucidating an alternative or counternarrative that encourages shifts in understanding. As the renowned Haitian anthropologist Michel-Rolph Trouillot puts it, "While some of us debate what history is or was, others take it in their hands."[42] Casting aside conventional historiographic methodologies while contraposing archival materials with imagined interior lives, the writers explored here provide other ways of knowing the African American celebrities who were often the canvases on which postbellum racial hierarchies and epistemologies were drawn. In the process, they destabilize the authority of archival documents (or of any one mode, including imaginative literature) to paint a comprehensive picture of the post–Civil War culture industry, as well as its residues and aftereffects.

Indeed, we must always recognize the inherent limitations of archives when we consider how we know what we know about marginalized historical figures. In recent years, archives have thus become not just a resource for research but also a central subject of investigation, with scholars, including archivists themselves, increasingly questioning the reliability of documents and artifacts preserved, in many cases, by white patriarchal power structures as authoritative sources.[43] As the archivists Terry Cook and Joan Schwartz state, "Archives have the power to privilege and to marginalize. They can be a tool of hegemony; they can be a tool of resistance. They both reflect and constitute power relations."[44] Additionally, as Irma McClaurin, founder of the Irma McClaurin Black Feminist Archive puts it, "Archives are where histories are recorded and written, but even at their best, they are imperfect reflections of an imperfect world. Inequities in whose writings are collected produce inequities in whose histories become known, and the failure of vision of one generation becomes failure for the next."[45] In renowned scholar Saidiya Hartman's own confrontation with archival erasures, she employs a practice she terms "critical fabulation," whereby she "imagine[s] what might have happened or might have been said or might have been done" in an effort to make the lives of the enslaved, including their acts of resistance, legible.[46] At the same time, within this history "written with and against the archive," Hartman is "unable to exceed the limits of the sayable dictated by the archive."[47] Confronting similar elisions, the historian Marisa J. Fuentes argues that it is not possible to shore up historical fragments into a tidy narrative of a people whom the archive long ago deemed disposable and unremarkable. "We cannot redeem or rescue them" (in her case, enslaved Barbados women), Fuentes points out, "but we can reconsider their pain."[48] Employing distinctly creative modes and methodologies, contemporary novelists and poets, I argue, reconsider underrepresented emotional and psychic experiences, exposing in the process both the fictions produced and the histories erased by the archive.

Examining representations of historical athletic and artistic performances similarly requires attention to that which cannot feasibly be set down in, say, the ledger or the vault. To this end, Diana Taylor's *The Archive and the Repertoire: Performing Cultural Memory in the Americas* (2003) exposes the false bifurcation "between the *archive* of supposedly enduring materials (i.e., texts, documents, buildings, bones) and the so-called ephemeral *repertoire* of embodied practice/knowledge (i.e., spoken language, dance, sports, ritual)."[49] As I suggest, Matejka, Young, Walker, Jess, Allen, and Phillips do not see the archive and the repertoire as mutually exclusive as much as equally valuable in their attempts to reanimate the public performances, backstage tensions, and interior lives excluded from forms of documentation governed by empirical dictates. As Taylor argues, "Each system of containing and transmitting knowledge exceeds the limitations of the other. The live can never be contained in the archive; the archive endures beyond the limits of the live."[50] Moreover, this book's novelists and poets "take seriously the repertoire of embodied practices as an important system of knowing and transmitting knowledge,"[51] and they use the printed page to set archive and repertoire in dialogue and counterpoint, revealing new truths about the first wave of Black celebrities in ways that translate to the twenty-first century.

It is beneficial to situate this literary turn not just toward archival and historical memory but more specifically toward the postbellum epoch in the sociohistorical context of the 150th anniversaries of the beginning and end of the Civil War (1861–1865), of Abraham Lincoln's 1863 Emancipation Proclamation, and of the passage of the Thirteenth, Fourteenth, and Fifteenth Amendments to the Constitution. For many people, the 2008 election of Barack Obama, the first nonwhite man to call the White House home, signified the culmination of these achievements as well as the racial progress engendered by the Civil Rights and Black Power movements. Obama, many falsely believed, was embodied proof that the United States had overcome endemic racism. While Phillips's novel *Dancing in the Dark* and Young's poetry collection *To Repel Ghosts: The Remix from the Original Masters* (both published in 2005) preceded the widespread "postracial" pronouncements that accompanied Obama's meteoric rise to political prominence, these works were written during a period in which the notion that the United States had moved beyond race had begun to gain considerable credence.

Eduardo Bonilla-Silva terms this fallacious logic "color-blind racism": "Much as Jim Crow racism served as the glue for defending a brutal and overt system of racial oppression in the pre–Civil Rights era, color-blind racism serves today as the ideological armor for a covert and institutionalized system in the post–Civil Rights era."[52] Further, what Carol Anderson terms "white rage" began conflagrating in response to the election of a Black man to the White House, harking back to the white-supremacist backlash to Reconstruction-era measures to enfranchise and empower African Americans. As Anderson explains, "The trigger for white rage, inevitably, is Black advancement. It is not the mere presence of Black people that is the problem; rather, it is Blackness with ambition, with drive, with purpose, with aspirations, and with demands for full and equal citizenship."[53] Accordingly, the writers in *Black Celebrity* journey back, not to the antebellum era so prodigiously and poignantly recounted in the aforementioned neo-slave narratives,[54] but instead to an era in which the pattern of white retribution in the face of perceived Black social mobility took hold. As Douglas A. Blackmon notes, "In every aspect and among almost every demographic, how American society digested and processed the long, dark chapter between the end of the Civil War and the beginning of the civil rights movement has been delusion."[55] Offering some clarity in the face of these delusions, the literary works considered here and, in turn, this book peel away the layers of white subterfuge and duplicity on the one hand and reveal Black modes of self-expression and resistance on the other.

Several literary and cultural critics have also drawn needed attention to the decades following the end of the Civil War but preceding the Harlem Renaissance, elucidating the fertile ground that was laid for the tropes and themes that would shape the modern canon of US literature and culture. Andreá N. Williams observes, "Especially during the period that [Charles] Chesnutt designates as the 'post-bellum, pre-Harlem' era—marked at one end by the Civil War and Black emancipation and, on the other, by Harlem's population growth around the First World War—Black artists established important institutions, networks, and artistic trends. However, the legacies of these postbellum, pre–Harlem Renaissance writers have been overlooked."[56] The decades following the Civil War receive far less critical and popular attention compared to the Harlem Renaissance, even while, as Williams also notes, the most trumpeted figures of the 1920s and '30s relied on Chesnutt and his contemporaries in their "quest for New Negro expression."[57] In *The African American Roots of Modernism: Reconstruction to the Harlem Renaissance* (2011), James Smethurst likewise contends, "The period of the 1880s and 1890s, then, was decisive in the development of American modernity, both anxious and triumphal, and the fundamental elements of that modernity were the often-violent establishment and maintenance of Jim Crow and the disenfranchisement of African Americans."[58] Similarly, in the collection of essays *Post-Bellum, Pre-Harlem: African American Literature and Culture, 1877–1919* (2006), editors Barbara McCaskill and Caroline Gebhard describe "a period of high aesthetic experimentation and political dynamism," suggesting that the Harlem Renaissance was not so much a sociocultural groundswell as much as a natural outgrowth of artistic activities that began during and after Reconstruction.[59]

Examining the period from a cultural studies perspective, Daphne Brooks's *Bodies in Dissent: Spectacular Performances of Race and Freedom, 1850–1910* (2006) theorizes the tightrope act that nineteenth- and early twentieth-century Black performers walked, both appeasing a white-supremacist logic and subverting the degradation that it entailed. Postbellum Black artists and entertainers, she argues, "combined a diverse array of cultural tools to voice the rich and resonant contours of black identity formation with all of its contradictions and conceits. Through their efforts, they waged a battle to reverse the crisis of representational timelessness projected onto blackness."[60] Brooks terms these dissenting performances "Afro-alienation acts," whereby "the condition of alterity converts into cultural expressiveness and a specific strategy of cultural performance."[61] As the present book argues, when Walker, Young, Matejka, Jess, Allen, and Phillips inhabit the personae of postbellum minstrel and vaudeville figures or boxing and jockey stars, they recount this history from the perspective of those who were on the cultural front lines as Reconstruction-era promises were yanked mercilessly back. At the same time, these writers focalize interior thoughts, anxieties, and desires, as well as acts of resistance to white supremacy and stereotypes of Black inferiority, showcasing divergent strategies for negotiating public life that continue to resonate with Black celebrity experiences in the current era.

Jess's *Olio*, Phillips's *Dancing in the Dark*, and Allen's *Song of the Shank* confront the long tradition of white ravening for Black culture, especially music, and the simultaneous degradation of its producers. As Kip Lornell observes, "Emancipation not only brought freedom (of a sort), it also slowly drew African American expressive culture into the mainstream. Music and popular culture in the United States have been utterly transformed as a result of this complex, sustained, and ongoing process."[62] Greg Tate adds, "In a world where we're [African Americans] seen as both the most loathed and the most alluring of creatures, we remain the most co-optable and erasable of cultures too."[63] This disregard for Black lives but deep attraction to the cultural by-products of racial oppression is a long-standing American tradition. As Imani Perry succinctly puts it, "The love of black culture with the simultaneous suspicion and punishment of black bodies is not unusual. Nor is the public fascination with the perceived depravity or dangerousness of black artists, who are simultaneously loved."[64] Jess, Allen, and Phillips trace these patterns of fetishization and exploitation to the mid- to late nineteenth century, when those patterns were set in place to be reenacted for decades (even centuries) to come. Importantly, however, they probe the interiority of historical figures, reimagining the ways in which those figures were, to quote Brooks, "experiment[ing] with culturally innovative ways to critique and disassemble the condition of oppression."[65]

Moreover, as Young's *To Repel Ghosts: The Remix from the Original Masters*, Walker's *Isaac Murphy: I Dedicate This Ride*, and Matejka's *The Big Smoke* suggest, similar racial dynamics were at work on the racetrack and in the boxing ring. In particular, the images and narratives of the jockey Isaac Burns Murphy and the boxer Jack Johnson were appropriated and misused in order to shore up notions of white identity and alliance in the decades immediately following the Civil War. The scapegoating of these individuals, in turn, furnished a cultural script for the uneven relationship between white power structures and Black athletes that continues to hold sway. As Patrick B. Miller observes, "The white counterpoint to black athletic accomplishment has all too often involved a calculated reinterpretation of the meanings of sport, revealing the racism that, though discredited time and again, has nevertheless shown few signs of retreat. These responses to the achievements of black athletes have effectively shifted the terms of debate from the democratic notions of a shared (athletic) culture to invidious distinctions based on blacks' innate talents in certain sporting activities."[66] That is, sports—one of the most highly visible and long-standing arenas for Black male socioeconomic mobility—is also the site for public reification of pseudoscientific notions about Black men's inherent physical, rather than mental, endowments. As Drew Brown puts it, "Social constructions of Black masculinity, especially those found in sport, continue to dwell amidst negative racial stereotyping, which consequently helps maintain the social vilification of Black males."[67] Correspondingly, the persona poems of Young, Matejka, and Walker reimagine the psychological and emotional responses of athletes who were some of the first to endure the ramifications of this racial scaffolding.

Inhabiting the personae of these postbellum athletes, these contemporary writers also elucidate parallels with the twenty-first-century social landscape. We need only look to many football fans' reactions to former San Francisco 49ers quarterback Colin Kaepernick and other like-minded fellow players, as they sat or kneeled as the national anthem played before the start of NFL games. This silent, peaceful protest was designed to draw attention to racial discrimination within the criminal justice system and, by extension, the nation at large. In 2017, President Donald Trump encouraged

NFL owners to fire these players: "Wouldn't you love to see one of these NFL owners, when somebody disrespects our flag, to say, 'Get that son of a bitch off the field right now, out, he's fired!'"[68] When players and owners responded with signs of unity and various forms of protest against both systemic racism and the president's incendiary remarks, the NFL's predominantly white fan base expressed its ire in ways that hark back to the scapegoating of Jack Johnson and Isaac Burns Murphy. As Intisar Seraaj and Christina Zdanowicz reported, "Fans burned jerseys; clubs disinvited athletes and some government agencies also made headlines for their reaction."[69] Eventually, the NFL more or less acceded to the base instincts of these fans (not to mention Trump), with NFL commissioner Roger Goodell announcing a new policy in May 2018: "A club will be fined by the League if its personnel are on the field and do not stand and show respect for the flag and the anthem."[70] Meanwhile, Kaepernick was maneuvered out of professional football after the 2016 season, reaching a multimillion-dollar settlement in 2019 in a joint case with his teammate Eric Reid that accused the thirty-two NFL teams of colluding to exclude them from the sport.[71]

Also in 2019, the hip-hop mogul Jay-Z and his company, Roc Nation, agreed to manage the NFL's social justice initiatives in exchange for creative control over the Super Bowl entertainment program and other high-profile events—an agreement that has polarized players and fans, some of whom have branded Jay-Z a sellout and some of whom see the move as a positive outgrowth of take-a-knee protests.[72] Regardless of where one stands on this development, the partnership signals a new chapter in the long-standing history of interconnectedness between Black entertainment and sports, as well as the political significance of these arenas for African Americans. Michael Eric Dyson observes, "Americans who are angry with Kaepernick often forget how black entertainers and athletes have used their fame to break down barriers of discrimination. Ray Charles helped to desegregate concert halls; Jackie Robinson integrated an entire sports league."[73] As the literary portraits here demonstrate, Black athletes and artists were trailblazers long before the mid-twentieth century, persevering against both the white gaze and "white rage" and often paying considerable personal costs for their cultural work.

As a brief case study of how contemporary writers reconstruct the complexities of Black celebrity history, let us turn to John Keene's exquisite short story "Cold" from his collection *Counternarratives* (2015). Here, Keene reanimates the aforementioned turn-of-the-twentieth-century "coon" songwriter Bob Cole, whose current cultural obscurity is linked not only to the caprice of time and circumstance but also to what is now perceived as the ignominious genesis of his fame in the first place. As Julian Lucas notes, "Remembered now, if at all, as a footnote or an embarrassment, he [Cole] is neither an overlooked hero to rescue from erasure or a tragic martyr."[74] In Cole's repertoire of popular tunes, he perpetuated prevailing racist stereotypes, while he also carved out a crucial (and remunerative) space for African Americans in a burgeoning postbellum entertainment industry. As Lynn Abbott and Doug Seroff remind us, "Black minstrels were professional stage performers who gathered coin and gained admiration from both blacks and whites"; moreover, these performers "made no pretense to 'elevate the Negro on the stage.'"[75] In other words, Cole, like his Black minstrel colleagues, was cashing in quite literally on the post–Civil War attraction to Black musical and comedic revues, slyly and subtly subverting dominant images of Black incapability but not demonstratively propagating a racial-uplift platform, which would become more or less de rigueur during the Harlem Renaissance of the 1920s and '30s. As Keene's "Cold" suggests, trafficking in anti-Black caricatures and stereotypes also took a psychological and emotional toll, as the Cole personage becomes increasingly haunted by his own denigrating tunes and commits suicide by the story's end. "No coon no more nobody knows the trouble I've seen," Cole thinks to himself as the icy waters of the Catskill Mountains area drag him under.[76]

In fact, "Cold" begins with the first inklings of this unraveling, as Keene, utilizing the second person, narrativizes Cole's acute feelings of alienation at the hotel that "has welcomed you, your mother, almost all who'll pay, permitting stays without incident."[77] Nevertheless, "The New Yorkers, city dwellers or upstaters, native or immigrant, do not so much as blink when they see you, staring mainly at the cut of your full dress suits and shoes, your mother's elegant day ensembles and summer gowns, as if viewing an exhibit.

Only one or two of them has ever known whom they were looking at, or, for that matter, uttered more than a simple slur."[78] Despite Cole's outsized impact on the culture industry, white Americans do not recognize the famous songwriter but instead both ogle and scorn the upwardly mobile Black population that he and his nattily dressed mother signify. Meanwhile, in Keene's rendering, Cole remains haunted by the vehicles—"that cooning and crooning minstrelsy copping a mountain of green"—that made this mobility possible.[79] Lyrics to Cole's music, such as "*All the hot dressed Coons*" and "*twenty pick-a-nin-nies playing 'round the cab-in door,*" among others, similarly appear alongside Keene's prose.[80] They provide a score, so to speak, for Cole's ruminations on what he comes to view as a Faustian bargain, while reminding readers of the denigrating caricatures that postbellum white Americans in particular flocked to see and hear.

Keene's second-person narration likewise places readers in Cole's fragile state of mind, inviting them to consider the psychological and emotional struggles of the first emancipated generation of Black Americans, who quickly discovered that in order to ascend the economic ladder, they would have to continue to cater to the proclivities and prejudices of white supremacists. As such, Keene not only encourages readers to recognize Cole's "subjectivity from beyond the boundaries of public expressiveness" but also implicates us (the "you") in this tale, collapsing the distance between the postbellum era and the twenty-first century.[81] Rather than scorning or heroicizing Cole, "Cold" communes with this once-heralded songwriter, mourning his suicide and considering what his experiences in the limelight might tell us about our own age, in which Black performers from hip-hop artists to comedians are encouraged to traffic in stereotypes. As Jelani Cobb laments, "debasement of black communities is entirely acceptable—required even—by hip-hop's predominantly white consumer base."[82] Moreover, in reference to Dave Chappelle's famed *Chappelle's Show*, Cobb describes the racial corner into which the comedian ultimately felt he had painted himself in skits that deployed anti-Black stereotypes with the hope that his audience would be savvy enough to understand the difference between confronting and endorsing racist caricatures: "An effort to deflate a stereotype instead affirms one. A comedian brought down by a single snicker from a single white man he realizes is laughing *with* the blackface devil not *at* him."[83] In 2005, Chappelle abruptly canceled his enormously popular show's third season and, temporarily at least, removed himself from the scrutiny of the public eye. As Constance Bailey notes, "One of the reasons cited was that he [Chappelle] felt he was reinforcing stereotypes instead of deconstructing them, which was not his intent."[84]

Transporting us back to the early twentieth century, Keene suggests that these racial dissonances were concretized during the decades following the Civil War and that, though the strategies have evolved along with the audience's expectations, in many respects the racial Catch-22 for Black artists remains intact. Abbott and Seroff, among other cultural critics and historians, have begun to dig figures such as Cole out of the dustbin of history, but Keene is especially deft at drawing readers into Cole's largely unexplored inner life, while questioning and reframing traditional evidentiary modes of history-making. As Keene noted in a recent interview, "In *Counternarratives* I place history as a linear, factually-based practice under pressure; the monovocality of a master narrative must yield not just to those voices that leap into the breach but to the very idea that such a thing is possible at all."[85] With his experimental narrative style—including the second-person "you" that places contemporary readers in Cole's fraught state of mind—Keene foregrounds his (re)construction of the past, while implying that all historical accounts are inflected with the subjective outlooks of their creators. "Cold" demonstrates, therefore, the unique capacity of creative recuperations to expose, qua Jacques Rancière and Diana Taylor, the limitations of the archival and historiographic methods by which we know US cultural history, to self-reflexively reimagine the psychic and emotional tableaux of postbellum artists (and athletes), and to show us the resonances between the paradoxical experiences of late nineteenth- and early twenty-first-century Black stars.

In the first three chapters of this book, I explore the ways in which contemporary poetry collections by Kevin Young, Adrian Matejka, and Frank X Walker journey back to the postbellum sporting arena in order to, in the spirit of Rancière's people's history, excavate the voices and perspectives of the Black athletes who were some of the first to experience the racial hypervisibility and personal invisibility that has characterized African American celebrity ever since. At the same time, Young, Matejka, and Walker draw attention to their own representational choices, implying the constructed nature of all historical narratives. I also attend to these writers' use of archival materials as a touchstone for mining the complex interiority of postbellum stars such as the first Black heavyweight champion, Jack Johnson, and the three-time Kentucky Derby winner Isaac Burns Murphy. In the process, Young, Matejka, and Walker indicate parallels with popular (mis)conceptions of contemporary Black athletes, as well as current efforts to combat the hegemonic forces that imperiled predecessors like Johnson and Murphy.

In chapter 1, I consider Young's collection *To Repel Ghosts: The Remix from the Original Masters*, arguing that Young uses persona poetry, ekphrasis, and interpolated archival materials in order to destabilize the white-supremacist ideologies and power structures with which Jack Johnson and his heavyweight champion successors, especially Joe Louis and Muhammad Ali, contended. Ekphrastically reimagining the painter Jean-Michel Basquiat's experimental portraits of famous Black boxers, Young traces the paradoxes of fame for athletes and artists of African descent from the postbellum period across the twentieth century, using the resonant staccato rhythm of a boxing jab as well as rich double entendres to elucidate the emotional experience of, as the Johnson persona puts it, spending "my life fighting— / crossing color / lines I never drew."[86] Bridging what Taylor described earlier as the gap between the "*archive* of supposedly enduring materials" and the "*repertoire* of embodied practice/knowledge," *To Repel Ghosts* both troubles and supplements conventional boxing histories. In the process, Young implies the connections between Johnson's and his successors' vexing experiences in the limelight and those of contemporary Black athletes, thereby subverting a teleological reading of US cultural history.

Chapter 2 turns to Matejka's collection *The Big Smoke*, which further advances what Rancière terms a "different sensorium" about Johnson in particular and the transhistorical continuities of Black celebrity in general. Whereas Young uses triadic lines replete with enjambed puns that draw out the paradoxes of Black athletic fame, Matejka voices the perspectives of a range of figures, including the heavyweight champion's first wife, Etta Duryea, who committed suicide in Johnson's Café de Champion, as well as several of his lovers, all of whom he is alleged to have physically abused. Matejka especially exposes the violent consequences of the boxer's relentless pursuit of hegemonic masculinity, which was always already foreclosed to Black men. When Matejka reimagines Johnson's inner life, he also retrains readers' attention so that we are drawn into the transoms of the boxer's mind rather than fixating on his overdetermined body. In distinct ways, Matejka and Young thus encourage readers to confront the fear, fascination, and rage that Johnson inspired in white audiences—a constellation of conflicting racial responses that often informs the public's treatment of current Black athletes.

Chapter 3 highlights these through lines by examining Walker's *Isaac Murphy: I Dedicate This Ride*, a collection that ventriloquizes the three-time Kentucky Derby winner Isaac Burns Murphy; his wife, Lucy; his horse-racing mentor, Eli Jordon; and his parents, James and America. Probing their interior thoughts, Walker reorients the hegemonic gaze so that postbellum history and culture are seen through the imagined perspectives of these figures who have been virtually wiped clean from cultural memory. In the process of recounting Murphy's immense triumphs at the racetrack and his and other Black jockeys' subsequent exile from the sport that they once dominated, Walker also denaturalizes popular conceptions of what constitutes predominantly "white" and "Black" athletic spaces, inviting readers to consider the suppressed histories that explain the *how* and the *why* of sociocultural segregation. Reimagining embodied experiences (or what Taylor refers to as the "repertoire") alongside archival accounts that reveal the white bias against Murphy and his loved ones, Walker retells a "heretical" history of horse racing, voicing interior thoughts and feelings that were never set down in written records. Walker is especially attentive to the double-edged experience of Black participation in sports, whereby Murphy and other famous Black jockeys were perceived to be both upsetting racial hierarchies and confirming stereotypes about Blacks as more physically than mentally endowed, setting the stage for sports to become a primary site for Black social mobility on the one hand and white-engineered exploitation on the other.

In the book's three subsequent chapters, I turn my attention to contemporary creative recuperations of nineteenth-century musicians and vaudeville and minstrel performers, suggesting that the love-hate relationship that white America currently enjoys with famous Black artists has its genesis on the postbellum stage.[87] Continuing to draw on theorists such as Rancière and Taylor while also taking cues from Jeanne Scheper's concept of "playing in the archive,"[88] I consider the innovative techniques that Caryl Phillips, Jeffery Renard Allen, and Tyehimba Jess have devised to interpret and even listen to alternative histories of postbellum, pre–Harlem Renaissance performers. As Jennifer Stoever asserts, "Since the establishment of slavery and the codification of Jim Crow laws in its wake, listening has greatly impacted how bodies are categorized according to racial hierarchies and how raced subjects imagined themselves and negotiated a thoroughly racialized society."[89] Phillips, Allen, and Jess attune readers to these sonic color lines and the racially essentialist listening patterns that underpin them by making use of what Rancière described earlier as *dissensus*, or the process of "putting together two separate worlds."[90] Interlacing archival materials with creative portraits, these writers advance "new configurations between the visible and the invisible, and between the audible and inaudible, new distributions of space and time,"[91] thereby defamiliarizing inherited truths and realizing instead a palimpsestic approach to Black celebrity history that makes the connections between past and present legible.

Chapter 4 examines Phillips's representation of Bert Williams, George Walker, and their wives, Charlotte Louis ("Lottie") Williams and Aida Overton Walker—a groundbreaking artist in her own right—in his novel *Dancing in the Dark*. "Playing" with archival documents (to borrow Scheper's apt phrase), Phillips recuperates the multiple impulses at work in the photographs, recordings, and transcripts of these figures' performances, recovering them from the margins of history, in which they have often been cast as either racial pawns and traitors (or both). Using free indirect discourse, Phillips inhabits these performers' interior thoughts and feelings, illuminating the double bind they faced when they invested in the entertainment industry as a way out of the abject poverty to which the vast majority of postbellum African Americans were subjected. As Phillips demonstrates, Williams, Walker, and Overton Walker had to capitulate to denigrating stereotypes in order to mollify the fears and biases of their white audiences, while they were also expected to represent their race in empowering ways. In Phillips's reimagining of Williams's, Walker's, and Overton Walker's inner desires and frustrations (even musings), he suggests that they wanted to be treated as artists and with the dignity that their white counterparts enjoyed. Subverting the sonic color line while reorienting the gaze away from these figures' bodies and toward the Quashian "quiet" of their minds, Phillips similarly offers another way to conceive of Black fame—one focused on what is concealed from a white-dominated fan base.

Chapter 5 considers Allen's acclaimed *Song of the Shank*, a novel that recuperates the paradoxical celebrity experiences of Thomas Greene Wiggins (1849–1908), known by the stage moniker "Blind Tom." "Tom had a huge cultural impact," Tim Armstrong notes; "his London programme [1880] suggested that he had been seen by more people than any living person, and he was written about by, among many others, Rebecca Harding Davis, Mark Twain, and Willa Cather—the last both in factual accounts and in a fictional version of him ('Blind D'Arnault') in *My Ántonia*."[92] Even while Tom enjoyed international fame, his physical and purported mental disabilities were used as legal justification for the actions of the Bethune family, who had enslaved him and his family to maintain lifetime custody rights to the pianist and his lucrative career.[93] Making use of free indirect discourse, Allen inhabits the perspective of a variety of figures in Tom's life, while tracking endemic forms of nineteenth-century cultural and sonic dissonance, whereby white audiences were both flocking to witness Tom's musical acumen and continuing to debase him as subhuman. At the same time that Allen focalizes wide-ranging perspectives, he never inhabits Tom's persona, highlighting the near total erasure of the pianist's perspective from historical records. Further, Allen's nonlinear timeline combined with his fantastical setting of Edgemere and reproductions of both contemporary artworks and denigrating promotional materials all draw attention to the creative choices involved in the construction not only of *Song of the Shank* but also of historical narratives more generally. Subverting conventional historiographic methodologies, Allen crafts a multimodal fusion of the archive and the repertoire that offers fresh epistemological (and sonic) insights about the US entertainment industry.

Chapter 6 explicates Jess's poetic portraits of "Blind Tom," Bert Williams, George Walker, Sissieretta Jones (the "Black Patti"), and Christine and Millie McKoy (the "two-headed nightingale"), among a host of others, in his Pulitzer Prize–winning collection *Olio*. Rather than attempting to recover these artists' repertoires, Jess pays tribute to their musical mastery by putting his own lyric dexterity on display, arranging his persona sonnets and contrapuntal poems so that they can be read in myriad ways—vertically, horizontally, and diagonally, as well as backward and forward. At the same time, Jess's meticulously crafted poetics draw attention to his *re*presentation of these artist-ancestors' personae for his own creative purposes, suggesting the ways in which history is not simply handed down but carefully arranged to advance particular perspectives. Jess's multimodal—what Rancière might term "heretical"—poetry not only forecloses the possibility of viewing the past through a monosemous lens but also encourages readers to confront their own participation in this history by physically tearing out particular pages and making Möbius strips and cylinders and other geometric shapes. In accordance with Quashie, Jess too evinces "quiet" thoughts, challenging the media tendency to overemphasize the Black celebrity body and to neglect the complexities of the mind. Reminding us of why these now-obscure Black celebrities still matter, *Olio* underscores the disjuncture between archival materials and lived experiences, and the sedimentation of now long-practiced social scripts, whereby white Americans avidly consume Black culture while remaining complicit in the systemic degradation of people of African descent.

When Jess visited one of my undergraduate classes shortly after the publication of *Olio*, a student asked him how he managed the anger he must have felt after researching the racialized trauma that figures such as Sissieretta Jones and Millie and Christine McKoy, among others, experienced as Black spectacles subject to the fetishizing and prejudices of white audiences. Reflecting on this question, Jess noted a peculiar optimism that set in when inhabiting these figures' perspectives. When they were born enslaved, he suggested, they had no reason to believe that they would ever become legendary artists who would inspire not only his own award-winning poetry but also the productive intergenerational, interracial conversation with which we were all engaged. One never knows what hopeful transformation may be on the horizon, and creatively recuperating the dead is one of the ways in which we are reminded of both how little has changed and how much still can.

1

"MY BLACK BODY THROWN FREE"

The Legacy of Jack Johnson in Kevin Young's To Repel Ghosts: *The Remix from the Original Masters*

John Arthur ("Jack") Johnson entered the boxing ring during the late nineteenth century, when, as Gerald Early notes, "professional boxing was metamorphosed into an American sport, serving a particular and powerful set of collective psychic needs."[1] White men invested in boxing as a vehicle for affirming their racial supremacy, often refusing to compete with Blacks for fear of destabilizing a carefully constructed racial scaffolding.[2] In 1908, Jack Johnson disrupted all of this, first by traveling to Australia to challenge and defeat the reigning heavyweight champion Tommy Burns and, two years later, by defeating the "Great White Hope," Jim Jeffries. In his personal life, he also broke color lines and codes, sleeping with and marrying white women and flaunting his riches at a time when African Americans were being lynched for the smallest (even perceived) infraction against a white patriarchal order. Consequently, as Johnson's biographer Geoffrey C. Ward puts it, "Most whites (and some Negroes as well) saw him [Johnson] as a perpetual threat—profligate, arrogant, amoral, a dark menace, and a danger to the natural order of things."[3] Defamiliarizing these caricatures, the poetic collections that this and chapter 2 take up—Kevin Young's 2005 *To Repel Ghosts: The Remix from the Original Masters* (chapter 1) and Adrian Matejka's 2013 *The Big*

Smoke (chapter 2)—revivify Johnson, shedding fresh light on his spectacular athletic success coupled with the public opprobrium that resulted from his disruption of the racial status quo. Looking back at Johnson's career, Young and Matejka likewise illuminate the development of a white-engineered playbook for Black celebrity that has been cast with various actors ever since.

Young's *To Repel Ghosts: The Remix from the Original Masters*, first published as *To Repel Ghosts: Five Sides in B Minor* (2001),[4] creatively recuperates Johnson's life and career alongside the late-twentieth-century painter Jean-Michel Basquiat, among a wide range of iconic African American athletes and musicians who appear on the artist's canvases. At first blush, Basquiat and Johnson share little in their background and experience. The effete, eccentric Basquiat was born in Brooklyn in 1960 to parents of Haitian and Puerto Rican descent. He became a well-known figure in the downtown, and mostly white, New York art scene, dated Madonna, played the role of deejay in Blondie's "Rapture" video, and famously collaborated with Andy Warhol before dying of a heroin overdose at the age of twenty-seven. Despite the time and circumstances that separate this pathbreaking painter and boxer, Young's ekphrastic poems position Johnson as the forebear of Black fame (or infamy), the fulcrum around which subsequent Black celebrities, including Basquiat, pivot as they negotiate conflicting feelings of defiance and alienation as Black men under the scrutiny of the white public's baleful gaze.

Despite Young's stature as a renowned poet, a nonfiction writer, poetry editor of the *New Yorker*, former director of the Schomburg Center for Research in Black Culture, and current director of the Smithsonian's National Museum of African American History and Culture, *To Repel Ghosts: The Remix from the Original Masters* has received only modest critical attention. The collection has been trumpeted for its breadth and innovation but understudied with regard to its archival and historiographic implications. In a brief piece in the online journal *Post45*, the poet Stefanie Wortman highlights Young's contributions to the ekphrastic tradition, noting, "By producing readings of the paintings, as well as by sampling them through both direct quotation and description, Young seems to deepen his thinking about issues that connect his experience with

Basquiat's, particularly the place of African American men in history."[5] In a book chapter on three of Young's early collections—*To Repel Ghosts: Five Sides in B Minor* (2001), *jelly roll* (2003), and *Black Maria* (2005)—Rick Benjamin highlights the poet's deft formal fusion of "Dante's terza rima and the hip hop or pop artist's approach to archiving history."[6] As noted in the introduction, Howard Rambsy II recently examined *To Repel Ghosts: The Remix from the Original Masters* alongside Tyehimba Jess's *leadbelly* (2005) and Adrian Matejka's *The Big Smoke* (2013) in a chapter of his monograph *Bad Men: Creative Touchstones of Black Writers* (2020). Rambsy contends that Young's collection "broke new ground in poetic meditations of black cultural figures" by "embed[ing] explorations of other black cultural figures within its overarching examination of the project's daring star painter [Basquiat]."[7] In my own previous reading of *To Repel Ghosts: The Remix from the Original Masters*, I focused briefly on Young's poetic representations of Billie Holiday and Robert Johnson, arguing that Young's invocations tracked twenty-first-century reappraisals of blues icons as complex artists, rather than the supposedly natural performers that they have often been presumed to be.[8]

In this chapter, I further examine Young's archival-historical work, suggesting that he utilizes the affordances of lyric, persona, and ekphrastic poetry to creatively recuperate Jack Johnson in particular but also the athletes that succeeded him. Alluding to Basquiat's abstract depictions of Black boxers in his paintings, Young opens up new ways of understanding Johnson, his heavyweight successors Joe Louis and Muhammad Ali, and, by extension, a range of Black athletes. While Young's title *To Repel Ghosts*—itself lifted from Basquiat's 1986 painting with the same title[9]—signals the warding off of spectral violence, neither the painter nor the poet is interested in repelling ghosts as much as engaging them in a dialogue about the sociocultural shifts that both have and have not occurred for US citizens of African descent. Indicated by Young's subtitle (and the new edition of the original 2001 collection that it signifies), his methodology is to remix a wide array of materials, fusing what Diana Taylor refers to as "the archive (i.e., texts, documents, buildings, bones)" and "the so-called repertoire of embodied practice/knowledge repertoire (i.e., spoken language, dance, sports, ritual)."[10] Young also suggests that fame for Black men (and women) always cuts more than one way, entailing social mobility but also deeper levels of white scrutiny and scorn. Formally realizing these paradoxes through prolific use of enjambment, Young does not attempt to account for all of the facts about Johnson (or the other athletes and artists he invokes) but instead focuses on what the cultural theorist Jacques Rancière refers to as "the truth of things as opposed to the chatter and lies of orators."[11]

When Young inhabits Johnson's persona, he is also interested in shifting the gaze away from the boxer's body and toward what Kevin Quashie describes as "quiet expressiveness."[12] As Young departs from persona poetry in his subsequent portraits, he similarly implies the challenge of recuperating the interiority of figures whose images and narratives were either overdetermined or underrepresented by a media landscape that consistently elides the diverse experiences of African America. With Young's clipped, staccato-style stanzas, he replicates the sound of Johnson's quick jabs at his opponents, evincing the ways in which Johnson's treatment "as both a venerated and denigrated figure" re-sound in subsequent Black athletes' and artists' careers.[13] Indeed, unlike the poetry collections and novels examined in the chapters ahead, *To Repel Ghosts* not only gestures toward implicit parallels between the experiences of the first wave of Black celebrities and their athlete and artist successors but also tracks them by invoking Jack Johnson alongside twentieth-century athletes, musicians, and painters (specifically Basquiat) who gained fame after him. Eschewing tidy timelines affirming teleological progress, Young's multimodal poetry makes it clear that, even as more contemporary figures are casting off the legacy of white exploitation and anti-Black scapegoating, transhistorical patterns often recur for African Americans in the limelight.

"Stud, Buck, Black"

The opening poem, "Negative," sets the stage for this intergenerational dialogue by introducing the notion of postracialism—or at least a refusal of racial codes and roles, as the poem title implies. Cataloguing a series of inversions of stereotypes, Young imagines "white back-up / singers, ball-players & boxers all / white as tar."[14]

A few stanzas later, Young poses the question, "Is this what we've wanted / & waited for?" a query he answers in the final stanza by affirming that, despite the ocular shifts, the capitalist regime that has always orchestrated these racial stratifications and taxonomies is firmly intact:

> Only money keeps
> green, still grows & burns like grass
> under dark daylight.[15]

For the members of Johnson's generation, professional options were mostly limited to manual labor and, for the lucky few like Johnson, the sporting arena or perhaps the minstrel or vaudeville stage. A few generations later, Basquiat found success as a painter, and, of course, Young himself is an acclaimed poet, implying that the racism and inequalities endemic to the postbellum era have been rectified, hence the humorous inversions of the prototypically "Black" roles. Yet Young's series of poems about Johnson and, later, Basquiat complicate this redemptive historical narrative, exposing the tension that both boxer and painter felt between their own personal and professional desires and the expectations of the US public that they abide by certain gendered and racialized codes of behavior.

Johnson is the only figure, including Basquiat, whom Young ventriloquizes, implying that his celebrity experiences established the blueprint for the precarious public reception of the other athletes and musicians invoked here. While Basquiat's iconic boxer portraits, such as *Jack Johnson*, *St. Joe Louis Surrounded by Snakes*, *Cassius Clay*, and *Untitled (Boxer)*, are characterized by flat outlines of upper torsos, boxing gloves, and crowns, Young uses the printed page to give them emotional depth and sociocultural context. To this end, the twenty-six-page poetic sequence "Jack Johnson" begins with the eponymous title and description of Basquiat's painting—"JACK JOHNSON / *1982, acrylic & oil paintstick on canvas*"—followed by an epigraph from Denzil Batchelor's biography *Jack Johnson and His Times* (1990) that reads, "Jack decided that being a painter was less of a vocation than he had supposed. He would be a boxer instead."[16] Bestowing a crown on Johnson, Basquiat exalts this icon as royalty. In turn, Young illuminates the commonalities between boxer and painter as both racially hypervisible in the limelight and depersonalized in a structurally racist United States.

Moreover, this section's ekphrasis, biographical research, and enjambed persona poetry represent Young's interweaving of archive and repertoire in order to defamiliarize hegemonic, monologic readings of US cultural history. The first poem in the sequence, "Black Jack (B. 31 March 1878)," begins with Young inverting the white gaze in order to voice Johnson's imagined understanding of the multiple and conflicting ways he is seen and understood:

> Some call me spade,
> stud, buck, black. That last
> I take as a compliment—
>
> "I am black & they
> won't let me forget it."
> I'm Jack
>
> to my friends, Lil'
> Arthur—like that King
> of England—to my mama.[17]

In Young's portrayal, Johnson has access to social mobility through boxing, but he is, like his enslaved parents before him, still objectified by stereotypes ("spade, / stud, buck") and a systemic disregard for Black lives. Rendering the experience of what W. E. B. Du Bois terms "double consciousness"—"two-ness,—an American, a Negro; two souls; two thoughts, two unreconciled strivings; two warring ideals in one dark body"[18]—Young implies Johnson's deep awareness of the denigrating stereotypes projected onto him. Young's Johnson is also careful to distinguish between these epithets and his own self-image, underscoring his refusal to internalize white-supremacist notions of Black inferiority. Using enjambment, Young thus makes it clear what it feels like to identify as "Jack / to my friends," while remaining cognizant that the US public views him as subhuman, which the disempowering statement "I'm Jack" affirms.

As the poem concludes, Young continues to juxtapose Johnson's hypervisibility and notoriety in the public sphere with Johnson's, in Quashie's terms, quiet "inner life," including his "desires, ambitions, hungers, vulnerabilities, fears."[19] According to Young, Johnson's private moments are not always preoccupied by what Du Bois describes as the "warring ideals" produced by anti-Black racism; instead, the boxer considers the allure and inherent risks within his chosen vocation:

> the ring, you gamble—
> go ahead then dealer,
> hit me again.[20]

Daring and brave, Young's Johnson persona not only is tenacious but also thrives on the thrill of chance. Beneath this self-possessed assertion, Young includes an excerpt from a 1923 Bohun Lynch column in the journal *Knuckles & Gloves* that nonetheless reveals the racial animus that Johnson was up against: "With money in his pocket and physical triumph over white men in his heart, he displayed all the gross and overbearing insolence which makes what we call the buck n[*****] insufferable."[21] Reproducing these white-authored portraits alongside Johnson's own imagined perspective, Young contraposes glimpses of the boxer's public image and private thoughts, which Young suspects moved between the alienation of double consciousness and what Quashie conceptualizes as quietude.

"Black Jack (B. 31 March 1878)" also reveals what Jamal L. Ratchford describes as a long-standing dynamic in which white-dominated media outlets, "ill-concerned or unknowledgeable about the reality faced by black athletes," have propagated images of Black athletes "that privileged the experiences of white Americans."[22] Drawing attention to this pattern, Young neither relies on the archive (in this case, white-owned periodicals) as a stable form of knowledge about famous Black Americans nor dismisses it as irrelevant. Rather, juxtaposing archival documents with what Taylor refers to as the repertoire of embodied experiences, Young encourages readers to approach historical and, by extension, recent accounts of Black athletes with heightened attention to the source and context of the information. Rancière conceives of this artistic mode of destabilization as "dissensus," which "re-configure[s] the fabric of sensory experience" and thus disrupts dominant modes of thought.[23] Focalizing Johnson's interior world and using enjambment to suggest the multiple meanings and paradoxes that accrued to him, Young represents the boxer anew, thereby undermining the one-dimensional portrait propagated by periodicals like *Knuckles & Gloves*.

Young shows that the boxer not only used his physical strength to knock out opponents in the boxing ring but also devised ways of publicly putting the lie to white-supremacist rhetoric that sought to circumscribe the lives of all African Americans. For example, as Young makes clear in "The Upset (26 December 1908)," Johnson, in order to become the heavyweight champion of the world, traveled to Australia to fight the reigning champion, Tommy Burns, forcing him out from behind the shield of segregation:

> no more
> color lines to hide
> behind.[24]

The final lines of the poem also imagine the fear lodged deep in white spectators after Johnson defeated Burns—"the police / rush in like fools"—and the rippling panic that spread among whites in the United States and United Kingdom: "like water, my wide wake."[25] "Wake," as many of the terms in Young's lines, takes on a double meaning, indicative of both the aftershocks of Johnson's achievement and the impending doom that it spelled out for him, as victory meant that he was now a marked man. Below this final stanza, Young cites the canonical American author Jack London admitting, "Personally I was with Burns all the way. He is a white man, and so am I. Naturally I wanted to see the white man win."[26] Rather than weaving London's words into the poem or manipulating them in any way, Young transposes them unadulterated, showing the way that the white community—even its most learned members—denigrated African Americans. Via London's press clipping, Young underscores the hegemonic perspectives that have shaped historical understandings of Johnson (and all famous Black men), implying the necessity of creatively recuperating both archive and repertoire in order to remake history in ways that do not perpetuate what Rancière described earlier as "the chatter and lies of orators."

Through Young's innovative poetics (combining historical fragments, ekphrasis, and persona poetry), he demonstrates that, despite Johnson's prodigious achievements, he would never gain respect from people outside the Black community. This experience is not strictly historical either. As Abby Ferber notes of the athletic landscape today, "Black athletes may be seen as potentially threatening to the notion of White male superiority"; at the same time, "depictions of African American athletes may also reinforce the traditional hierarchy by reifying stereotypes of their animal-like nature, emphasizing their sexuality, aggressiveness, and physical power."[27] In addition, "sports broadcasts . . . have depicted black athletes as having physical superiority, whereas white athletes have been depicted as possessing intellectual superiority."[28] Examining the career of LeBron James, we can readily see these patterns at work, as well as his awareness of the double-edged nature of Black athletic success. For example, when James used his celebrity platform to amplify the concerns of the Black Lives Matter movement, he was ridiculed by the right-wing media. In response, James launched a three-part Showtime series *Shut Up and Dribble*, the title of which is an overt rejoinder to the calls of the right-wing pundit Laura Ingraham specifically and conservative NBA fans and commentators more generally.[29] Tracing the origins of these racial scripts and Black players' defiant responses to them to the decades following the Civil War, Young adumbrates the cultural tissue that binds an epoch that brandished its white supremacy to one that touts colorblind meritocracy; moreover, he uses persona poetry to voice a counternarrative to the white media's depiction of Johnson in particular and Black athletes more generally.

In "The Crown (4 July 1910)," Young continues his ekphrastic dialogue with Basquiat by engaging with the spare *Jack Johnson* portrait, which features the boxer wearing a crown and raising his right, gloved arm in victory, while his face is a series of dark lines, an inscrutable oval set against the white expanse of the canvas. Investing this Johnson sketch with three-dimensional emotional and psychological depth, Young elucidates the ramifications of winning "the crown" in the boxer's storied fight against the so-called Great White Hope, Jim Jeffries. That the date of the fight is July 4 speaks volumes about the national stakes, particularly in regard to the whiteness that in 1910 was a prerequisite for enjoying the full benefits of US citizenship. Young highlights the contradictory nature of Johnson's powerful blows, which enabled his economic prosperity ("Jeffries was cash / by round one") and at the same time antagonized white supremacists:

> the Whites
> couldn't have
> me running
> their show, much less
> own the crown.
> Called for my head.[30]

The word "running" has particular resonance here, recalling the desire for escape among enslaved African Americans like Johnson's parents, as well as the feelings of entrapment that the heavyweight champion experienced, even as he reigned supreme in the ring. As Dave Zirin reports, "After Johnson's victory, there were race riots around the country—in Illinois, Missouri, New York, Ohio, Pennsylvania, Colorado, Texas, and Washington D.C. Most of the riots consisted of white lynch mobs attempting to enter Black neighborhoods and Blacks fighting back. This reaction to a boxing match was the most widespread simultaneous racial uprising in the U.S. until the riots that followed the 1968 assassination of civil rights leader Dr. Martin Luther King Jr."[31] Incorporating and interpolating headlines about this racialized violence—"that Independence / Day," "JOHNSON WINS / WHITES LYNCH / 70 ARRESTED"—Young conveys the double-edged sword of victory for Johnson and other Black celebrity athletes.[32]

Young also draws on the repertoire here, concluding the poem by citing a verse from a "*Traditional*" song that sums up these contradictory feelings of triumph and anguish:

> The Yankees hold the play,
> The white man pull the trigger;
> But it makes no difference what the white man say,
> The world champion's still a n[*****].[33]

Spotlighting the bittersweet nature of Johnson's victory, "the white man" is still in power, but in boxing, the champion is "a n[*****]." In other words, Young mobilizes these archival resources and remixes them into his poetry, indicating the importance of sports for Black advancement but also the intractability of social stratifications and structural racism that no boxer, musician, or lone Black star of any sort is capable of single-handedly dismantling. That lyric lines stand alongside newspaper clippings and a vernacular song likewise exemplifies the process of creative recuperation, whereby the conventional hierarchy between empiricism and the imagination, as well as the artificial binary between archive and repertoire, is swept aside to make room for a multimodal engagement with Black cultural history that exceeds the biases and (il)logic of white hegemony.

Additionally, in citing a range of perspectives on Johnson's fame, Young shows how little control the boxer wielded over his public image and narrative, as well as the immense pressure that he and other Black athletes (and famous figures) were (and are) under as they were and are transformed into embodiments of Black America writ large. As Benjamin notes, "Young charts the rise and fall of the artist-icon with a montage that reads like a history lesson, a cautionary tale, the boxer [Johnson] accounting for himself at the same time that others speak both for and against him."[34] In this regard, Young reproduces responses to Johnson by the foremost postbellum Black leaders—Booker T. Washington and W. E. B. Du Bois—inviting readers, as he did with the Jack London excerpt, into the archive with him. Not unsurprisingly, Washington and Du Bois offer radically different assessments of Johnson's achievements and behavior, and Young's side-by-side citations evince the additional social pressures Johnson and his successors endured. To illustrate, Young quotes Washington's remarks to the United Press Association that Johnson "is another illustration of the most irreparable injury that a wrong action on the part of a single individual may do to a whole race"; moreover, "No one can do so much injury to the Negro race as the Negro himself.'[35] On the one hand, Washington's assessment seems to blame Johnson for the anti-Black scapegoating that clearly led to his arrest and conviction. On the other, Washington conveys the challenge faced by all Black Americans in the limelight: they are always already denied individuality. Du Bois is much more sympathetic toward Johnson, pinning the outrage over his behavior on the racist attitudes of white America: "Some pretend to object to Mr. Johnson's character. But we have yet to hear, in the case of white America, that marital troubles have disqualified prizefighters or ball players or even statesmen. It comes down then, after all, to this unforgiveable blackness."[36] Although Du Bois and Washington are characteristically distinct in their diagnoses, both suggest the enormous impact that Johnson had on the struggle for racial justice in the early twentieth century.

Using the lyrical landscape to reimagine Johnson's "quiet" thoughts and contraposing them with these historical citations, Young also encourages readers to appreciate Johnson's complexities, as well as the multiple perspectives layered into but not always visible within the archival vault. As Christina Sharpe explains in *In the Wake: On Blackness and Being* (2016), "I am interested in how we imagine ways of knowing the past, in excess of the fictions of the archive, but not only that. I am interested, too, in the ways we recognize the many manifestations of that fiction and that excess, that past not yet past, in the present."[37] Correspondingly, as Young journeys back to Johnson's early-twentieth-century experiences, he reminds us of the through lines between the pressures the boxer faced and those of Black professional athletes today, not to mention artists like Basquiat and even Young himself. While Johnson has not been shunted to the backwaters of US cultural memory, as have many of the other postbellum, pre–Harlem Renaissance figures this book examines, the undue public scrutiny he faced as a Black celebrity athlete was not adequately redressed in the century that elapsed between his watershed victory over Burns and the publication of Young's persona poems.

In the final poem in the Johnson sequence, "The Race (D. 10 June 1945)," Young represents Johnson taking stock of his life, highlighting both the racist propaganda and pressures to represent "the race" that pervaded his self-image: "Despised by whites / & blacks alike," "Gave Negroes / a bad name— / shame," and "Only good / Negro is dead / broke," to name only a few of the lines that suggest Johnson's keen sense of the agendas of both white hegemonic power structures and the architects of racial uplift. Young likewise educes Johnson's vacillation between feelings of anguish and accomplishment that accompanied becoming the first Black heavyweight champion:

> Big bucks. I spent
>
> my life fighting—

crossing color
lines I never drew

up dreamt. I put
the race on
check—track—no Jack,

no Joe
Louis. . . .[38]

Delivering enjambed puns in the staccato-style rhythm of Johnson's boxing jabs, Young imagines the boxer's exasperation that the US public reduced him to the stereotype of the "Big [Black] buck," while he also made "Big bucks" that challenged a white economic stronghold. Similarly, Johnson laments the "color lines" that he "never drew" but was nonetheless forced to cross in order to gain socioeconomic mobility, as well as to challenge the injustices of second-class citizenship. While Booker T. Washington and other African American leaders may have felt ambivalent or even hostile toward the boxer's public persona, Johnson, via Young, takes pride in the groundwork that he laid for the second Black heavyweight champion, Joe Louis, among others, to achieve success in white-dominated arenas.

As the poem ends, Young reenacts Johnson's death, shedding further light on the burden of racial hypervisibility and personal invisibility. On June 10, 1946, Johnson died in a high-speed crash fueled by his frustration at being told at a diner outside of Raleigh, North Carolina, that he could only be served in the back. As Ward recounts, "Johnson took the wheel of his latest high-powered automobile, a Lincoln Zephyr, and roared along the highway. . . . He lost control. The car swerved across the white line, left the road, and slammed into a telephone pole."[39] Young, in turn, conveys Johnson's final sense of relief that this "pole / of power—utility—" will end his embattled lifetime of challenging the ideology of white supremacy: "my black body / thrown free."[40] While Johnson was legally always a "free" man, unlike the chattel slavery into which his parents were born, he experienced the frustration of attempting to avail himself of the first-class citizenship rights that were never actually on offer to people of African descent. He may have defeated white boxing legends and married white women, but, as Young's persona poetry deftly shows, Johnson was never able to *feel* fully free in a society that constantly reinforced myths of Black inferiority.

The former US poet laureate Natasha Trethewey—a pioneer in historical persona poetry in her own right and one of Young's colleagues from his early years in the Dark Room Collective—sees her work as recuperating "things that have been forgotten and erased": "Sometimes it's more like what Robert Hayden wanted to do, which was to correct some of the misapprehension about history, African American history in particular. . . . So part of what I'm trying to do is tell fuller versions of history."[41] As with Trethewey, Young invests in persona poetry to complicate historical memory and, in *To Repel Ghosts* specifically, to tell a fuller story of the first Black heavyweight champion. Fusing the archive and repertoire, including citations from periodicals and ekphrastic allusions to Basquiat, Young also unsettles dominant historiographic methodologies while reminding us of why Johnson's experiences matter for contemporary understandings of the links between the sociocultural landscapes of the United States' past and present.

"The Details of Transactions Not Reported"

As the collection segues into the next section, "Famous Negro Athletes," Young moves away from persona poetry, and the interior excavation of Johnson's life and career that it entails, and tracks the impact that Johnson's groundbreaking success in the ring, as well as his persecution outside it, had on the Black celebrities who followed him. At the same time, Young continues to draw on ekphrasis, enjambment, and the emotive economy of poetry in order to, similar to Rancière and Taylor, subvert monologic modes of history-making, while implying the constructedness of all narratives of the past, including his own. As Taylor points out, "As opposed to the supposedly stable objects in the archive, the actions that are the repertoire do not remain the same. The repertoire both keeps and transforms choreographies of meaning."[42] In Young's representation of the Black athletes who followed Johnson, he "both keeps and transforms" the trace of Johnson's experiences within and beyond the ring, re-sounding his jabs through the staccato-style rhythm of his stanzas that continue throughout "Famous Negro Athletes" and the collection as a whole. Moreover, while Basquiat's portraits of Joe Louis and Muhammad Ali are captivating tributes, Young infuses them with new valences, reconfiguring (or "remixing") them in order to elucidate the sociopolitical challenges of the limelight for Basquiat and other Black athletes and artists and thereby collapsing the distance between the postbellum, pre–Civil Rights and post–Civil Rights eras.

Young's "Famous Negro Athletes" section begins by quoting Basquiat from "Report from New York: The Graffiti Question," in which the painter admits, "In those days I never had enough money to cover a whole canvas. I wouldn't be surprised if I died like a boxer, really broke, but somehow I doubt it."[43] Such an admission echoes the aforementioned title page of the "Jack Johnson" section, in which Young quotes Denzil Batchelor's *Jack Johnson and His Times*: "Jack decided that being a painter was less of a vocation than he had supposed. He would be a boxer instead."[44] As Basquiat's comments imply, he was keenly aware of the exploitation of Johnson and other Black boxers whose ephemeral victories in the ring did not translate into financial security or social acceptance. These perils of Black fame are what unify *To Repel Ghosts*' diverse cast of characters across time and space, suggesting the continuity in vexing experiences for Black celebrities, whether they pursue sports, music, or, for that matter, painting.

Continuing with the short, enjambed stanzas used in the Johnson section, Young implies that the boxer's experiences reverberate across the twentieth century and into Basquiat's foray into the 1980s downtown New York art scene:

> B anomaly—
> anomaly he be—
> caught between
>
> a hock
> & a hard race—
> From the peak
>
> you can almost see[45]

Basquiat is an "anomaly" here—a Black painter in an elite white world, not unlike Johnson's own isolating singularity as a Black boxer challenging Burns and then Jeffries and, by extension, the entire white sports establishment. Playfully subverting the adage "between a rock and a hard place," Young also refers to the difficulties that Basquiat experienced both as a starving artist who might be forced to "hock" his possessions and as a figure forced to assume the burden of racial representation ("a hard race").

As the poem continues, so too do the parallels between Basquiat and Johnson, particularly as Young imagines both men struggling against the pernicious forces of racial oppression. Invoking Homer's *Odyssey*, Young represents Basquiat as "Lashed / to the mast / the hero rides,"[46] implying the stature of the painter and, by extension, the boxer in the pantheon of Black icons. At the same time, their prodigious accomplishments do not inoculate these figures from racial discrimination. For example, Young segues from this Odysseus allusion to the infamous tale of Johnson being denied passage on the *Titanic*:

> luxury, no matter
> how heavy
> his pockets, how full
>
> still no one will let
> Gentleman Jack
> Johns'n board this Titanic—[47]

Blacks may be "permitted" to achieve fame and socioeconomic success, Young affirms, but such breakthroughs will not dismantle the anti-Black status quo. Moreover, beginning the poem with Basquiat and ending it with Johnson—not to mention the title's reference to "Negro Athletes"—Young tracks the continuities in their racialized experiences, troubling the narrative of progressive change in the decades separating Johnson's postbellum period from Basquiat's and Young's own post–Civil Rights era.

Likewise emphasizing a long tradition of resistance, the poem's final stanzas recall the blues singer Leadbelly's "Titanic," which begins, "Jack Johnson want to get on board, / The Captain said, 'we ain't hauling no coal.'" After the ship "ran into that great iceberg,"

Leadbelly reports that the boxer was grateful to have been denied a ticket: "Jack Johnson heard the mighty shook. / Might 'a' seen him doin' the Eagle Rock."[48] Young's poem imagines Johnson's unexpected good fortune, even as he suggests that the boxer's defiance did little to erode the structural forces that continued to imperil Basquiat and other Black men and women:

> O how the ship will rock
> when it meets
> that giant block
>
> of ice—doing
> the Eagle Rock—
> It's not what
>
> you can see
> —the white—
> that kills, but what you cannot[49]

In Young's riff on Leadbelly's tune, Basquiat stands at the center, carrying with him the knowledge of both Odysseus and Johnson. The painter is "ignoring the sirens," while he is also aware that no amount of "luxury" will prevent racial discrimination.[50] As David J. Leonard avers, the "sports world . . . routinely redeems, forgives, and humanizes white athletes, all while criminalizing and policing black athletes."[51] While Basquiat (and Young himself) are artists, not athletes like Johnson, the poem implies that they are similarly refused redemption, forgiveness, and, ultimately, humanization. The poem's final lines thus offer a cautionary addendum by suggesting that, despite Johnson's and, later, Basquiat's refusal to countenance anti-Black racism, there are forces beyond their control ("—the white—") conspiring to maintain systemic inequities.

In "St. Joe Louis Surrounded by Snakes," Young enriches his alternative lyrical history (and historiography) by showing the ways in which the public scrutiny of Johnson furnished a cultural script for the next Black heavyweight, Joe Louis, whereby triumph or defeat was inextricably linked to the capability or incapability of all people of African descent. Here we also see Young's attention to the interplay between the archive and the repertoire, as he draws on official accounts and Basquiat's identically titled painting *St. Joe Louis*

Surrounded by Snakes and interpolates them with his enjambed lines, which emphasize the multiple meanings we might infer from Louis's boxing career. That Young does not inhabit Louis's perspective, as he did previously in his Johnson poems, also points to Louis's lack of voice in a white-dominated sociocultural landscape in which only his body—not the "quiet" of his mind—seemed to matter. In this sense, Young suggests that the United States had made scant progress toward racial equality since Johnson's day, thereby undercutting teleological narratives that would place Black American athletes on a neat timeline of equitable change.

Mimicking Basquiat's appropriation of popular phrases and capitalized graffiti-style lettering, Young likewise makes use of ekphrasis to suggest the overdetermined nature of Louis's fights, which, much as was the case for Johnson, became representative of the success or failures of the Black community as a whole:

> MUST NOT YIELD.
> One night only—
> SCHH VS. SCH
>
> Hindenberged
> home, a hero.
> Uber—
>
> mensch
> © 1936
> KING
>
> FEATURES
> SYNDICATE—A
> Rematch
>
> against Saint
> Joe Louis,
> the whole of Harlem
>
> listening. All
> or nothing.[52]

Riffing on Basquiat's painting, which features a haloed Louis in the foreground with several men with devious grins flanking him, Young elucidates both the high political stakes and social vulnerability with which the boxer contended. Young especially alludes to the racialized social consequences of Louis's 1936 loss to and subsequent 1938 victory over the German boxer Max Schmeling, years when racial segregation was still legally sanctioned at home and the Nazis' fascist platform was gaining a stronghold in Europe.[53] Anthony O. Edmonds argues that Louis the individual was more or less lost amid the symbolic values projected onto him during this time: "'Joe Louis as a public symbol is more meaningful than Joe Louis as a fact.' Nowhere was this symbolism more vibrant than at the intersection of race and national identity, especially in the 1930s and early 1940s."[54] Using his enjambed lines to suggest the multiple ways in which to view this history, Young creatively recounts not the "real" Louis but rather the complex field of signification with which the boxer contended.

At the same time, Young retrains the gaze away from what Louis's victory meant for "might and manliness against the forces of fascism" and focuses instead on the repertoire of Black feelings accompanying Louis's eventual triumph over Schmeling:[55]

All the flags
of Harlem USA
raised

like fists.
Jubilee.
The Brown

Embalmer
in this corner
BOXED (X 3)[56]

A metonym for Black America, Harlem's proud embrace of Louis and other "Famous Negro Athletes" reframes their victories as acts of resistance to the United States' entrenched racism. Young places Louis's victory, for instance, alongside other pivotal moments, such as the emancipation of enslaved Black Americans (Jubilee) and, later, the Black Power salute given by the sprinters Tommie Smith and John Carlos at the 1968 Olympics in Mexico City. Playfully subverting Louis's moniker, the Brown Bomber, Young underscores the danger the boxer faced as a figure who, according to the long-standing pattern of white fetish and fear of Black athletes, was essentially boxed into a corner "(X 3)" as a result of his success.

Augmenting both Basquiat's titular reference to and sketch of the "snakes" surrounding Louis, Young's enjambed lines formally evince the paradoxes of Louis's success in the ring. On the one hand, Louis had ascended to royalty by defeating Schmeling, who had come to be seen as an embodiment of the ideology of white supremacy; on the other, his success made him vulnerable to exploitation:

> his gloves down.
> CROWN.
> Trainers round
>
> his neck like towels
> halo
> hiss his cauliflower ear.[57]

With "his gloves down," Louis becomes prey to the trainers and other vested authorities who wished to capitalize on the boxer's success. We can read these sweat-drenched towels as either a souvenir of Louis's triumph (a "halo") or reminiscent of the noose-like constraint ("Trainers round / his neck like towels") placed on him now that he has inadvertently become representative of the entirety of African America, as Johnson was before him. Young observes in his endnote for this poem, "Gentleman Joe pictured in the corner of a room, slight slouch, by photographer Irving Penn would seem to be one inspiration for this painting. The snakes in BSQT's title refer to the Brown Bomber's managers and others—for Louis, tho he made millions, in the end welcomed folks to Vegas from a wheelchair & died impoverished."[58] Lyrically reframing Louis's career from a contemporary Black perspective, and via Basquiat's portrait, Young offers an alternative "truth of things," to refer back to Rancière, illuminating in particular the ways in which Louis was caught up in a recurring pattern (or repertoire) of objectifying, exploitative, and also defiant acts that can be traced back to Johnson.

"Monarchs," the poem that follows, more specifically highlights Young's interest in excavating Black experiences that are not readily available in historical documents. As the archivist Marlene

Manoff asserts, "If the archive cannot or does not accommodate a particular kind of information or mode of scholarship, then it is effectively excluded from the historical record."[59] "Monarchs" suggests these epistemological flaws in historiographic methods that rely too heavily on tangible artifacts and records, particularly since Black figures and experiences were often excluded from the vaults and annals on which US social memory is constructed. Evincing these omissions, "Monarchs" reproduces only partial lineups for the famed Negro League baseball team the Kansas City Monarchs from 1920 through 1945—for example, 1929 lists Newt Allen, Bullet Joe Rogan, and Tom Young, while 1932 only lists James "Cool Papa" Bell.[60] Moreover, some Monarchs' positions and places of birth are listed ("Paige, Leroy 'Satchel' P Mobile"), whereas for others, only the position is listed ("Washington, 'Blue' 1b").[61] While many Negro League historians have dedicated themselves to the task of reconstructing full rosters and statistics,[62] Young's gaps and elisions represent the effacement of Black experiences in the records of US life.

"Monarchs" concludes by exposing precisely these archival silences: "Before Baird sold the franchise [in] 1955, he sold / 8 Monarchs to the majors & 4 to the minors. / The details of transactions not reported."[63] Not unlike Young's earlier account of the white mob violence that erupted in the aftermath of Johnson's 1910 victory over Jeffries—"JOHNSON WINS / WHITES LYNCH / 70 ARRESTED"[64]—this dispassionate reporting of Baird's financial transactions bespeaks of the archive's inadequacies when it comes to the lives and (mis)fortunes of Black athletes and other figures. Put another way, Young reminds readers that "rather than verifiable truths, the archive—and its silences—house the very questions that unsettle us."[65] The white team owner Baird's sale of Monarchs players to white-owned major and minor league teams is reminiscent of slavery, and the transactions themselves are "not reported." By reproducing these scant records on the printed page, Young underscores the systemic erasure of Black points of view, even when it comes to sports—one of the few arenas in which African Americans have had opportunities (albeit inconsistently) to climb the socioeconomic ladder. Paired with poems about Johnson, Louis, and Basquiat, among others, "Monarchs" thus demonstrates the key role that *To Repel Ghosts* plays in reanimating the repertoire, as well as writing back against racial biases within the archives and dominant narratives of US history more generally.

"Red Wash—Fists Up"

The collection's subsequent two poems, "Muhammad Ali by Andy Warhol" and "Cassius Clay by Basquiat," take up similarly significant epistemological concerns by constructing a multimodal, intergenerational, and interracial dialogue about the visual representations of Black athletes. Like many of the poems in *To Repel Ghosts*, these poems are ekphrastic, furnishing new understandings of Basquiat's and Andy Warhol's paintings by pointing out the implications of the colors, lines, and images that convey each artist's interpretation of the cultural meaning of Ali. As the poet Vievee Francis notes, ekphrasis poetry engenders "the possibility of engagement with the art (and its referents as well as the artist), the poet writing in response to the art, and any other poets who have also responded to the art," thereby allowing for "fresh modes of acknowledgment and interrogation."[66] This is precisely the polysemous approach that Young adopts as he draws on an array of allusions to Ali's life and career, while thematizing not only the final image stretched onto each painter's canvas but also the ways in which these Ali portraits reflect distinctly racialized interpretations of the meaning of iconic figures of African descent. Further, utilizing an ekphrastic mode, Young self-reflexively acknowledges that his is not the only interpretation but rather another way to approach Basquiat's canvas and the celebrity boxers that they feature. As such, Young points to the necessity of viewing US cultural history capaciously, using all of the various modes at one's disposal rather than relying on the white-dominated media or institutional archives for truths about Black athletes, artists, and individuals from all walks of life.

Young interprets Warhol's 1977 painting, which combines acrylic, silkscreen, and ink, as an homage to Ali; yet his descriptions (augmented by a return to the boxing-jab rhythms of the Jack Johnson series) also suggest the white anxieties that were projected onto both heavyweight champions. As Early avers, "No black athlete since the reign of Jack Johnson (1908–15), the first black heavyweight champion, so enraged most whites, and more than a few blacks, with his opinions and the way he chose to live his life."[67] Although Young does not register this racial animus in Warhol's portrait, he does suggest some of the reasons that many Americans condemned Ali, specifically for his refusal to "know his (subordinate) place."[68] With Young's characteristic enjambment, he begins "Muhammad Ali by Andy Warhol" with a series of references to Ali's notorious braggadocio and public harassment of his opponents—"loose / talker. Your / mama"—and then segues into an interpretation of the symbolic significance of Warhol's chosen image:

> Colorful
> in Warhol
>
> 's red wash—
> fists up.[69]

In Warhol's portrait, the boxer is featured, much like in a promotional photograph for one of his fights, as an intimidating man with his "fists up" and the suggestion of the blood ("red wash") that he will exact from his opponent in the ring.

Young also remixes this history in order to reflect his own post–Civil Rights reading of Black boxing, including the final years of Ali's career, which have notable parallels with the tragic ends for Johnson, Louis, and Basquiat. Early further notes, "On March 8, 1971, he [Ali] lost to undefeated Philadelphian Joe Frazier, Ali's archrival and the man he most ridiculed throughout his career, in a close fifteen-round decision at Madison Square Garden in what was the richest, most publicized sporting event in American history. The fight was so brutal that both men were hospitalized after, Frazier for several weeks. It was Ali's first defeat."[70] Frazier and Ali would fight two subsequent times, with their 1975 bout "so savage that it was thought that neither [boxer] should fight again."[71] Young lyrically restages this public bloodbath, suggesting Ali's unwillingness to relinquish his role as the fiercest (not to mention funniest) Black athlete:

> Battled Frazier—
> *that ugly gorilla*
> (whose grandmother

had blond hair
down to here) enough

times to shorten both
their lives. Hospitalized.[72]

Young takes readers behind the slick surface of Warhol's silkscreen painting to reimagine the racialized cultural scripts that compelled both Ali and Frazier to battle each other almost to the death for the heavyweight crown. While Young does not criticize Ali and Frazier for their chosen profession, he does humanize the tragic aspects of their experiences in the limelight ("enough / times to shorten both / their lives. Hospitalized"). These men "battled" each other rather than dismantling the white power structures that deemed it permissible for Frazier and Ali to become boxing champions (by the 1960s, anyway) but not to excel in other fields. As Ratchford points out, "Because of the historical legacy of American institutional racism, sports became a central strategy for socioeconomic vitality and success for many African American men at the expense of the pursuit of success in education, public policy, and business."[73] He adds that "it could be argued that American society valued inclusion of African Americans in sports more than in its broader society."[74] Interpreting Warhol's representation of Ali, Young alludes to these dynamics, implying that Ali's iconicity is directly linked not only to Johnson's and Louis's celebrity but also to white America's acceptance of Blacks into particular cultural spaces, such as the boxing ring, which has tended to perpetuate rather than erode racial stereotypes of Blacks as more physically than mentally capable.

As "Muhammad Ali by Andy Warhol" continues, Young considers the ways in which a white fascination with the "other" and with Black men more specifically as both exotic and menacing may have informed Warhol's portrait. Through Young's ekphrastic rendering of the canvas, he reorients this hegemonic perspective, producing what bell hooks terms "an oppositional gaze" that reconfigures "history as counter-memory":[75]

Lips fat
as their bank

as bacon. Swelled
heads. His skin

tone brown,
even, mixed

by an assistant—
still the lips

are his, not stock
or air-

brushed. Full.
No smile.[76]

Young's comparison between Ali's lips and "bacon" alludes to the animality projected onto Black Americans. As Young envisions the process of constructing the painting, whereby the "skin / tone" is "mixed / by an assistant," he calls attention to the layers of separation between the boxer and white spectators like Warhol to whom Ali was likely both fascinating and frightening. Young notes, for example, that the lips are painted in earnest ("not stock / or air- // brushed"), but there is also "No smile," implying the suspicion that this heavyweight champion, as with Johnson before him, invoked in a US public not especially interested in teasing out Ali the complex (and even "quiet") man from derogatory myths circulating about Black male criminality.

Alternatively, in Young's reading of Basquiat's Ali portrait, "Cassius Clay by Basquiat," he underscores the boxer's challenge to hegemonic power structures, stitching a common thread that binds Johnson, Ali, and Basquiat. Reframing white America's understanding of Ali as "the 'wrong type' of black" who needed to be "'put in his place,'"[77] Young sees in Basquiat's work an identification with Ali's iconoclastic approach that was self-righteous, boastful, and above all else defiant of the white-engineered codes of conduct for Black male athletes. The poem commences with Ali's own words of affirmation, resonating, albeit briefly, with the first-person accounts of Johnson's alternating self-confidence and psychic pain as a spectacularized Black man: "*I'm pretty! / I shook up / the world!* Clay shouts."[78] Rather than the "brushed. Full" lips Young observes in Warhol's painting, here Ali self-identifies as "*pretty!*" both cutting against the grain of caricatured attributes (i.e., full lips) imputed to people of African descent and the conflation of whiteness with beauty.

Additionally, Ali, like Johnson before him and Basquiat and Young after him, refused to be grateful to white America for "permitting" him to become famous, resisting the role of Black supplicant and, as noted in both this and the previous poem, paying a very public price for it. Not unlike the legal consequences of Johnson's defiance of white-supremacist codes, "in June 1967, Ali was convicted in federal court of violation of the Selective Service Act and sentenced to five years in prison and fined ten thousand dollars. . . . For the next three and one-half years, Ali, free on bond while appealing his case (which he eventually won unanimously on appeal to the U.S. Supreme Court on a technicality on June 28, 1971), was prohibited from boxing."[79] Young formally conveys the context of Ali's courageous act through enjambed lines:

> —Army taking away
> his right to fight
>
> when he won't fight
> them Viet Cong[80]

The multiple meanings of "fight" here are suggestive of the two battles that Black athletes have long been waging, between their putative opponents and a US government and society that has systematically thwarted their inclusion in the body politic. The poem's staccato rhythm reinforces this long-standing pattern by echoing the jabs in the boxing ring that, since Johnson's breakthrough, allowed for Black socioeconomic mobility while facilitating greater public scrutiny and often contempt. Remixing Ali's explanation for refusing the draft ("Viet Cong / who've done him / nothing wrong") with his own colloquialisms ("Houston, we gots / a problem"), Young also interlaces the archive and the repertoire in order to imply the residue of both in the contemporary landscape.[81]

We need only recall the NFL's 2018 decision to fine teams whose players do not stand for the national anthem to be reminded of how little has changed. As Michael-Shawn Dugar observes, the NFL "told the players not to disrespect the anthem and keep any acts of protest in the locker room, where no one can see them. It's a notion that makes about as much sense as being forced to stand for a song that ends with a line about the 'land of the free.'"[82] As

Young's creative recuperation of Black athletes suggests, expressing individuality and resisting the racial status quo always comes at a high cost for African Americans. Ali's highly publicized defiance and punishment were in many respects a replay of Johnson's Mann Act conviction, and professional football players are only the latest figures to be caught in the crosshairs of white America's fear of public resistance to its sociopolitical stronghold.

As Taylor notes of the repertoire of performances, "We've seen it all before."[83] Nonetheless, "the frictions between plot and character (on the level of narrative) and embodiment (social actors) make for some of the most remarkable instances of parody and resistance in performance traditions in the Americas."[84] While Ali and his boxing predecessors (not to mention Basquiat) are not actors, arguably the sports arena is its own theater, with these figures working within the same repertoire of complicity, parody, and resistance as do their counterparts on more traditional dramatic stages. Young makes use of ekphrastic poetry to recover these dynamics, while infusing the flat canvases of Basquiat's paintings with his own twenty-first-century lyric ruminations. The conclusion of "Cassius Clay by Basquiat" is especially concerned with the ways in which Black male athletes (and other African American celebrities) have, at least since Johnson's day, transgressed the behaviors demanded of their assigned roles:

> Ali, now he could hit you
> into next year—
> but apart from the flogging,
>
> his flaunting, were the taunts
> challengers heard ringing
>
> *Uncle Tom! Come on*
> *Come on White America!*
>
> even above the ten count
> & crowd—his undented smile—
>
> that smarts still.[85]

While Basquiat honors Ali, Young imagines a discursive repertoire for Basquiat's canvas that helps to explain why a hip celebrity painter invested so deeply in boxing icons and other "Famous Negro Athletes." Ali and others, Young implies, charted an alternative course for Black fame that actively resisted white control. The poem's final lines underscore this rich tradition of public and "quiet" expressions of agency that link Basquiat, his athlete heroes, and Young, who "smarts" and "smile[s]" with his nimble lyricism.

Whereas traditional histories and biographies are wedded to empirical methodologies, Young's double entendres, ekphrastic engagements with Basquiat's paintings, interpolated archival materials, and the staccato rhythm of a round of boxing jabs work in choreographed conjunction, opening up new, transhistorical ways of engaging the Black icons who embody what it means to stand center stage but to remain socially and politically marginalized. For instance, in much the same way that former San Francisco 49ers quarterback Colin Kaepernick was maneuvered out of the National Football League by owners who simply did not offer the player a contract,[86] Johnson was not denied the right to box but rather convicted of the unrelated Mann Act. In turn, Ali's public commitment to the Black Muslim faith arguably led to his being drafted to serve in Vietnam; for his refusal, he was charged with violating the Selective Service Act and only acquitted on a technicality. As previously noted, Joe Louis spent his retirement years mired in financial woes and pursued by the Internal Revenue Service. Upon his death in 1981, he was employed at Caesars Palace in Las Vegas, where he worked from his wheelchair as a "greeter." A different kind of ignominy befell Basquiat, who died of a drug overdose at the age of twenty-seven. The common denominator that unites these disparate figures is the paradox of Black (male) celebrity: on the one hand, their public platforms enabled their shared resistance to the mechanisms of white supremacy; on the other, that same hypervisibility made them vulnerable to the (white) US public's contempt and censure.

By calling forth and remixing traces of the archive and the repertoire, *To Repel Ghosts* shows us the ways in which white America performed this same script with different actors, thereby implying the continued resonance of these prescribed roles and players' resistance to them in the contemporary landscape. Moreover, as Rancière notes, "in literature, intentions don't count. If the author has to say what he's doing, that means he hasn't done it."[87] Through Young's multimodal approach, which utilizes an economy of rich staccato lyricism, historical fragments, ekphrastic possibilities, and enjambment, among other strategies, his poetics pressure progressive narratives of US cultural history while elucidating the complexities of Black fame. Further, *To Repel Ghosts* exemplifies creative writers' crucial role in exposing and exceeding the limitations of traditional historiographic methods. Young, as with his contemporaries considered in the pages ahead, makes use of the imagination to consider the embodied acts and interior thoughts that are not often part of the written record, especially for individuals subject to intense public scrutiny and degradation. In chapter 2, we will see Adrian Matejka's collection *The Big Smoke* (2013) revivify other aspects of Jack Johnson's public and "quiet" (à la Quashie) personae, underscoring the continued resonance of his experiences for understanding the discursive interplay of race, gender, and fame in the sporting arena.

2

"MORE OF A MAN THAN YOU"

The Many Faces of Jack Johnson in Adrian Matejka's The Big Smoke

In Jack Johnson's 1927 autobiography, *Jack Johnson—In the Ring—and Out*, he reflects on his remarkable life and career: "In looking back over the years of my tumultuous career, I am astounded when I realize that there are few men in any period of the world's history, who have led a more varied or intense existence than I."[1] While Johnson was notoriously boastful, neither his estimation of his sociocultural impact nor his sense of the broader meaning of his story is an exaggeration. As we learned in chapter 1's examination of Kevin Young's *To Repel Ghosts: The Remix from the Original Masters* (2005), Johnson's paradoxical celebrity experiences as the first Black heavyweight champion set the stage for a wide range of Black artists and athletes to be both celebrated and pathologized. His fungibility as a figure who loomed larger than life in the white-supremacist imagination and yet whose individual humanity was routinely unrecognized furnished a script for the treatment of famous citizens of African descent that has remained stubbornly intact even over a century after Johnson first claimed his heavyweight title.

In this chapter, I examine Indiana Poet Laureate Adrian Matejka's creative recuperation of Johnson in his award-winning collection *The Big Smoke* (2013)—winner of the Anisfield-Wolf Book Award and a finalist for both the 2013 National Book Award and the 2014 Pulitzer Prize. While Matejka does not cite Young's *To Repel Ghosts* as an influence, his more comprehensive portrait of the heavyweight champion, as well as Johnson's wives and lovers, complements and significantly extends Young's portrait while affirming persona poetry as a resonant vehicle for reimagining early Black celebrity in general and Johnson in particular. For instance, Matejka noted in an interview that he was reading an array of his contemporaries' persona poems as he was entering the consciousness of Jack Johnson: "There are so many project books I admire. . . . I just want to list a few (and there were many more than this) that I read for inspiration while I was working on *The Big Smoke*: Gabrielle Calvocoressi's *Apocalyptic Swing*, Tyehimba Jess's *Leadbelly*, A. Van Jordan's *M-A-C-N-O-L-I-A*, Quraysh Ali Lansana's *They Shall Run: Harriet Tubman Poems*, Oliver de la Paz's *Names Above Houses*, and Patricia Smith's *Blood Dazzler*."[2] This list suggests that, while Johnson is Matejka's primary subject, he is working in community with other poets to embody perspectives that both are rendered one-dimensionally in more conventional histories and are especially relevant to making legible the residue of the past on present constellations of race and gender.

Moreover, as with the collections Matejka cites, *The Big Smoke* has been critically applauded but not extensively studied. The critic Ryan Sharp's 2019 article on the collection has begun to fill in this gap by placing *The Big Smoke* within a broader conversation about African American persona poetry and archives. Sharp highlights Matejka's interlacing of his research with his imaginative understanding of Johnson to arrive at a more complex portrait of this African American icon: "both the found and the imagined exhibit the same capacity for truth and meaning-making and, as a result, neither is privileged."[3] As previously noted, in *Bad Men: Creative Touchstones of Black Writers* (2020), Howard Rambsy II considers *The Big Smoke* alongside Young's *To Repel Ghosts* and Tyehimba Jess's *leadbelly*, calling attention to their lyric rendering of the complexities of the bad man trope in African American culture. As Rambsy argues, "*The Big Smoke* further enriched poetic domains concerning bad men, providing poets with even more blueprints for producing chronicles in verse of sensational and defiant African American cultural figures."[4] Extending Sharp's and Rambsy's analyses, I consider the archival and historiographic implications of Matejka's collection. In particular, I argue that *The Big Smoke* lyrically braids together what Diana Taylor conceives of as "archive" and "repertoire" in order to shed new light on Johnson's legacy. Taylor notes that the repertoire "enacts embodied memory: performances, gestures, orality, movement, dancing, singing—in short, all those acts usually thought of as ephemeral, nonreproducible knowledge"; further, "as opposed to the supposedly stable objects in the archive, the actions that are the repertoire do not remain the same. The repertoire both keeps and transforms choreographies of meaning."[5] While Matejka's collection is textual, not a live performance, the poems therein reenact and rescript both interior, affective experiences and written documents, thereby infusing new meanings into the "choreographies" of Johnson's life.

As I contend, *The Big Smoke* is not as much concerned with recounting Johnson's biography as with exposing the archive as a site of ideological contestation and epistemological instability, while attempting to reimagine the voices and perspectives that hegemonic forces have shunted aside. Matejka's "Notes" provide a profitable glimpse into his creative process, explaining, for example, "Jack Johnson was a natural fabulist and never let the truth get in the way of a good story, so I used his autobiographies *In the Ring and Out*, *Jack Johnson Is a Dandy*, and *My Life and Battles* as organizational resources for the collection's narrative."[6] In addition to his riffs on Johnson's own accounts, Matejka cites a range of biographies that "were crucial to the development of this project,"[7] but, as with the other poetry collections and novels that the present book takes up, historical and archival sources do not determine the repertoire of psychological and emotional truths brought to bear on *The Big Smoke*. "An aesthetic of quiet," Kevin Quashie notes, "is not incompatible with black culture, but to notice and understand it requires a shift in how we read, what we look for, and what we expect, even what we remain open to."[8] Focalizing Johnson's inner life, *The Big Smoke* retrains readers' attention so that we are drawn into the transoms of the boxer's interior landscape, rather than fixating on his overdetermined body.

As Matejka recalibrates and supplements his sources with lyric imagery and persona poetry, he also suggests absences in both popular discourse and conventional historiographies about Black celebrity. As Jacques Rancière points out, literature can play an integral role in redistributing this power over cultural memory and providing other portals to the past: "In short, literature provides a different sensorium, a different way of linking a power to perceptibly affect and a power to signify. Now, a different community of sense and of the perceptible, a different relationship between words and beings, also means a different common world and a different people."[9] Accordingly, *The Big Smoke* reframes dominant understandings of Johnson, tracking implicit through lines between the paradoxes and perils he experienced in the postbellum limelight and those of Black athletes today. Matejka specifically highlights the consequences of the boxer's efforts to become "a man *with* power, and a man *of* power."[10] For example, the Johnson persona proclaims, "I'm pure-blooded American / of the first rate," while his first wife, Etta Duryea, admits, "hit hit hit. No / babies, thanks to Papa's [Johnson's] hits."[11] Inhabiting the personae of Johnson, his alter ego ("the Shadow"), Etta, and his lovers, Belle Schreiber and Hattie McClay, Matejka illuminates the suffering that the heavyweight champion inflicted through his violent and ultimately futile attempts to be recognized as an empowered man in a structurally racist nation. Through Matejka's *re*presentation of Johnson's archive and repertoire and a Rancièrean "different common world" more generally, he evinces the ramifications of both anti-Black racism and toxic masculinity, especially as they collide and intersect in the United States' past and present sporting arenas.

"I've Heard This Same Song My Whole Life"

While Kevin Young's lyrical portrait of Johnson began in medias res with the boxer already the most notorious Black man in the world, Matejka journeys back to the beginning of the boxer's career, reimagining his justification for boxing in the first place. *The Big Smoke* charts the boxer's remarkable experiences from a poverty-stricken young man to the internationally renowned (and, in some circles, despised) heavyweight champion and finally to his retirement years, when he was forced to perform a caricature of his former self in Hubert's Museum and Flea Circus. In many ways, these twists and turns mark the zenith-to-nadir trajectories of Black experiences in the postbellum period, and thus it is no wonder that

Matejka, following Young, finds in Johnson a story worth retelling. As Louis Moore argues of postbellum Black boxers, "For a black man, boxing gave him release from the daily indignities he suffered because of his race. It allowed him, in other words, to be a man."[12] Via Johnson's first-person perspective, Matejka's poetry recounts these circumstances, suggesting that Johnson was more or less forced to use his body in order to survive in a late-nineteenth-century social landscape characterized by "the ongoing exploitation and control of blacks."[13]

As noted in chapter 1, Johnson was born in 1878 in Galveston, Texas, to two ex-slaves, Henry and Tina ("Tiny"), and his childhood was spent in the crosshairs of the sociocultural and political struggles over the newly granted Black citizenship rights ushered in by Reconstruction and the white-supremacist backlash that resulted in a curtailing of those rights throughout the early years of Johnson's life. While boxing offered Johnson social mobility, his participation in the sport was double-edged from the start, particularly as "before the Civil War it was a common, if barbaric, betting practice for white slave owners to force Black slaves to fight to the death in a makeshift boxing ring."[14] Recounting Johnson's entry into the postbellum boxing arena, Theresa Runstedtler describes the same dehumanizing practices: "White promoters often trolled the rail yards in search of itinerant Black youths to participate in these bloody free-for-all fights. Usually three or more blindfolded African American boys were pitted against each other in the ring. A Springfield man had approached Johnson about trying his luck in such a fight. Still without a manager to underwrite his expenses and arrange his matches, the half-starved Johnson agreed to participate in a battle royal in exchange for food, housing, and a $1.50 purse."[15] While historians have laid bare this brutal history of exploitation, Matejka's opening section, titled "Hurt Business," is adept at rendering Johnson's repertoire of inner thoughts and feelings, particularly regarding the pain and humiliation that even Johnson's own autobiographies shy away from.

The opening poem, "Battle Royal," illuminates the transmogrification of the cruel and unusual sport of bear baiting to "battle royals," or the pitting of blindfolded Black man against each other in a ring:

I believe you need
eyes more than you need teeth

in a fight, but losing either makes
a bear a little less mean. Once baiting

was against the law, some smart
somebody figured coloreds fight

just as hard if they hungry enough.[16]

Telling the story from Johnson's perspective, Matejka underscores the dehumanizing experience of being forced to subject oneself to the predatory fantasies of "some smart" white men. Moreover, reversing the white gaze, boxing (and sports more generally) is reimagined not as a meritocratic pipeline to economic stability but rather as an arena for further subjugation:

When the bell rang,
it seemed like I got hit from eight
directions.[17]

Despite the abjectly violent circumstances, Johnson puts all of his physical force into winning, "because the man said only / the last darky on his feet gets a meal."[18] Many readers of this poem will recall the famously surreal first chapter of Ralph Ellison's *Invisible Man* (1952), in which the narrator (the "invisible man") similarly participates in a "battle royal" staged for the entertainment of the southern town's white male gentry. These resonances speak to, as Rancière noted earlier, the importance of literature for illustrating not only the facts of racial spectacles but also the affective dejection for those who endure them.

From Johnson's vantage point, Matejka provides a starkly realist account of the reasons—namely, hunger—why the man who later became the first Black heavyweight champion of the world was motivated to engage in such a brutally humiliating performance. That is, "Battle Royal" traces a genealogy of such spectacles to the late nineteenth century, whereby Black people were striving to survive in an economy designed to perpetuate their exploitation. As Runstedtler avers, "Even today, the hypervisibility of black athletes has not translated into increased black political power or racial equality more generally. Instead, this hypervisibility has become a frequent point of critique for white conservatives and certain members of the black middle class. There has been a tendency to blame black youth, particularly those from poor and working-class backgrounds, for their overinvestment in the cultural arena and, in particular, for their supposed 'sports fixation.'"[19] Returning to the period in which such racialized double standards were incubating, readers are able to consider why scores of African Americans enter a sporting arena in which, statistically speaking, they have little chance of financial success and, if they do become professionals, they risk becoming, to borrow a felicitous phrase from William Rhoden, "forty million dollar slaves."[20]

Elucidating Johnson's interior thoughts, Matejka likewise shows him struggling to establish a sense of self disentangled from the derogatory images of Black men circulating in the postbellum era, while relentlessly pursuing the mantle of hegemonic masculinity that was always already foreclosed to him. In "Shadow Knows," the first of several "Shadow" poems to come, Matejka riffs on the shadow boxing that Johnson engaged in as part of his training, whereas his alter ego voices the feelings and aspirations that the boxer could not publicly express without white scorn and potential retribution:

> *None of that* yassuh,
> boss & *watermelon rind*
> *smile for us.*[21]

Instead, Johnson desires "*high- / styling clothing, gold rings*," as well as "*More women than coats / White women in our architecture.*"[22] All of these patriarchal, capitalist pursuits will be acquired through sports: "*We want to be / prize fighting's main attraction.*"[23] On the one hand, Matejka imagines Johnson casting off the trappings of racist caricatures such as the docile, happy-go-lucky Sambo; on the other hand, Johnson's desire to display the acquisition of jewels and white women—both presented as commodities—implies his internalization of hegemonic notions of success in the United States.

Similarly, in the poem "Courtship," Matejka emphasizes Johnson's investment in dominant conceptions of masculinity, which, as Michael Kimmel notes, are especially bound up in "power, success, wealth, and status," including the ability to dominate women.[24] The Johnson persona boasts to Hattie McClay of the riches he will bestow on her:

> We can bathe
> in champagne, dry
> ourselves with hundred-
> dollar bills.[25]

Johnson's flaunting of both his money and his affection for white women like McClay was an especially daring move considering that "nearly seven hundred Negroes had been lynched in the United States since 1900, some simply because someone had whispered that they had been 'too familiar' with white women."[26] Despite these attempts to gain entry into the coveted circle of masculine dominance and respect, Johnson, as Matejka underscores, lacked the prerequisite whiteness.

To evince this point, Matejka mobilizes newspaper headlines to the poetic page, drawing readers into the archive of the United States' sporting life to expose the endemic racism that dogged Johnson and all other citizens of African descent, as well as to question the authority of empirical histories to excavate the complexities of Black celebrity. The poem title "TEXAS AUTHORITIES WILL PROSECUTE THE CHAMPION IF HE TAKES WHITE WIFE" demonstrates the fear and loathing that Johnson engendered when he crossed the lines drawn to reinforce white male dominance. Matejka provides the full citation in his "Notes": "The title is a byline excerpt from the *Chicago Tribune* (March 12, 1909). The full byline is 'Beware Mr. Jack Johnson: Texas Authorities Will Prosecute the Champion if He Takes White Wife to That State.'"[27] As Matejka incorporates these historical accounts into his lyrical landscape, he enjoins readers to face the biases inscribed into the official records of US history, both debunking the myth that a "just the facts" approach is neutral and using the poetic landscape to voice the alternative perspectives undocumented in mainstream (white) periodicals such as the *Chicago Tribune*. For example, Matejka's Johnson counters the racism embedded in a criminal justice system that would arrest him for marrying the woman he loves—"I have the right / to choose who / my mate will be"—defamiliarizing the logic of segregationists and reminding contemporary readers that there was no era in which such prohibitions against love were justified.[28]

Another poem later in the collection, "Carefree as a Plantation Darky in Watermelon Time," functions similarly, exposing the limitations of the archive when it comes to constructing cultural memory and making use of persona poetry to advance a counternarrative. Matejka's "Notes" cite "the *Baltimore American* (July 2, 1910)" as the source for this headline, which refers to Johnson's victory over Jack Jeffries, the former heavyweight Jim Jeffries's younger brother. Making use of this repugnantly racist headline as the poem's title, Matejka then segues into the Johnson persona's interior monologue of the fight, not only inverting the white-supremacist gaze but also, echoing Taylor, debunking the myth that the archive is "unmediated" and thus more historically valuable than the repertoire.[29] The Johnson persona notes, "I put Jack down at the beginning of Round / Five. Naturally, I was surprised to find I was / a ten-to-four underdog to the older Jeffries," suggesting that the white press as well as sports enthusiasts were motivated more by racism than by an objective appraisal of these boxers' abilities.[30] Via Johnson's interior thoughts, Matejka similarly evinces the boxer's utter loneliness as a man who has enormous talents but who is feared and loathed (not to mention underestimated) by a racist US public: "If I felt any better, I'd be afraid of myself. I'm so fast I only got my shadow / to spar with."[31] Rather than relying solely on Johnson's autobiographies, white media accounts, or the imaginative persona that Matejka inhabits, *The Big Smoke* places them in dialogue, underscoring the need to view past and present through this multimodal lens. As Sharp describes, Matejka establishes "a nonhierarchical relationship with the imagined, and although the found might have a superficial appearance of objectivity, both the found and the imagined exhibit the same capacity for truth and meaning-making and, as a result, neither is privileged."[32] "The languages of law, contracts, insurance documents, newspapers, and art historical writing," Wendy W. Walters adds, "are as open to interpretive pressure as the creative text itself. This reexamination enables us to posit and imagine pasts that exceed material documentation, and helps make clear that the past actually does exist in the present."[33] Showing the prejudices underwriting the materials utilized to construct narratives of US cultural history, *The Big Smoke* illuminates instead "a different community of sense and of the perceptible," as Rancière might put it.

Further, the biases that Matejka exposes remain embedded in the ways that today's white-dominated media covers Black athletes. For example, in an effort to confront and reconcile structural racism, John Eligon and Brandon K. Thorp's recent article "Missed in Coverage about Jack Johnson, the Racism around Him" investigated the *New York Times*'s coverage of Johnson: "'The big black' and 'the big negro' are just two of the phrases that *The New York Times* used to describe Jack Johnson." Additionally, Johnson's race "permeated how the newspaper covered every detail of his life, from his boxing to his legal troubles to his demeanor and success." Eligon and Thorp likewise note their discomfort in the lack of change in the white media's response to tenacious Black athletes from Johnson's era through our own: "Today, people still seem to struggle with black athletes who are outspoken. So while the harsh and sometimes racist tone of the coverage came as no surprise, it was jarring still."[34] Such acknowledgments of historical bias, which are few and far between, confirm the danger of relying solely on official records (or archives) to explain the experiences of famous Black men, seemingly not only in the postbellum period but also in the twenty-first century.

Through *The Big Smoke*, an epithetic title that in and of itself affirms the extreme animus that Johnson was up against, Matejka engages readers in a form of creative reckoning, which allows other voices and perspectives to come to the fore. As Rambsy notes, "By offering Johnson's inner thoughts in contract to the printed slurs, Matejka gives the boxer a space to produce counterstatements to the degrading coverage."[35] Indeed, while Matejka's poetic portrait is no more verifiable than a strictly historical account is, he utilizes self-reflexive, multivalent strategies that offer a more complex picture of Johnson as neither hero nor menace but instead as a simultaneously courageous and flawed individual. Matejka ruminates, for example, on the physical abuse that appears to have been an integral part of Johnson's romantic liaisons. Matejka's "Notes" explain, "One file worth mentioning is the Department of Justice File 164211. The file catalogues the government's case in Johnson's

1913 Mann Act conviction and the subsequent surveillance of Johnson once he fled the United States. Though the incidents related to the trial do not directly appear in the book, the Belle Schreiber interview poems are a response to documents included in the file."[36] In the poem "Fisticuff Difficulty," Matejka transcribes an "*Excerpt from Belle Schreiber's interview with Agent T.S. Marshall. October 30, 1912*," drawing on this testimony to both document other perspectives on Johnson and to illustrate the inherent biases and gaps in archival records typically relied on to narrativize US cultural history. Marshall asks Belle, "*Since he's a Negro and a prize fighter, you knew he had a violent temperament*," to which she replies, "I knew violence was in him, but I didn't know what he was capable of. One time, he took me to see Etta in the hospital. She was asleep and her face was lumpy like a sack of potatoes. He told me, 'This is what happens if you don't do what Papa says.'"[37] In response to the next question, "*Did you ever fear for your life?*" Belle recalls, "Papa never said he was sorry after he beat me. He'd smile that gold smile and say, 'I'm a prince, ain't I?' Then he'd go soak his hands in cold water."[38] Giving voice to women's experiences on the sidelines of the boxing arena—accounts that are often ignored in sweeping narratives about male competition—Matejka evinces the dark and troubling consequences of Johnson's quest for hegemonic masculinity; at the same time, Matejka shows the white power structure's obsession with finding and publicizing information that would strip the heavyweight champion of any public dignity he might have accrued through his victories in the ring.

Rancière notes that poetry is especially adept at illuminating "the directions thinking in general can take, along with their political implications."[39] Read this way, it is not only *The Big Smoke*'s exposure of violence against women that is key here but also its destabilization of a purely empirical approach that, on the one hand, elucidates the mechanisms by which hegemonic versions of history are produced ("the directions thinking in general can take") and, on the other, interpolates and supplements these narratives with imaginative alternatives. For instance, Matejka augments his archival findings with lyrical letters from Hattie to Belle, further complicating the portrait of both the "Black brute" propagated by white authorities and the valiant "prince" advanced by Johnson himself.

In *Jack Johnson—In the Ring—and Out*, the boxer asserts, "My marriages and my loves have been sincere. They have been clean. The women who have come into my life have been honored, and lovingly protected by me. To them I have given the utmost consideration and kindness; to none of them have I been cruel, and never was I lacking in my responsibilities for their welfare and happiness."[40] Yet, in Matejka's "Letter to Belle (September 15, 1909)," Hattie writes, "Being with Papa makes me feel important. He does not beat me much either. When we are together he always has one of those big hands on my tit or around my throat. It is just play for us. Make sure it is the same for you."[41] Both women were sex workers—"sporting women," as the Johnson persona calls them—and Matejka shows Hattie and Belle's (albeit temporary) alliance to be forged along class and gender lines with their shared desire to gain social stature through their affairs with Johnson.[42]

Moreover, in Belle's testimony to "*Agent T.S. Marshall, October 30, 2012*," recounted in the poem "Introductions," she relishes the memory of the attention Johnson lavished on her, making it clear that such respect was unique for a woman of her stature: "Once we were together, he rented an apartment for me near the lake. He paid for everything and called me 'Mrs. Jack Johnson.' He introduced me that way wherever he went."[43] At the same time, Matejka evinces Johnson's nearly unrelenting abuse, as well as his unwavering belief in patriarchal codes. As Johnson puts it in "Cooking Lessons," "Belle, I wouldn't put my hand on you if you'd do what I say."[44] Johnson also justifies his behavior by asserting, "Belle, a woman is still / a woman & the female mind / is much slower than a man's."[45] Highlighting Johnson's domestic crimes, as well as his sexist attitudes, Matejka expounds on the facets of Johnson's life that often go unnoted both in the boxer's own narratives and, as Sharp points out, "within a cultural narrative prone to either heroization or vilification for Johnson's complexity and fallibility."[46]

Thus, Matejka invites readers to consider Johnson as a multifaceted figure, whose experiences as a victim of the wrath of white supremacy as well as a perpetrator of violence against women have twenty-first-century resonances. In *Black Sexual Politics: African Americans, Gender, and the New Racism* (2004), Patricia Hill Collins traces a genealogy of Black male attempts to cast off historical stereotypes by gaining entry into an exclusive white patriarchy that has been designed to foreclose their entry: "The fact of Blackness excludes Black men from participating fully in hegemonic masculinity because, if they do so, they decenter the assumed Whiteness of those installed in the center of the definition itself. . . . The best that Black men can do is to achieve an 'honorary' membership within hegemonic masculinity by achieving great wealth, marrying the most desirable women (White), expressing aggression in socially sanctioned arenas (primarily as athletes, through the military, or law enforcement), and avoiding homosexual bonding."[47] As Matejka demonstrates in his representation of Johnson, this pattern, whereby Black male athletes internalize the ideals of hegemonic masculinity and strive (and ultimately fail) to parlay their celebrity into social respect, was set in motion during the postbellum period.

Matejka likewise underscores the high price that Black athletes pay for such failures—a common thread tying together the lyric portraits in *The Big Smoke* with today's sporting landscape. Responding, for example, to the public opprobrium and NFL sanction against the former Baltimore Ravens star Ray Rice, Dave Zirin notes, "The video of Ray Rice punching his then-fiancée Janay and knocking her unconscious not only launched a national discussion about domestic abuse and the NFL's near-pathological serial cover-up of violence against women, but also a parallel discussion about violence against women in 'the black community,' as if black athletes—and black men in general—were uniquely predisposed to hurting the women in their lives."[48] Michael Rosenberg adds that "NFL teams will gladly take five men who act and think like Colin Kaepernick before signing Kaepernick himself, just as they often take players who commit domestic violence but want nothing to do with [Ray] Rice. Teams are not taking any kind of political or moral stand. They just don't want to be associated with a symbol."[49] That is, Rice's intimate partner abuse was not an anomaly in the NFL, but he has, like the former San Francisco 49ers quarterback Colin Kaepernick, become an embodiment of behavior (whether it is antiracist protests or intimate partner violence) that white NFL executives and fans would rather not countenance. These recent episodes resonate with the turn-of-the-twentieth-century nexus of sports, hegemonic masculinity, and fame that Johnson was negotiating, whereby Black athletes engage in the same kinds of behavior as their white counterparts but are subject to additional and often excoriating public scrutiny.

Matejka's "Shadow" poems are especially illustrative of the psychological trauma incurred by such experiences in the limelight, as the Johnson persona struggles to cast off stereotypes of Black incapability and inferiority. In the third iteration of the poem "Shadow Boxing," for example, Johnson tells his imagined interlocutor,

> I want to put you out
> of the Flyer, watch you
> go end over end into the roots
>
> & old leaves like Belle did
> last time she sassed. She'd
> still be on the side of the road
>
> if I hadn't wanted a piece
>
> of her that day. . . .[50]

Johnson's desired means of expelling the self-doubt that his "Shadow" signifies is especially revealing of his frustrated aspiration to affirm his masculinity in a postbellum society bent on foreclosing all opportunity and respect for Black men. First, the Johnson persona notes his expensive car—his Flyer—a commodity that exemplifies his socioeconomic claim to manhood, and second, he notes his absolute dominance over Belle Schreiber, whom he can abuse, abandon "on the side of the road," and use for his sexual pleasure without repercussions ("if I hadn't wanted a piece / of her that day"). In analogizing Johnson's desire to root out his inferiority complex with his physical abuse of Schreiber and other women, Matejka shows the ways in which the ideology of hegemonic masculinity may be perpetuated by the very individuals victimized by it. By the poem's end, the Johnson persona tells the shadow, "you're / not even a man at all," to which the Shadow retorts, "*More of a man than you, Mr. Heaviest Negro in / the World. Least I'm honest.*"[51] Read as the voice of the white patriarchal order that Johnson has internalized, the Shadow refuses to accept both Johnson's assertions of manhood and his title of heavyweight champion of the world. Instead, he is the "*Heaviest Negro*," weighted down by racial stereotypes and the public spectacle of being the most notorious and vilified "Negro" the world over.

In "The Shadow Knows," Matejka revisits these anxieties, with the Shadow telling Johnson, "You can wreck an auto & buy / a new one the next day" and "change clothes / five times a day," but that does not change the boxer's "*unconditionalness / of blackness.*"[52] Reframing W. E. B. Du Bois's 1914 assessment of Johnson's Mann Act conviction in the *Crisis*—"Some pretend to object to Mr. Johnson's character. But we have yet to hear, in the case of white America, that marital troubles have disqualified prizefighters or ball players or even statesmen. It comes down then, after all, to this unforgiveable blackness"—Matejka highlights the racial litmus test that has long been used to deny access to the United States' mythical meritocracy.[53] Moreover, as Matejka shows, the hegemonic masculinity that Johnson relentlessly pursued was never on offer to him, despite his many attempts to possess everything coveted by privileged white men.

Although over a century has transpired, we continue to witness this pattern, as Black athletes, following in Johnson's footsteps, attempt to navigate the alternating racial hypervisibility and depersonalization that accompanies the limelight. For example, the golf legend Tiger Woods devised his own term to describe his multiethnic background—"Cablinasian," which combines "Caucasian," "Black," "American Indian," and "Asian"—attempting to chart an individualized course, only to be subjected to the same kinds of racial debasement perpetuated against Johnson. In 1997, the golf legend Fuzzy Zoeller observed of Woods, "That little boy is driving well and he's putting well. He's doing everything it takes to win. So, you know what you guys do when he gets in here? You pat him on the back and say congratulations and enjoy it and tell him not to serve fried chicken next year. Got it?"[54] Such racist paternalism did not dissipate even as Woods became one of the most accomplished golfers of all time and, like Johnson, married an upper-class white woman (Elin Nordegren). In 2008, "Golf Channel anchor Kelly Tilghman joked with former golf champion Nick Faldo that young players should 'lynch him [Tiger Woods] in the back alley.'"[55] As Matejka demonstrates, Johnson, too, was forced to endure a wide range of vitriolic taunts and threats as a Black man in the then-white-dominated sport of boxing. No matter how assiduously Johnson attempted to abide by dominant masculine norms, he, like Woods and scores of other Black male athletes, was never able to bask in the unconditional adoration reserved for famous athletes of European descent.

Placing archive and repertoire in dialogue, in "A Great Maltese Toying with a White Mouse," Matejka continues to educe the feelings of frustration with white supremacy that Johnson had to publicly conceal. The poem recounts what Johnson "*told the reporters*" and then offers his polite approach to his fight with then–heavyweight champion Tommy Burns. Careful not to further fan the flames of anti-Black sentiment, Johnson, in Matejka's portrait, both lauds his opponent for his fortitude and expresses his gratitude to law enforcement for saving Burns from undue injury:

> He was a game man & showed
> no inclination whatsoever to quit.
> My fists were better in every round
> & I landed punches I thought
>
> would bring him down. Like a great
> pachyderm, he refused to stop.
> & because he was so game, I was glad
> The police ended the fight.
>
> I wanted to be heavyweight
> champion, not injure Burns seriously.[56]

Strategically avoiding any description of the fight that would confirm stereotypes of Black men as menacing or inordinately aggressive, Johnson's public remarks leave Burns's dignity intact, even while he affirms his superior performance. In his autobiographical reflections about the fight, Johnson similarly affirms, "I was supremely glad I had attained the championship, but I kept this feeling to myself. I did not gloat over the fact that a white man had fallen. My satisfaction was only in the fact that one man had conquered another, and that I had been the conqueror."[57] Matejka reproduces these sentiments unmediated before juxtaposing them with what he imagines to be the boxer's actual feelings about suddenly becoming the most famous (and most feared) Black man in the world.

The second section of "A Great Maltese Cat," titled "*What I really meant*," imagines the bravado that Johnson felt compelled to suppress:

> That man made me chase him from Texas
> to England, then all of the way
> to Australia before he would fight me.
> Four-flusher. He didn't win the title.
>
> He just happened to be white & in the right
> place, like somebody striking gold. I put him
> down, but gently, in the first round so he'd
> know what was to come when he got a knee.[58]

In contrast to the cautious tone that Johnson struck in his public account of the fight, Matejka *re*presents the boxer's defiant attitude toward a white-supremacist boxing establishment (and society) that was anything but meritocratic. Put another way, Johnson, as with his Black contemporaries and successors, had to be "twice as good" in order to become heavyweight champion, and Matejka's first-person account of the Johnson-Burns fight reminds us of the origins of this script that has been performed many times over.

The collection's "Shadow" poems are adept at elucidating the Johnson persona's Du Boisian double consciousness—the "sense of always looking at oneself through the eyes of others, of measuring one's soul by the tape of a world that looks on in amused contempt and pity"[59]—but Matejka also "uses [poetic] form to tell a story quietly, which is to tell it with the expressive complexity of the inner life."[60] In poems such as "Out of the Bath," the force of whiteness "as everything and nothing" does not disappear,[61] but Matejka refocuses readers' attention on Johnson's "quiet" mind rather than the physicality that tends to overdetermine how we know what we know about African American athletes in particular and Black celebrities in general. In this poem, Matejka's tercets unfold a private exchange between Johnson and Etta in which the jocular, sensual, and aesthetic commingle to produce a poignant scene of domestic intimacy:

> Etta thinks I'm out driving & she gets
> out of the bath to reach the towel I moved
> as a joke. I didn't expect to be in our rooms
>
> when she finished bathing. But I am,
> watching while her foot searches marble
> uncertainly, like a foal working the hard
>
> way up to standing. Etta is singing, *Donna*
> *s'avanza, donna s'avanza*, from "Stride
> la vampa." Her voice sounds like water.[62]

That Johnson has played this childish trick on his wife reveals a tender side neither captured by the popular images of a fierce fighter nor quelled by the reality that the couple have to "pay / the colored tax" and stay "in hotels / that will have [them]."[63] Johnson's knowledge of the song and his keen attention to the sound of his wife's voice—later noting, "I could / accompany her if I had my bass"—similarly underscores his aesthetic sensitivity.[64] Whereas he may be reduced to his physicality in the ring and in the press, this poetic scene highlights his surreptitious admiration of his wife and their shared appreciation for the "high" art of opera. As Quashie notes, "the black subject . . . often seems to be known even before he or she arrives," and "Out of the Bath" remind us of the private, inner life that is missing from Black celebrity discourse, both historically and contemporarily.[65]

At the same time, in several poems told from Etta's perspective, Matejka voices her disappointment with the course of her marriage, affirming that she was yet another victim of Johnson's unfulfilled desire to prove his dominance in a society that viewed his manhood as a threat. Geoffrey C. Ward notes, "Glamorous, well-spoken, and unattached, she [Etta] brought a new elegance and refinement into Johnson's life. . . . Perhaps, because of Etta's background and bearing, Johnson seems to have been more taken with her than he had been with any of her predecessors."[66] In Matejka's rendering, however, Etta is subject to both his infidelity and his abuse and becomes increasingly despondent as a result. In "Fidelity," Etta laments, "He grabbed my arm / like it was an engine wrench."[67] Moreover, in "Aristocracy," she initially plots her revenge—"If I had a gun, I'd treat Papa / like a duck in a Long Island / duck hunt"—only to determine that her own destruction is what she truly desires: "What I want is a metallic way back to before."[68] The corresponding poem, "Compromises," again features Belle's imagined testimony to Agent T. S. Marshall, with her affirmation of Johnson's objectification and denigration of all of his romantic partners: "Papa never cared about any of us. From her last actions, Etta seemed to finally understand that fact."[69]

Supplementing the many narratives of Johnson's marriages and affairs with these imagined testimonials, Matejka revises Johnson's own public statements on his wife's suicide, enriching it with an emotional dimension absent from a strictly historical recounting of the circumstances of Etta's untimely demise. For example, in Johnson's aforementioned autobiography *Jack Johnson—In the Ring—and Out*, he recalls,

> On that day that the end came, we had entertained some friends. Etta and I had arranged to accompany them to the train on which they were to leave the city. When the time came for their departure, my wife pleaded a headache, and begged that she be excused from going to the train. She said good-bye to our friends cheerfully and promised to meet them later. I went with them to the train and when I returned home, I found the street in front of our apartment filled with crowds of people. Police wagons were drawn up and I experienced a chill that almost numbed me. When I arrived friends told me to hurry upstairs that something had happened to Etta. Those ominous words gave me the worst fright but dreading what I was to find. She lay on the floor, her beautiful hair long hiding her face. Near her was a revolver.[70]

Johnson's story reads much like a statement to the police in which he states his alibi and evinces the shock of discovering his wife's body. He does not especially emote about his grief, and he conspicuously avoids discussion of any actions that may have led to Etta's despair.

By contrast, in Matejka's poem "*Il Trovatore*," a reference to the heavyweight champion's favorite opera, a gutted Johnson reels from the guilt he feels for his abuse and infidelity. While this imagined response is no more verifiable than Johnson's autobiography or even press accounts are, Matejka uses the lyric landscape to, qua Rancière, educe "a different sensorium" about the boxer's grief that supplements the facts preserved in archival records:[71]

> The first time I heard the aria,
> it was like sun up after the Great Storm.
>
> The woman's voice rising, then rising
> more as if the want of it all wouldn't
>
> allow her another breath. Like roadwork
> when you've punched yourself out.
>
> Like Tommy Burns catching my gut hook.
> Like the first time I saw Etta.
>
> Like the sound of the crowd in Reno
> when Jeffries couldn't go on. Like going
>
> up the steps of the Café de Champion
> after the crash of a gunshot in Etta's
>
> room. Like finding Etta on the floor,
> a halo of blood getting bigger.[72]

Matejka's anaphoric "Like" statements portray Johnson as a man attempting to reconcile his traumatic loss, grasping at other pivotal moments in his life in order to make sense of the violence that has unfolded. In fact, the comparisons to Johnson's two most stunning defeats, of Tommy Burns and Jim Jeffries, suggest that Etta's death was a result of his abuse, and the poem concludes with Johnson reeling from Etta's gutting last words: "a libretto on the heels of her last breath: *You did this, Papa. You did this.*"[73]

Here we have access to a multidimensional Johnson, who on the one hand uses his athletic prowess to dominate other men and women and on the other invokes the aria in *Il Trovatore* as a key emotional reference point, revealing a quiet "watcherless" sensitivity mostly concealed from the public.[74] Whereas in *Jack Johnson*, the boxer takes no responsibility for Etta's suicide—"Our relations up to the last were joyful and peaceful. She never complained of anything and never gave any intimation that she was weary of life"—Matejka sheds further light on Johnson's feelings of guilt and anguish, implying that he was at least partially to blame for her despondency ("*You did this, Papa. You did this*").[75] Juxtaposing Johnson's adherence to and deviations from the discourse of hegemonic masculinity, Matejka elucidates the boxer's inner conflict as a figure who could not express the full range of his emotional life for fear of losing his tenuous grasp of manhood in a society in which all Black men were either belittled as "boys" or criminalized as "brutes."

As Matejka's persona poetry repeatedly emphasizes, Johnson's attempts to gain the respect and admiration of white society—becoming heavyweight champion, buying expensive automobiles, operating popular nightclubs, and publicly demonstrating his control of white women—only ended in further tragedy and alienation. This trend has continued in the contemporary sporting landscape, and in terms of the kinds of intersections between race and gender taxonomies and stereotypes that Matejka elucidates. As Abby Ferber contends, "The disproportionate media coverage focused on violent or sexual assault charges brought against Black male athletes, compared with similar charges against White male athletes, reifies this stereotype of Black men as inherently dangerous and in need of civilizing."[76] As noted earlier, Black male athletes are no more likely to assert their dominance over women than their white counterparts are, but they are disproportionately linked to and admonished for such behavior, perpetuating their marginalization and stereotypes of Black inferiority more generally. In creatively recuperating Johnson alongside his wives and lovers, Matejka suggests the ways in which his postbellum experiences laid the blueprint for the experiences of today's Black male athletes, whereby their "public personalities come to embody the full spectrum of male pathology."[77]

In the longest poem in the collection, "The Battle of the Century," Matejka recounts, in the style of the boxing press's round-by-round accounts, the epic 1910 fight between Johnson and Jeffries, which Young similarly restaged in chapter 1. In Matejka's poem, readers see the ways in which archival traces can be mobilized and reconfigured to, as Rancière noted earlier, make a "different common world" legible. As Taylor also argues, "the archival, from the beginning, sustains power." Its enduring materials, she continues, appear to "exceed the live," whereas the repertoire of embodied acts and ephemera are dynamic and thus not easily fixed in time and space.[78] Attentive to the ways in which this reliance on documentary evidence has muted subaltern perspectives, Matejka's "The Battle of the Century" lyrically reperforms this historic boxing match, drawing our focus to the mise-en-scène of the song and stage in which multiple and competing agendas were at work.

In this reenactment, Johnson is calling the fight, rather than a white announcer, thereby reimagining this sporting history from the vantage point of the famous man who stood center stage but whose humanity was routinely devalued. As Ken McLeod notes, "The spectacularization of Black athletic and musical masculinity is a form of commodity fetishism that renders invisible the labor of Black athletes and musicians so they may simply be read as specimens."[79] Matejka subverts this objectification by breathing regenerative life into Johnson's labor, as well as the feelings, thoughts, desires, and frustrations that the boxer did not express to a US public that was fascinated by but especially fearful of his body. In the section "Round Two," Matejka illuminates both the racial animosity that Johnson endured and the formidable challenge to white supremacy that he enacted in the ring:

> Jim Corbett paced outside the ring
> like one of those circus tigers before
> the man with the whip shows up.
> He kept yelling *n*[*****] as if name-
> calling could move me when Jeffries
> couldn't. Corbett must not have heard
> the band playing "All Coons Look
> Alike" when I split the ropes.
> I've heard this same song my whole life.[80]

Matejka inverts the white gaze so that we as readers are able to gawk at the horrors perpetuated by Corbett (a nineteenth-century boxing legend) and the white-supremacist attitudes he signifies. Thus, instead of Johnson becoming a dehumanized spectacle, it is Corbett who appears as an untamed "circus tiger" stalking the ring and hurling racial epithets. Corbett's uncensored trash-talking is also notable in the context of the current discourse about race and sports. As David J. Leonard notes, "Bravado and confidence, like rage, is unacceptable in association with blackness. Whiteness plus brashness is not only acceptable but also desired and celebrated."[81] While over a hundred years have passed between the Johnson-Jeffries matchup, Matejka's "The Battle of the Century" reminds us of the origins of this racialized double standard when it comes to athletes' taunts and boasts.

The song introducing this epic matchup, "All Coons Look Alike," further suggests the complex racial dynamics at play within and beyond the postbellum boxing ring. Composed by the African American songwriter Ernest Hogan, this immensely popular tune appealed not only to white Americans but also, as Yuval Taylor and Jake Austen note, to Blacks because it "painted a picture of masculine liberation completely opposed to the actual condition of blacks of the era"; Taylor and Austen add, "The conventional explanation for the popularity of coon songs is that these images of violent, sexual, dangerous black men justified the segregation and oppression of an era of lynching and peonage. But this doesn't explain why so many coon-song performers and writers were black. The protagonists of these [coon] songs emerge *happy* and *triumphant* rather than getting punished, as would be expected in music used to justify oppression."[82] Arguably, "All Coons Look Alike" exemplifies a double-voiced strategy, whereby Hogan and others within his fin de siècle circle were capitulating to dominant stereotypes of African Americans while simultaneously adumbrating a more liberated future (dual impulses that I explore at length in chapter 4). In many ways, such a strategy parallels with Johnson's own commitment to boxing—a sport that on the one hand confirmed denigrating caricatures about Black men's naturally violent tendencies and on the other provided an opportunity to upend the ideology of white supremacy through besting men like the "Great White Hope" Jim Jeffries. Reenacting this watershed sporting event, Matejka engages readers in the repertoire, peeling away some of its intricate sociocultural layers within both sports and music and, in the process, drawing attention to Black Americans' strategic negotiation of white hegemony.

"The Battle of the Century" similarly interpolates the archival record by recounting each round of the Johnson-Jeffries fight but allowing Johnson's perspective to reign supreme. Through fifteen rounds, Matejka portrays Johnson as restrained in his approach to Jeffries, who is unable to match his challenger's strength as well as his nimble movements in the ring. For example, in "*Round Nine*," the Johnson persona reports,

> Jeffries's mouth was so swollen he looked
> like the newspaper versions of me. Through
> those cartoon lips, he tried to talk: *Ain't I*
> *got a hard old head?* I hit him with two rights
> & agreed: *You certainly have, Mr. Jeffries.*[83]

In Matejka's rendering, the Johnson persona is aware of the white mob violence he will incite if he humiliates Jeffries, with the calls of "*Don't let the n*[*****] *knock him out!*" ringing in his ears.[84] Thus, he maintains the upper hand until Jeffries is finally finished: "As the seconds helped him up, I heard Jeffries saying, / *I couldn't come back, boys. I couldn't come back*."[85] Reminding readers of the symbolic significance of Johnson's victory over the "Great White Hope," Matejka counters the rhetoric of the white sporting press by giving primacy to Johnson's vantage point.

Moreover, the Johnson persona's comment about "those cartoon lips" subverts denigrating representations of Johnson in the media, implying both the biases stitched into archival records and the key role that lyric poetry can play in exposing and offering alternatives to such degradations. For instance, in the July 8, 1910, edition of *Chicago American Sports*, the long-standing sports journalist and cartoonist Tad Dorgan depicts Johnson as a minstrel figure with abnormally large white eyes and mouth who, as the byline suggests, "Kidded with Sparring Partners When Training for Big Go." The bottom of this caricature features three "trainers," also painted in a minstrel style, shooting craps and making crass comments such as "Oh You Mister 10—You Big Dick—Roll Over While You're Warm."[86] Even while this image features Johnson as a renowned pugilist, the reporter uses the opportunity to depict Johnson as physically and mentally inferior. The image of the trainers shooting craps also reinforces stereotypes of Black men as criminals to be feared by a supposedly morally virtuous white America. This is the white-supremacist environment in which Johnson rose to fame, and Matejka's portrait of him as a skillful athlete offers a rejoinder to press accounts reliant on these endemic stereotypes.

The collection's final poem, "Hubert's Museum & Flea Circus (1937)," further complicates Johnson's image by portraying his embrace of his spectacularized image, appearing "After Congo the Wild Man's / caterwaul & Seal the Seal-Finned Boy's handclaps."[87] In some ways caricaturing his former elegance, "Jack Johnson / comes out. Dog-eared blue suit & blue beret. Red wine / sipped through a straw: *What would you like to know?*"[88] Perhaps compromising his dignity and perhaps subverting the expectations of the audience for this traveling circus (and probably both), Johnson is an aged Black boxer striving to remain financially solvent in an economy designed to thwart Black socioeconomic mobility. In fact, this portrait brings the collection full circle, as it began with Johnson's participation in the "battle royal," whereby in order to feed himself, he acceded, as he does in this vaudevillian show, to white demands for Black subservience.

As Anne Anlin Cheng observes of the visual archive of Josephine Baker (another star to emerge in the post-Reconstruction, pre–Harlem Renaissance era), "The issue is less the distinction between immutable and mutable traits, or between essence and superficiality, and more about how these two sets of signifiers constitute one another. In the end, it is not a question of who is the fetishist and who the fetishized, but rather how both the colonial/racist imagination and its antidote share a predicament of embodiment."[89] As Matejka shows, Johnson was similarly entangled in this web of racialized visual signifiers and their slippages. Reimagining Johnson's interior thoughts, Matejka suggests the boxer's awareness of this conflicting minefield of interests, as well as his attempts to imagine a self not predicated on the colonial/racist imagination—in other words, the alternating feelings of hypervisibility and invisibility that his "Shadow" alter ego signifies. For Matejka, Johnson is neither stereotype nor archetype but a multifaceted, complex individual, whose desperation to gain respect as a man caused several women in his life irreparable harm. Therefore, *The Big Smoke* makes prolific use of persona poetry not in the service of hagiography but rather as a vehicle for destabilizing a monologic understanding of Johnson in particular and Black celebrity history more generally.

As Matejka braids together archive and repertoire, his readers are likewise invited to undergo a shift in perception, whereby we may more productively interrogate both how we know what we know and the means by which we know it. Saidiya Hartman observes in her recent portrait of turn-of-the-century Black Americans that she "learned to work with the mess of the archive, to *creatively disorder* the institutional fictions and the violent abstractions authorized as fact and truth."[90] Similarly drawing on and disordering a range of archival materials, Matejka defamiliarizes the conventional conclusions drawn about Johnson, implying, for instance, that he used the fears that whites had of him to his advantage, refusing the prescribed codes of behavior for Black men as a means of generating the notoriety necessary to become an international celebrity. Yet he also paid a hefty personal price for this strategy, forever striving to shield himself from a baleful white gaze and grappling with feelings of alienation and self-doubt as a result. Extending the cultural work of *To Repel Ghosts: The Remix from the Original Masters*, *The Big Smoke* creatively recuperates these affective experiences, charting alternative histories of the postbellum period and suggesting the connective tissue between the racialized and gendered norms sedimented during the postbellum sporting arena that, though perhaps less immediately visible, undergird many social codes and cues today.

In this regard, Ferber underscores the sociohistorical continuity when it comes to the public treatment of Black men:

> Black male bodies are increasingly admired and commodified in rap, hip hop, and certain sports, but at the same time they continue to be used to invoke fear. Black men are both held in contempt and valued as entertainment. Yet this is really nothing new. Black men have been defined as a threat throughout American history while being accepted in roles that serve and entertain White people, where they can ostensibly be controlled and made to appear nonthreatening. Furthermore, within the contemporary context of color-blind ideology, the embrace of Black athletes helps White fans to assure themselves that America really is not racist after all.[91]

Correspondingly, Matejka makes an implicit connection between the anxiety and loathing that Johnson engendered in white spectators during the early twentieth century and similar feelings of fetish and fear in response to Black athletes today. As Nicole Fleetwood notes, "Professional sports and their commoditization of the black athletic body also bring us face-to-face with the psychic and physical violence of the racial state that continually attempts to dominate and manipulate black bodies."[92] While *The Big Smoke*'s focus is historical, it makes the connections to the current era clear. That is, African Americans' outsized impact in particular sports, namely, basketball and football, in many respects "sustain[s] the traditional view of blacks as essentially physical and thus primitive people."[93] Moreover, Black excellence displayed in the sports arena fits into a colorblind or postracial narrative about racial progress and meritocracy that Matejka's links between past and present work to dispel.

In the process, *The Big Smoke* supplements the work that historians and cultural critics have performed on Johnson's behalf by reaching beyond what may be found in the official vaults. To this point, Rancière argues that biography specifically and history in general are no more reliable in regard to their epistemological truths than is imaginative literature: "The ambiguities of biography are not a simple matter of methodology internal to a discipline. They go to the heart of the very regime of writing that makes the science of history possible—literature. To say that history has no truck with literature is simply to say that it doesn't want to know that that's what it's doing."[94] For Rancière, literature gives historical writing its lifeblood, even as the latter often distinguishes itself as a "science" rather than an "art." Matejka's revivification not only of Johnson but also of Etta Duryea and Belle Schreiber provides a salient example of the kind of sociocultural work that creative writing does on behalf of marginalized figures and histories. That is, Matejka draws on the facts of Johnson's life as outlined in biographies and the boxer's own autobiographies, but, rather than feeling constrained by empirical data or anxious about disciplinary ambiguities, Matejka interlaces archive and repertoire, creating a polysemous portrait of an icon that the white US public was hyperaware of as a threat yet knew almost nothing about as a sentient ("quiet") individual.

The Big Smoke similarly suggests what Johnson's story foretells about the contradictions of Black fame, as well as the continuities between the postbellum, pre–Harlem Renaissance period and our own time—eras characterized by progressive social change on the one hand and regressive commitments to the doctrine of white supremacy on the other. For example, Serena and Venus Williams have long experienced intersecting forms of racism and sexism in the predominantly and historically white sport of tennis. In a recent interview with the hip-hop artist Common, Serena explained, "[It's] hard as a black woman and being someone who's black in America, representing this country when I'm playing and when I'm doing things."[95] Like Johnson before her, Serena, as well as her sister Venus, is not simply displaying her exceptional talent on the court; "she is always signifying, representing, and otherwise embodying not only the hopes and dreams of the black community but also the fears, anxieties, and hatred of white America."[96] In chapter 3, Matejka's contemporary Frank X Walker inhabits the perspective of the jockey Isaac Burns Murphy, who also gained considerable renown (and notoriety) during the decades following the Civil War. As with Matejka, Walker's lyrical portraits of Murphy and his loved ones offer another way to know and feel Black celebrity, a way that is focused on the emotional and psychological repertoire that is continuously effaced by a society that has long fixated on the Black body.

3
"THE STING OF RACE AND SPORT"
Revivifying Isaac Burns Murphy in Frank X Walker's Isaac Murphy: I Dedicate This Ride

In 1997, the sports historian David K. Wiggins lamented, "The most frustrating aspect of my work on [Isaac Burns] Murphy was trying to get inside the mind of this famous jockey to determine his thoughts regarding his profession, racial discrimination, and a host of other matters. As is the case with some of the other early black athletes, there are no extended interviews, personal reminiscences, or autobiographies."[1] In the biography *The Prince of Jockeys: The Life of Isaac Burns Murphy* (2013), Pellom McDaniels III expressed similar concerns: "Absent Murphy's own account to deconstruct, it is impossible to know all of what he experienced during his lifetime."[2] The once-famous jockey Isaac Burns Murphy (1861–1896) is virtually unknown today, his cultural memory shunted to the backwaters in a contemporary era in which Black jockeys are an anomaly. In this chapter, I explore the ways in which Frank X Walker's poetry collection *Isaac Murphy: I Dedicate This Ride* (2010) steps into the breach, creatively recuperating Murphy's interiority and supplementing archival records that are focused almost exclusively on his feats at the racetrack. As Ben Carrington argues, "Only rarely has the black athlete spoken, or been allowed to speak. It is normally spoken for."[3] By contrast, Walker mutes the perspectives of white authorities and instead gives imaginative voice to Murphy's private thoughts, fears, desires, and frustrations. Importantly for a poetry collection focused on a male athlete, Walker also illuminates the perspectives of a range of other figures, including Murphy's wife, Lucy Murphy, and his mother, America Burns, making these nineteenth-century Black women's lives legible, while implying the racialized and gendered biases undergirding our national archives, in which these individuals and others like them barely appear.

Howard Rambsy II observes that "the personae or masks that black poets regularly choose to adopt allow them to provide commentary on African American history and society and participate in a longstanding tradition of speaking in the tongues of various black people."[4] As with Kevin Young (chapter 1) and Adrian Matejka (chapter 2), Walker extends this tradition, adopting the personae of Murphy and his loved ones in order both to honor their achievements and to suggest parallels between Murphy's experiences with fame and those of Black athletes today. A founding member of the Affrilachian Poets and the 2013–2014 Kentucky poet laureate, Walker also has deep roots in the region in which horse racing has long been a preeminent sport. Moreover, there are notable parallels between the historical silence regarding Black jockeys and the effacement of Black experiences in the mythos of Appalachia—a region typified in popular culture as the province of working-class people of European descent. In this regard, the Affrilachian poets' website offers the following conceptual history:

> The term "Affrilachia" was originally coined by Frank X Walker. In reference to the region of Appalachia, a mountain range stretching over thirteen states along the East Coast of the U.S. from Mississippi to New York, Affrilachia is an ever-evolving cultural landscape poised to render the invisible visible. Affrilachia embraces a multicultural influence, a spectrum of people who consider Appalachia home and/or identify strongly with the trials and triumphs of being of this region. Since 1991, the Affrilachian Poets have been writing together, defying the persistent stereotype of a racially homogenized rural region. Through their writing and the very existence of their enclave, the Affrilachian Poets continue to reveal relationships that link identity to familial roots, socio-economic

stratification and cultural influence, and an inherent connection to the land.[5]

Corresponding to these efforts to "render the invisible visible," Walker noted in a 2014 interview with JoAnn LoVerde-Dropp, "In Murphy's case, the degree to which African Americans participated in and in many cases dominated thoroughbred racing is so invisible that it rarely comes up."[6] Through his persona poetry, Walker attempts to right this wrong, encouraging readers to reexamine the overwhelmingly white makeup of horse racing and other whitewashed arenas and suggesting that there is nothing *natural* about the process by which US cultural spaces become racially homogeneous.

Despite this collection's significance with regard to lyrically reimagining "the greatest jockey in the history of thoroughbred racing," it has received scant critical attention.[7] This chapter begins, therefore, a conversation about the importance of *Isaac Murphy* for shedding needed light on this three-time Kentucky Derby winner, for elucidating persona poetry's archival-historical salience, and for drawing attention to the through lines between the pendulum swings of adoration and dehumanization that Murphy endured in the decades following the Civil War and the fraught relationships that current Black celebrities are forced to negotiate. For example, in 2017, the Los Angeles home of LeBron James—arguably the most acclaimed contemporary professional basketball player—was defiled with a racist slur. As James lamented, "No matter how much money you have, no matter how famous you are, no matter how many people admire you, being black in America is tough. . . . We got a long way to go for us as a society and for us as African Americans until we feel equal in America."[8] As Walker's poetry suggests, Murphy could easily have spoken these same words, demonstrating the fallibility of progressive narratives of US history, especially with regard to the treatment of African Americans, even in a sports industry in which they have made an impressively outsized impact. As Hanif Abdurraqib writes of the tennis superstar Serena Williams, who contends with the intersecting forces of anti-Black racism and sexism, "There is really no measurement for how America wants its black athletes to be. Oftentimes, they are asked to both know their greatness and know their place at the same time."[9] Abdurraqib's point rings true in a transhistorical sense, for Murphy and his twenty-first-century descendants are held to an entirely different standard than their white counterparts are—a standard that demands that their individual success not challenge the inequitable race and gender status quo. In centralizing horse racing, Walker also reminds us that players of African descent may dominate some of the most visible and celebrated sports in the United States—namely, basketball and football—but their absence from certain playing fields and from the front offices of others suggests the residue of the postbellum period, in which athletics was an alluring but ultimately unreliable arena for Black social mobility.

My reading of Walker's *Isaac Murphy* is further framed by Jacques Rancière's understanding of imaginative literature's role in disrupting purportedly commonsense ways of excavating the past, as well as Diana Taylor's emphasis on the highly mediated nature of the archive and the dominant narratives that lay claim to its documents and artifacts. As Taylor puts it, "What makes an object archival is the process whereby it is selected, classified, and presented for analysis."[10] Also recognizing the limitations of archivally generated knowledge, Rancière argues that literature "has its own politics, or rather its own metapolitics. On the one hand, literature reads signs written on bodies, on the other, it loosens bodies from the meanings people want them to take on."[11] Walker's persona poetry "loosens" Murphy and his family members from the archive's hegemonic gaze by reimagining what Taylor refers to as the repertoire of embodied experiences.[12] While Walker's representations of these figures are no more "real" than a biography or other historical account is, *Isaac Murphy* utilizes poetic license to culturally productive ends, especially evincing what Kevin Quashie describes as the "inner life unable to be expressed fully but nonetheless articulate and informing of one's humanity."[13] Focusing on the private thoughts and not the bodies of Murphy and his loved ones, Walker's creative recuperation works to restore multifaceted subjectivity to figures who were objectified during their own time and are mostly forgotten in ours. In the process, *Isaac Murphy* demonstrates how resonant the once-famous jockey's postbellum experiences are for grappling with the contemporary paradoxes faced by Black athletes, who are both vaunted for their physical feats and demeaned as individuals, expected to know their prowess but not to challenge systemic racial inequities.

"I Feel like I Own Isaac"

The collection's opening poem, "Murphy's Secret," serves as an introduction to the double-voiced tactics that Walker imagines Murphy had to employ in order to advance the cause of Black empowerment without unnerving white authorities who owned the racetracks and sponsored the sport. Rather than the spectacle of Murphy's races, Walker lyrically reimagines the jockey's private thoughts, which are "not entirely legible in a discourse of publicness."[14] The poem commences with Murphy's internal reflections on his strategic approach to distinct groups of onlookers:

> When folks find out I'm *him*
> they always want to know what I say to 'em.
> If they be white I tell 'em
>
> 'Run an run quick
> or they gone feed you to the n[*****]s.'
> An they usually laugh an leave be.
>
> If they be black I tell 'em the truth.
> I tell 'em how I cup my hand to a horse's ear
> how I let it catch some wind so they remember
>
> what it sound like to run full out,
> to know you not just a field hand or a work horse
> but beautiful an strong an smart.[15]

Walker suspects that Murphy told white horse-racing fans what they wanted to hear—in other words, that he did not see himself as the equal of white men, as his self-reference to the term "n[*****]" indicates. As Russel T. Wigginton explains, enslaved Black Americans had long been tasked with "the unattractive, arduous labor associated with maintaining horses. . . . Thus performing the undesirable duties, typically referred to as 'n[*****] work,' gave blacks an important presence in what quickly became an American pastime."[16] Walker's portrait recounts this history, showing that Murphy had to remain mindful of the vestiges of antebellum racial codes undergirding the sport of horse racing, striking a delicate balance between appeasing and defying the white-supremacist attitudes that pervaded *post*bellum US society. Murphy was likewise compelled to make such capitulations even while he was quickly becoming the most renowned jockey in the sport, as the first line indicates ("When folks find out I'm *him*").

In addition to recounting Murphy's precarious social position within the white community, Walker, consistent with Rancière's view of literature, "loosens" the jockey from a rather one-dimensional public portrait to speculate about the unvarnished self he revealed to other Black Americans. To this end, we as readers are drawn into the quietude of the Murphy persona's mind, as he explains his loving care for the horses with which he identifies, not because of the animalistic stereotypes projected onto Black people but instead out of a shared sense of the tension between servitude and liberation. "Murphy's Secret" ends, in fact, with Murphy affirming both his own and his horse's right to self-determination:

> When I'm up there I rub my hands against they neck
> lean into they ear, pretend I'm the wind an whisper
> 'Find yo purpose. Find yo purpose' an hold on.[17]

Murphy, Walker insists, was the most storied jockey of his generation because he treated his horses with dignity, respecting them as sentient beings instead of chattel pressed into the service of human wants and needs.

According to Walker, Murphy was also triumphant at the racetrack because of his desire to honor the sacrifices of his parents and the other formerly enslaved people who made his life and liberty possible. In the title poem, "I Dedicate This Ride," the Murphy persona conveys the debt he especially owes to his father:

> When I come barreling down the stretch
> I always think about my daddy, James Burns,
> a runaway slave turned soldier.[18]

In this link between past and present, Walker speaks to the initial hopefulness of the Reconstruction period, when figures like

Murphy were able to capitalize on the citizenship rights that the generation of the formerly enslaved fought and, in many cases, died to secure: "Just so their children could dream. / So I could ride horses and enjoy true quiet."[19] The phrase "true quiet" is particularly salient here. Walker underscores the significance of the life of the mind, which is often obscured when the archive of durable objects is the primary site for excavating Black cultural history. For Walker, unlocking this "quiet" allows for a deeply humanized portrait of Murphy that, in turn, implies what may be missing from contemporary discourse about Black athletes.

As Rancière notes, literature offers a way to mine the voices and perspectives shunted aside by hegemonic forces: "Literature pits a different politics against this democratic mise en scène. The principle of this politics is to return to its vanity the great racket made by the orators of the people, brought up on the voices in order to decipher the testimonies that society itself offers us to read, to disinter those society unwittingly and unintentionally deposits in its dark underground shoals. The noisy stage of the orators is opposed by the journey through the subterranean passages that hold its hidden truth."[20] Inhabiting not only Murphy's but also his family members' personae, Walker eschews dominant accounts ("the noisy stage of the orators") in order to uncover "subterranean" voices and truths. For example, "The Right to Bear Arms" focalizes the perspective of Murphy's father, James Burns, who proudly recalls his experiences fighting for the Union:

> we had us almost a hundred black officers,
> none bigger than captains,
> but all a us much bigger than slaves.[21]

Using persona poetry to offer another way to know US history, Walker implies that hegemonic narratives and the archival artifacts that lend them credence are not sufficient to account for the "hidden truth" of the Black men and women who forced the nation to realize its founding democratic creed.

In the same vein, Walker's "The Heart of the Matter" ventriloquizes Murphy's mother, America Burns, as she describes the white southern scramble to implement various forms of quasi-slavery in the wake of Union victory:

I took my babies to the city to live wit my daddy.
I heard the country was indenturin' up
colored chil'ren to they former masters.

A slavery trick if I ever heard one.
I refuse to let my chil'ren grow up in bondage
no matter what new name they was callin' it.[22]

The perseverance and sacrifices of the scores of Black people like America Burns who spent their lifetimes fighting for freedom often go unrecognized in histories that focus on Reconstruction's legal and sociopolitical battles or the accomplishments of the postbellum, pre–Harlem Renaissance era's most iconic African Americans, such as Booker T. Washington, W. E. B. Du Bois, and Ida B. Wells, among others. In reimagining the first-person outlooks of Murphy and his family, Walker shifts the perspective so that readers engage this period through the eyes of citizens of African descent whose lives have been rendered archivally mute, while adding emotional sustenance to their legacies.

In "Defining Wealth," Walker further emphasizes the significance of horse racing and other sports for Black Americans seeking both economic mobility and social respect that were not available in other white-dominated spheres—a reality that, though the sporting landscape has changed, has continued into the present. As Katherine Mooney contends, Black jockeys' "success and stature fueled hopes of the coming of a racially integrated America, founded on the idea that equality was entailed in the freedom attained in emancipation. For many Americans both white and black in the 1880s, that was a nascent society that seemed embodied in Isaac Murphy."[23] Horse racing eventually foreclosed these opportunities for Black men, but Walker revisits a liminal postbellum period in which this sport, at least tentatively, offered Murphy and others self-determination and the promise of meritocratic advancement. And whereas Mooney and other scholars elucidate this history through media accounts and other archived records, Walker makes use of the imagination to consider what it might have felt like to be Murphy, the jockey whose success at the racetrack gave Black Americans hope that dark skin pigmentation would no longer be a barrier to social mobility:

> In years around Lexington after the war
> young boys like me with the *right* attitude
> might look to wait tables at a nice whites-only hotel,
> work as porters, messengers, janitors or even stewards.
>
> But a few of us were lucky enough to serve
> Beautiful four-legged masters instead.[24]

Not quite as sanguine as Mooney, Walker dispels the myth that a fully integrated, equitable democracy was ever on the postbellum horizon. Yet he does suggest that sports—specifically horse racing—offered a rare opportunity to rise above the subservient roles carved out for newly emancipated Black Americans, and to "serve / Beautiful four-legged masters instead."

Indeed, reanimating what Taylor refers to as the repertoire of "embodied practice/knowledge (i.e., spoken language, dance, sports, ritual),"[25] as well as what Quashie describes as the "sovereignty" of the quiet mind,[26] Walker voices Murphy's proud reflections on the experience of guiding his horse to the finish line:

> So down the homestretch, I feel like I own Isaac,
> I own the horse, I own the race, and every time
> I cross the finish line in front of all the other riders,
> I feel like I own the whole day.[27]

Not beholden to anyone and not needing the "*right* attitude," Walker's Murphy persona finds in horse racing an opportunity to achieve self-determination—a sense conveyed through the repetition of the lyric "I." "Owning" himself and his surroundings makes horse racing an especially desirable arena for Murphy, and importantly, these are feelings that he does not have to express publicly. Instead, these are the "quiet" thoughts of self-possession and resolve that cannot be appropriated by white onlookers but that Walker's creative recuperation brings to life.

At the same time, in drawing us back to this late-nineteenth-century era in which Murphy identifies the racetrack as one of the few arenas in which he can pursue his dream of "serv[ing] / beautiful four-legged masters," Walker implies the complex role sports played in African American communities during the nineteenth century and, by extension, today. As Krystal Beamon and Chris

Messer argue, "Images of successful African-American athletes abound, but there are fewer numbers of culturally visible African-American male public role models successful in business or education, which perpetuates the stereotype that African-American males are primarily or even exclusively athletically talented."[28] In other words, it is not that citizens of African descent were in Murphy's day or are in our own more gifted in athletics; rather, hegemonic power structures have deemed it permissible for Blacks to dominate on courts, tracks, and fields while discouraging their success in other industries that might threaten a white sociopolitical and economic stronghold.

While *Isaac Murphy* elucidates these paradoxes for Murphy and his fellow Black jockeys, the collection is also attentive to the experiences of Black women, who have been shunted aside in an even more profound way than their male counterparts. Walker particularly highlights women's efforts to maintain Black familial and communal bonds, despite state-sanctioned efforts to rip them asunder. For example, America Burns neither penned a slave narrative nor chronicled her commitment to ensuring that Isaac and her other children remained free from predatory forces seeking unremunerated Black labor. With no paper trail, America's experiences have become, to borrow an eloquent phrase from the historian Douglas A. Blackmon, "as fragile as a scent in the wind."[29] Poetically reanimating her private reflections in "Come Sunday It's Derby," Walker emphasizes America's undocumented but nonetheless essential part in shaping her son's prodigious sporting career:

> He might not ever tell it to the papers
> but I'm the first person Isaac ever see ride.
>
> I'm the first person he watch
> get up at dawn
> fill a tub wit scaldin' water, soap an dirty clothes
>
> lock everything 'tween my knees
> bend over an grab somethin' by its ears
> race it up an down the washboard
> 'till I baptize the dirt right out.
>
> Everybody ride the hell outta somethin'.[30]

Inhabiting America's outlook using not the archive but instead an imagined repertoire of personal memories, Walker bears witness to her admirable work ethic and tenacity, which she imparted to her son, facilitating his ascendance to athletic fame. With America's observation that her son "might not ever tell it to the papers," Walker also calls attention to the information about Black cultural history that is absent from newspaper accounts and other archival records. Unconstrained by empirical strictures, Walker reanimates America's outlook, both implying the gaps in our knowledge and utilizing lyric persona poetry to excavate the "hidden truth[s]" that Rancière noted earlier.

The last line's emphasis on each individual's attempts at self-determination ("Everybody ride the hell outta somethin'") likewise prevents this poem and the collection as a whole from becoming an encomium to Black male achievement. While Walker celebrates Murphy as a pivotal postbellum figure, he also underscores the accomplishments of his family members, particularly his mother and wife, ensuring that labors and achievements dismissed by dominant histories as inconsequential receive their just due. Daina Ramey Berry and Kali Nicole Gross point out that "Black women fought oppression throughout the nineteenth century";[31] yet, as Angela Y. Davis notes, "With the sole exceptions of Harriet Tubman and Sojourner Truth, black women of the slave era remain more or less enshrouded in unrevealed history."[32] Redressing this effacement, Walker shows how Black women militated against both self-abnegation and white attempts to destabilize the Black family and, by extension, Black collective power. By inhabiting America's persona, Walker restores her humanity and subjectivity, moving figures and experiences that are even less legible than Murphy from margin to center.

Congruent with Quashie's emphasis on "quiet," Walker also draws attention away from the hypervisibility of the Black body in a white-dominated body politic and toward the reflective interiority of the mind. The poem "Nomenclature," for example, imagines America's explanation for her son's decision to change his last name from Burns to Murphy, signaling his and, by extension, the majority of African Americans' newly emancipated state. Braiding the archive and the repertoire, Walker begins with the epigraph "*Isaac*

Murphy's first recorded race was in 1875 under the name Isaac Burns" and then segues into America's imagined testimony:

> We was carryin' Burns, our slave name,
> when we first come to Lex'nin.
>
> But I guess it got too heavy for Isaac
> once he answered his callin' an needed to be
> as free in the saddle as possible.
>
> He tried on my family name
> in honor for my daddy, said it fit just fine.
> Been callin' himself Isaac Murphy ever since.[33]

Murphy's name change signifies the rebirth and renewal made possible by manumission and the hopes and promises bound up in Reconstruction ideals. As America describes, the name Burns is freighted by a tortured history of subjugation ("it got too heavy") that her son now feels at will to cast off. As Walker uses the historical record as a touchstone rather than his sole source of knowledge, he dwells on the affective resonances, underscoring the significance of the jockey's appellation not only for himself but also for his family; moreover, he redirects readers' attention to the microhistories (or what Rancière might term the "subterranean passages") of the postbellum era that, when this period is addressed at all, are often overshadowed by landmark events on timelines traced by men invested with structural power. In the process, Walker self-reflexively suggests his own artistic commitments, which regard linguistic choices (hence the poem's title, "Nomenclature") and voice (hence the poem's speaker, America Burns) as central to reclaiming the typically whitewashed history of horse racing in particular and postbellum Black American culture in general.

"The Power of Sports" further elucidates the cultural dissonances regarding Black participation in sports that were incubating during Murphy's era and still remain operative in the contemporary moment. As Carrington argues, "There are no races, only ways in which we see race. And sport continues to play an important role in the making and remaking of these ways of seeing."[34] Journeying back to the late nineteenth century, Walker illuminates the establishment of the post–Civil War sports industry as a key site for determining the racial codes and customs that have undergirded the US social landscape ever since. He evinces the respect and admiration that Murphy receives from white racing fans, while suggesting that his accomplishments do little to erode these same fans' investment in white supremacy:

> Men who might call a colored exercise boy
> every foul name they can pronounce
> and add more salt by placing dirty or n[*****]
> in front of it
>
> turn around and tip their hats to me
> as if everything I do during a race
> separates me from my blackness
> making me an honorary white man.[35]

This seeming contradiction, whereby whites love individual Black athletes ("tip[ping] their hats") but routinely denigrate Black people (weaponizing "every foul name they can pronounce"), remains deeply ingrained in US sociocultural attitudes and discourse. As Abby Ferber contends, "Images of successful Black athletes also provide a 'bootstraps' story, sending the message that these Black men have succeeded; therefore, there is no reason other Black men can't. . . . The vast reality of discrimination and institutionalized racism is erased from view."[36] This is precisely the danger that Walker's Murphy perceives in the postbellum era, demonstrating a long-term pattern of lauding Black excellence in particular arenas in order to preserve systemic white privileges on the one hand and justify the degradation that the vast majority of African Americans experience on the other.

Stripping away Murphy's characteristic poise, Walker further illuminates what Rancière refers to as the "metapolitics" of literature, not only tracking dominant responses to alterity but also offering other ways of knowing the lives of marginalized figures. As Walker explained in the aforementioned interview, "When I craft collections of persona poems, I'm building from source material gathered from memory, research and imagination. It's the emotional currency that comes from a first-person voice and the imagination that keeps it from just being another history text."[37] Accordingly,

"The Power of Sports" illuminates Murphy's feelings of frustration and rage at the endemic degradation that Black Americans were forced to tolerate, testifying to the wrenching psychic pain that persona poetry is so adept at capturing:

> They call me mechanical, stoic and all business
> at the track, but riding a horse fast is easy
> compared to my toughest job—holding rein
> over the large, angry, bitter colored man
> that lives inside.[38]

Evincing the emotional burden of racial performance, Walker recalls the metaphorical mask that Murphy's contemporary Paul Laurence Dunbar poignantly described in his 1895 poem "We Wear the Mask." Although Dunbar more specifically refers to a minstrel mask "that grins and lies," his focus on the subterfuge that Black Americans employ to conceal the pain of dehumanization—"We sing, but oh the clay is vile / Beneath our feet, and long the mile / But let the world dream otherwise"—resonates with this poem's portrait of Murphy.[39] William Rhoden notes that Murphy was called "the Machine" because he carefully concealed his emotions while he rode, projecting a "cool, unflappable control."[40] Yet the Murphy persona's admission—the "large, angry, bitter colored man / that lives inside"—pushes beyond the mask that Dunbar's poem evokes, which, as Quashie notes, has "little quality of an inner life."[41] In Walker's rendering, readers are invited to peer behind this "cool, unflappable" veneer to ruminate on what Ann Cvetkovich describes as the "complex accounts of what it *feels* like for people of color to live in the context of racism."[42]

Moreover, as Taylor notes of the repertoire of dramatic scenarios, we become "participants, spectators, or witnesses," which "precludes a certain kind of distancing."[43] While poetry is not a live performance, Walker's creative recuperation of both the mise-en-scène of the late-nineteenth-century racetrack and the interiority of its most accomplished athlete is akin to the scenario Taylor describes, particularly with regard to the relationship Walker establishes with us as readers. We are not passive observers, in other words, but instead witnesses who must grapple with the cultural dissonance that Murphy endured between acclaim and degradation, contemplating the continuation of those racialized experiences in our own time. As Walker emphasizes in "Blinders," no matter how much Murphy (and other African American athletes) achieve, they can never shed their Blackness and the attendant stereotypes that dark skin hues entail:

> I won the Derby at Latonia five times.
> Got four American Derby trophies.
> I took three at Churchill Downs.
>
> But at least twice a day
> somebody called me a n[*****].[44]

Walker invites readers to bear witness to the embodied experience of anti-Black violence that resonates with LeBron James's earlier lamentation about the defacement of his property. And as the legendary basketball player Kareem Abdul-Jabbar noted in response to the widespread Black Lives Matter protests in 2020, "Racism in America is like dust in the air. It seems invisible—even if you're choking on it—until you let the sun in. Then you see it's everywhere."[45] "Blinders" makes the endemic ideology of white supremacy visible, showing that Murphy's unrivaled success at the track, like James's and Abdul-Jabbar's on the court, did not ultimately shield him from racism. In so doing, Walker suggests the longstanding precarity of sports as a pipeline to wealth and especially political capital.

Moving from the "quiet" of the mind to concerns with the internalized white gaze—what Du Bois terms "double consciousness" —and resistance to anti-Black stereotypes,[46] Walker spotlights Murphy's efforts to use his public platform to contest racial disparities, creating further parallels between him and James, Abdul-Jabbar, and scores of other contemporary Black athletes.[47] In "Black Gentry," for example, the Murphy persona describes his subversion of caricatures performed routinely on nineteenth-century minstrel stages:

> I've been to a minstrel show. I know the opinion
> some folks have of colored men
> and I've seen some of my people believe themselves
> to be those same ragged fools.

> I don't jig or shuffle. I don't scratch my head
> and delight in my own ignorance.
>
> I wear the finest clothes—not to parade around
> the Colored Fair, but so strangers know I'm a gentleman.[48]

Confronting the cultural stereotypes of Black inferiority ("ragged fools") popularized in the ever-expanding postbellum entertainment industry, Walker represents Murphy as a man determined to prove that he is a dignified citizen, "a gentleman" worthy of respect. While such a portrait could be read as a tacit endorsement of respectability politics—the understanding that anti-Black discrimination can only be countered through the adoption of the codes and norms of the dominant white majority[49]—Walker is careful to illustrate Murphy's interest in combating, not acceding to, the ideology of white supremacy:

> When they see me traveling with my white valet
> from Kentucky to Saratoga to Chicago and back,
> they are forced to take pause, forced to look twice.[50]

Murphy, as Walker imagines him, was consciously using his success as a jockey to denaturalize expectations of Black servitude.

At the same time that Walker interprets Murphy's historical significance with regard to disrupting stereotypes, he underscores the jockey's frustration with members of the Black community who interpreted his display of wealth and privilege as a betrayal of his Blackness. In the aptly titled "Negritude Test," the Murphy persona notes, "many question my blackness / Accuse me of believing / I am white"; subverting fallacies about racial authenticity, Murphy asserts,

> But if the prerequisite for
> owning instead of renting,
> wearing suits instead of rags,
> eating ham instead of scraps
>
> and enjoying champagne over
> pot liquor is being white,
> then I'm as Irish as they come.[51]

Through this representation of Murphy's struggles against racist caricatures, Walker traces the origins of essentialist ideologies both within and without Black communities—ideologies that continue to constrain African Americans' self-expression. As Kwame Anthony Appiah contends, "If I had to choose between Uncle Tom and Black Power, I would, of course, choose the latter. But I would like not to have to choose. I would like other options."[52] Correspondingly, Walker shows that, in the late nineteenth century, being white became synonymous with socioeconomic mobility ("enjoying champagne over / pot liquor"), whereas being Black was equated with abject poverty ("rags" and "scraps"); and notions of authenticity were predicated on these racial configurations. Unraveling these threads in regard to one of the first Black athlete celebrities, Walker portrays Murphy as a multifaceted individual, not as a signifier of a homogeneous collective. By extension, Walker encourages readers to apply those lessons to the contemporary landscape, in which, as Appiah notes, similarly one-dimensional racial scripts are reinforced.

"They Say"

Importing archival documents into *Isaac Murphy*, Walker also "'brushes against the grain' . . . of monumental history in order that the ruins of the dismembered past be retrieved."[53] To this end, he exposes the denigrating nineteenth-century media portraits of Murphy and other African Americans, showing that fame and public approbation were always coupled with the rhetoric of racial inferiority. In "Colored Jockeys Show the Way," Walker reproduces a headline and excerpts from a story from the "*New York Herald, September 20, 1889*," in which the unnamed reporter reveals endemic anti-Black biases, while implicitly raising alarm bells about African Americans' domination at the racetrack:

> The sons of Ham outrode the children of Japheth
> with a vengeance, for not a single white boy
> was successful in guiding a winner past the judges.
>
> It was a field day for the dusky riders,
> and they forced their Caucasian competitors
> to take positions in the background.[54]

Deploying the word "dusky" and drawing on racist biblical interpretations that delineate distinct and hierarchical lineages for people of African and European descent, the *New York Herald* is not simply reporting factual truths. As Wendy W. Walters argues, "Where the archive records people as slave, coolie, and arsonist, black international creative writers set these languages mobile, aspirational, and open to the subjunctive, asking: what if they were rebel, lover, leader?"[55] Walker puts precisely these sorts of destabilizing questions to the documents he cites, indicating the archive's limitations when it comes to documenting the lives of Murphy and other postbellum African Americans, while pressuring the historiographic methods used to construct dominant notions of the past.

Further, "Colored Jockeys Show the Way" registers increased anxieties among Euro-Americans about the potential threat posed by Black Americans' attempts to avail themselves of opportunities in sports and other burgeoning postbellum industries. As Mooney argues, white nineteenth-century journalists and turfmen "sought to acknowledge the special position of black horsemen in ways that would strengthen racial subordination, rather than imperiling it amid debate over the relationship of freedom and equality for African Americans."[56] Inhabiting the perspective of Eli Jordan, Murphy's esteemed trainer, Walker exposes Black jockeys' precarious sociocultural position and the strategies used to eventually expel them from a sporting arena that they had effectively dominated:

> Between not hirin' blacks, made-up suspensions
> an accidents that left many black riders
> crippled or dead, I believe somebody
> in a back room somewhere made a plan
>
> to keep all the green,
> to make horse racin' a whites-only sport.
> So they forced us out a the business one by one.
>
> The first Kentucky Derby had thirteen black riders.
> A generation later you could hardly find one.[57]

Juxtaposing the *New York Herald* report with the imagined voices of Jordan, Murphy, and other Black men and women, Walker "loosens" these figures, to use Rancière's apposite term, from the degradations imputed to them in white-authored accounts. Walker further shows that Murphy was the original victim of what Rhoden refers to as "Jockey Syndrome," which "usually involves a series of maneuvers to facilitate racist outcomes, including the taking away of previously granted rights and the diluting of access through coercive power and force. . . . In short, the conspicuous success of black jockeys led to their demise."[58] Denaturalizing this process by which social spaces once populated by scores of Black jockeys came to be exclusively filled with "Caucasian competitors," *Isaac Murphy* uses the imagination to bring the history that Rhoden recounts to life. In the process, Walker raises critical questions about what contemporary Americans think of as traditionally "Black" and "white" cultural sites.[59]

Along similar epistemological lines, Walker calls attention to the scores of African American women whose names often do not appear in the dominant narratives of US sporting history but are nonetheless essential to it. In addition to voicing America Burns's experiences, Walker inhabits the perspective of Lucy Murphy, Isaac's wife, through whom he elucidates African American women's efforts to become socially mobile in the years following the Civil War. As many critics have noted, nineteenth-century Black women were systematically denied access to "the cult of true womanhood"—"piety, purity, submissiveness, and domesticity"—and at the same time subject to the dehumanizing stereotypes of the licentious jezebel and the asexual, subservient mammy.[60] Describing the pressure on nineteenth-century Black women writers, Hazel Carby writes, "They had to define a discourse of black womanhood which would not only address their exclusion from the ideology of true womanhood but, as a consequence of this exclusion, would also rescue their bodies from a persistent association with illicit sexuality."[61] Walker creatively recounts Lucy's negotiation of these pressures, by embodying the ideals of "true womanhood" while remaining resistant to the white-supremacist forces that sought to deny her and Isaac their dignity.

Through Walker's focus on Lucy's private thoughts, he likewise shifts readers' focus away from the objectified Black woman's body and toward the complexity of Lucy's interiority, what Quashie referred to earlier as the "sovereignty" of the quiet mind. In "Keeper of the Flame," Lucy reflects on the supportive role she plays in Isaac's life, noting, "he loved horses so much / I learned to love them too" and

> Men work hard to become the legends
> they create. But as hard as roosters work
> to lift that sun every day, it's hens
> that give them something to crow about.[62]

In addition to this emphasis on Lucy's femininity and commitment to her husband's needs, Walker highlights the significance of her domestic role as the mistress of her own home: "Once when my Isaac was traveling, I polished my silver. / Not some white lady's silver, but my own."[63] Lucy's investment in traditional gender roles is not a mark of a contemporary feminist stance, but it is especially notable within the context of nineteenth-century racial discourses that Walker has her asserting these signs of domestic refinement, offering a counternarrative to denigrating caricatures of Black women that continue to pervade US culture.

In the same way that Walker associates Lucy with the middle-class mores historically propagated as the exclusive province of white women, he inverts the white gaze in order to reimagine Lucy's resistance to the oppressive forces that sought to further marginalize her and her husband. In the elegiac "How to Break a Thoroughbred," for example, Lucy ruminates on the white backlash against Black participation that sullied Murphy's reputation and eventually cost him his place in the limelight:

> They say it was flipping.
> They say it was the champagne.
> They say he could no longer make the weights.
> They say he lost the desire to win.
>
> I say they thought he forgot his place.
> I say they needed to show us who was boss.
>
> They set out to break his spirit—
> but ended up breaking his heart.[64]

Juxtaposing the voice of "they"—the white power structure—with Lucy's "I" and "us," Walker penetrates the façade of the spurious reasons invented to justify the negative press that Murphy suddenly began to receive toward the end of his career. Indeed, Wigginton suggests that Murphy's increasing wealth and "ability to purchase a home in an exclusive white neighborhood" threatened a white economic stronghold, leading to various efforts to circumscribe the opportunities that he and other Black jockeys previously had to compete at the racetrack. McDaniels similarly notes that by 1890, "the once flawless professional jockey [Murphy] had become a pariah to whites"; he adds, "For Murphy in particular, and for African Americans in general, the decade would be marked by expulsion, alienation, exclusion, and the increased stigmatization of Black masculinity as corrupt and inherently menacing."[65] Exposing these trends from Lucy's imagined perspective, Walker subverts the authority of white journalists and the horse-racing establishment—what Rancière might term "the noisy stage of the orators"—that engineered Murphy's precipitous downfall.[66]

For Walker, it seems, availing himself of poetic license is necessary in order to excavate embodied experiences (or what Taylor terms the "repertoire") that were not set down in the written record. In so doing, readers may experience this postbellum history, however speculative, through the voice of a faithful wife mourning her husband's heartbreak and, more implicitly, the dashed dreams of Reconstruction and Black liberation. As Walker notes in a recent essay, "One of the more important things that I have learned after crafting multiple volumes of historical poetry can best be summed up with one of my mama's favorite sayings, 'There's two sides to every story and then there's the truth.' I always took that to mean that each witness has his or her point of view and opinion, but the truth is the sum total of everybody's point of view. I have come to see, even more discernibly, that the more points of view you add, ballasted by memory, research, and imagination, the closer to the truth you get."[67] Bringing all relevant materials, including the imagination, to bear on Murphy's story, Walker unfolds a series of truths about a once-trumpeted jockey who has long disappeared from popular cultural memory. In the process, Walker suggests that horse racing was a resonant site where the postbellum promise of meritocracy was tested and, ultimately, met with a trenchant national recommitment to white supremacy. On the first Kentucky Derby day in 1875, "a black jockey was almost predetermined to cross the finish line first, as 14 out of the 15 riders in the race were

African American."[68] By contrast, Mooney reports about the 2017 Kentucky Derby, "When the horses enter the gate for the 143rd Kentucky Derby, their jockeys will hail from Louisiana, Mexico, Nebraska and France. None will be African-American. That's been the norm for quite a while. When Marlon St. Julien rode the Derby in 2000, he became the first black man to get a mount since 1921."[69] This whitewashing of the racetrack and other social spaces often goes unnoticed, and Walker's collection performs the important cultural work of tracing this rise and fall of Black jockeys through horse racing's most accomplished African American.

Via Murphy and the postbellum promises and failures he signifies, Walker also troubles a redemptive timeline charting a progressive march forward toward racial equality. "Here Lies . . ." describes the ways in which Murphy's corpse was subject to the caprice of white segregationists and, later, to a post–Civil Rights desire for atonement, without considering what Murphy's own desires might have been. First, Murphy's ghost laments, "they stabled me in a stall at the African Cemetery," comparing his treatment to that of the horses that were treasured for their bodies and then discarded, while evincing the separate but unequal burial grounds common throughout the Jim Crow United States.[70] When winds of racial change began to blow through Kentucky, Murphy became a pawn in white attempts to publicly display their socially just stance. As McDaniels notes, "In January 1967, the vice president of the Kentucky Club Tobacco Company, Stuart F. Bloch, saw an opportunity to both gain publicity for his company and honor the memory of Isaac Burns Murphy. The idea was for the tobacco company to create a monument to Murphy and rebury him at Man o' War Park in Lexington, Kentucky. . . . Apparently, no one discussed the proposal with Lexington's African American community, which would be losing one of its symbols of achievement and success."[71] Walker describes this turn of events from Murphy's first-person perspective, emphasizing his lack of agency across this long expanse of time and thereby challenging teleological narratives of sports and, by extension, US history:

> Years later, my bones almost dust, they dug up
> what was left then placed me in the ground
> beneath a big monument next to Man o' War.

And if that wasn't respect enough they dug us both up
and buried us again at the Kentucky Horse Park.

I know I'm the only black jockey buried here.
And I know I finally got my name and face in stone.

But they left my Lucy back in the cold hard ground
next to an empty hole without me to share forever with.

Even in death I feel the sting of race and sport,
while I hover at the front doors of the Park—
like a ghost lawn jockey.[72]

"Even in death," Murphy is still objectified, used as a token to fend off calls for the complex and painful work of reckoning with the postbellum white-supremacist violence (gradual and immediate) that purged African Americans from the racetrack. And whereas McDaniels ably recounts this history, Walker creatively recuperates Murphy's and his family's interior lives in emotionally evocative, often "quiet" ways that suggest parallels with today's "sting of race and sport."

Additionally, Walker displaces the white authorities whose accounts made their way into the archive and focalizes instead the African American voices that were only documented in fragments and by proxy during the postbellum epoch and have not been well curated since. As Taylor notes, "The challenge is not to 'translate' from an embodied expression into a linguistic one or vice versa but to recognize the strengths and limitations of each system."[73] Walker's poetry puts recorded history and imagined embodied expressions in dialogue, "journeying into subterranean passages," as Rancière described, in order to uncover "hidden truth[s]."[74] Through this creative process, *Isaac Murphy* offers a blueprint for the paradoxical experience of many contemporary Black athletes, who are able to rise to sociocultural prominence and top economic brackets but remain alienated by anti-Black rhetoric and violence. As Drew D. Brown notes, "Sports can be viewed as a perpetuator of racial differences and a vehicle for widespread racism"; more specifically, "just as athletics can be used to 'liberate' Black males, it can also be used to perpetuate the images of Black masculinity that supported the stereotypes imposed by Whites."[75] To evince this point, Brown recounts the NFL commentator Gus Johnson's 2009 remark after Tennessee Titans running back Chris Johnson sprinted across the field: "He's got getting-away-from-the-cops speed."[76] Rather than a sign of his adroit athletic skill—no doubt a result of intense practice—Johnson's performance was used to publicly reify the caricature of Black men as inherently suspect and dangerous. Given the history that Walker recounts, it is deeply troubling but not especially surprising that Black athletes' achievements continue to be refracted through the lens of centuries-old stereotypes that affirm whiteness as normative and Blackness as alternatingly exotic and criminal.

Though many of the poignant insights and experiences in *Isaac Murphy* spring from Walker's imagination, they nonetheless offer crucial guidance for Murphy's twenty-first-century descendants. As McDaniels reminds us, "The white majority worked systematically to regulate and manage the narratives associated with people of African descent and their individual and collective histories, especially those that demonstrated blacks' ability to rise above their circumstances. To be born disconnected from one's history—past and present—is one sure way to confuse and alienate an individual's sense of destiny and purpose."[77] Walker, through his Rancière-esque lyrical history, invites readers to question the vestiges of slavery and Jim Crow that remain both within the whitewashed world of horse racing and well beyond it. As Michael Eric Dyson laments, "American sports, despite all of the black bodies that make it go, is still a profoundly white enterprise."[78] As with Murphy and other postbellum African American athletes who were able to compete interracially but were still treated as inferior, contemporary Black players' athletic prominence, especially in basketball and football, often serve to affirm white stereotypes of Black men's inherent physical gifts and, conversely, insufficient mental ones. The polyvocal, multivalent history that Walker represents in *Isaac Murphy* counteracts such willful effacement of Black ambition and excellence. In addition, Walker speculates about the desires, frustrations, and sociopolitical outlooks of Murphy and his loved ones, subverting the tendency to focus on Black celebrities' physicality while reminding readers of the private thoughts and embodied experiences that remain hidden from the exploitation of white America.

In considering the ways in which archive and repertoire become entangled in dramatic scenarios, Taylor notes that there is always the possibility of "friction between the social actors and the [assigned] roles," whereby transgressions may be staged and the ideologies of oppressive regimes subverted, even within a rather conventional framework.[79] In *Isaac Murphy*, Walker takes us back to a series of early sports scenarios in which Murphy was cast into a familiar role in which it was understood that he was permitted to climb the meritocratic ladder at the racetrack (albeit only temporarily), at least in part because his athleticism confirmed degrading ideas about Blacks as more physically than mentally endowed. At the same time, Walker recuperates embodied acts and interior thoughts that cut against the grain of this scenario for Black athletes, lyrically enlivening the repertoire in order to challenge the archival knowledge propagated by, as one example, the *New York Herald*. In the process, Walker implies that the tension between archive and repertoire in Murphy's sports "scenario" is one that has reconstituted itself on fields, courts, tracks, and sports arenas of all sorts ever since. As the NFL defensive end Michael Bennett asserts in his part memoir, part exposé *Things That Make White People Uncomfortable* (2018), "The reality is that I'm a Black man in America and I'm going to be a Black man in America long after I'm out of this [National Football] league. . . . It makes some people so angry to see us taking a stand (or taking a knee). I get that they watch football to escape, and they view us as entertainers, here to give them a break from the so-called real world. But we aren't machines. We are human beings."[80] When Walker revivifies Isaac Burns Murphy and his loved ones, he provides historical context for the vexing experiences of Bennett and others, evincing the recurring, reductive (even machine-like) parts that Black athletes are enjoined to play and the various ways—"quiet" and public—in which they refuse these dehumanizing scripts.

Walker's final poem in the collection, "Praise Song," written from his own point of view, exhorts the reader not only to take responsibility for Murphy but also to harness the power of his personal narrative as a source of untapped inspiration:

> Wrap your arms around his story,
> close your eyes,
> feel the wind whispering in your ears.

Grab the reins of any and everything
that makes your heart race.
Find your purpose. Find your purpose
And hold on.[81]

Not unlike the circular shape of the racetrack, Walker returns to the final lines of the collection's first poem—"'Find yo purpose. Find yo purpose' an hold on"—but the speaker is no longer Murphy but the poet.[82] As with Murphy's affirmation, which performed the double duty of encouraging himself and the horse he rode of their right to self-determination, Walker has made his way around Murphy's alternatingly triumphant and imperiling track, thereby making visible the through lines between the postbellum period and the contemporary epoch. Using the second person, Walker then passes this task onto us as readers. Our charge is to, recalling Rancière, "loosen bodies" from the hegemonic gaze and dispense with disempowering cultural scripts (or, as Taylor might put it, scenarios). Instead, we must dedicate our own ride, our "purpose," to making this a society in which the grit and tenacity of figures like Murphy and his family are a cherished part of the national narrative and that values the minds and hearts of Black citizens rather than merely the athletic potential of their bodies.

4
"THE OVERWHELMING EVIDENCE OF HIS ARTISTRY"

Wiping Away the Minstrel Mask in Caryl Phillips's Dancing in the Dark

The contemporary novelist Caryl Phillips, not unlike his poet counterparts in previous chapters (Kevin Young, Adrian Matejka, and Frank X Walker), who ably demonstrated the double-edged nature of Black participation in sports, represents the postbellum, pre–Harlem Renaissance entertainment industry as a site ripe for artistic self-expression, as well as for further racial objectification. Exemplifying Jacques Rancière's description of literature's role in countering hegemonic historical narratives with its own "truth talk,"[1] Phillips's novel *Dancing in the Dark* (2005) recuperates the once-famous, now culturally obscure nineteenth- and early-twentieth-century stars of the stage Bert Williams (1874–1922) and George Walker (1873–1911), as well as their wives, Charlotte Louis ("Lottie") Williams (1866–1929) and Aida Overton Walker (1880–1914), the latter a trailblazing (albeit underappreciated) dancer and choreographer.

"Fully engaged in contemporary issues," Karen Sotiropoulos avers, "Williams and his colleagues brought a black political agenda to their stage productions, even though they worked in commercial theater."[2] As Louis Chude-Sokei likewise observes, "although his name has faded into near-utter obscurity, Egbert Austin—'Bert'—Williams was arguably the first black performer who could be described as an international pop star" and "was rumored to make more money than the American president."[3] He "was acknowledged as the greatest stage comedian in late-nineteenth- and early-twentieth-century America," and likewise "in the period before Harlem's vogue, his was the only black recorded voice regularly and consistently available."[4] At the same time, "black minstrelsy is most often dismissed as either pathological or an unfortunate and pitiable sideline in the transition from a more passive political era into a much more self-assertive and militant one. This too helps obscure Bert Williams even further behind the mask that he could not escape."[5] Using this history as a springboard, Phillips's prologue begins by introducing Bert Williams's unacknowledged spectral presence in the contemporary cultural landscape in which, only a century earlier, he had such profound sway: "If you walk down Seventh Avenue today he is a man who never existed. On this broad Harlem avenue a torn curtain might stir in response to the tug of a hand. Dark hand, now waving."[6] Breathing new life into this faint whisper of a man, Phillips centralizes, as he put it in an interview, "the emotional texture of his [Williams's] life."[7] In addition to excavating Bert's interiority, Phillips elucidates Lottie's, George's, and Aida's emotional tableaux,[8] as they attempted to be recognized as artists in an era and a society prone to reduce them to embodiments of racist and gendered stereotypes.

While historians such as Sotiropoulos, Chude-Sokei, Cedric J. Robinson, and Daphne Brooks, among others, have mined the archives to illuminate these figures' outsized but undervalued impact on US musical and theatrical arenas, Phillips is not guided by the empiricism that governs more conventional historical representations. Instead, he makes use of the tools of imaginative literature both to fill in archival lacunae about these figures and to "reorder the archive's epistemological grammar."[9] In this respect, the novel accords with the methodology that Jeanne Scheper outlines in *Moving Performances: Divas, Iconicity, and Remembering the Modern Stage* (2016). Building on Diana Taylor's conceptions of the archive and the repertoire, Scheper advocates for an inclusive, innovative approach for recuperating marginalized performance histories: "If, as scholars or as consumers, or as fans, we aren't listening to or playing in the archive, or if the archive (understood as tangible, material, or official traces) and the repertoire (understood as ephemeral, embodied, or cultural practices) are not heard together, or the repertoire is ignored, forgotten, or misidentified, then the meaning of these figures (and the tropes, histories, and performances that accrue to their iconicity) is distorted, misrecognized, made illegible, and can, indeed, be lost forever."[10] Utilizing a range of narrative perspectives and modes, Phillips *plays* with traces of the archive and the repertoire in order to shed new light on the complex experiences of Williams, Walker, and Overton Walker (and to lesser extent Lottie Williams) as some of the first famous Black entertainers.

This chapter also extends the work of a number of other critics who have explored the implications of *Dancing in the Dark*. For example, Kathie Birat has considered the novel's depiction of the culturally empowering possibilities of African American performance as outlined by Houston Baker and in contradistinction to what Judith Butler conceives of as performativity, "which sees social behavior as an unconscious and all-encompassing performance."[11] Robert Nowatzki has likewise argued that the novel uses "minstrelsy to represent blackness and whiteness as identities that are constructed through performance."[12] Alternatively, Shauna M. Morgan Kirlew argues that Phillips's women characters, specifically his depictions of Aida and Lottie, "anchor the broader themes of the texts," while *Dancing in the Dark* demonstrates that "intimacy (or lack thereof) is linked specifically to the male protagonists' internalized white supremacy, which projects stereotypical images of black women, particularly as hyper-sexualized and conversely as unseen, unseeable, or undesirable."[13] Yuval Taylor and Jake Austen, on the other hand, find fault with Phillips's representations, particularly of Williams. Emphasizing the pride Williams took in his contributions to the minstrel tradition, Taylor and Austen critique Phillips's "portrayal of Williams as a depressed alcoholic with no offstage vitality."[14] There are certainly other ways to represent Williams (not to mention his wife and George and Aida) other than the portrait that Phillips advances, and the novel's juxtaposition of a range of materials and perspectives gestures toward these varied ways. Phillips, akin to this book's other contemporary writers, calls attention to the methods by which he reconstructs the past, implying the subjective interpretations that shape all historical narratives.

Dancing in the Dark lays bare the material gaps and epistemological limitations we must remain mindful of as we attempt to piece together what Toni Morrison, congruent with Rancière, describes as "a kind of truth. . . . Because facts can exist without human intelligence, but truth cannot."[15] Not purporting to recount all of the facts but instead focused on yielding truths, Phillips uses free indirect discourse to plumb Bert's, Lottie's, George's, and Aida's emotional and psychological states, including both the alienation brought about what W. E. B. Du Bois terms "double consciousness" and the "quiet" interiority that a US public which equates Blackness with public expression has long been reluctant to recognize. "Quiet," Kevin Quashie notes, "is the habitat of the inner life, a selfhood not based on race or gender but on the rages of the interior, a subjectivity sobered and armed by possibility."[16] Speculating about the imagined inner lives of these historical figures and *playing* with archival materials, Phillips eschews the one-dimensionality of the white gaze and reconceptualizes Bert, George, and Aida as artists and not the natural entertainers that the white public assumed them to be. In the process, the novel suggests the relevance of their experiences in current Black artists' negotiation of the limelight, especially regarding representational biases and constraints on self-expression.

"The Unwritten Contract"

Beginning the first chapter in medias res, Phillips introduces readers to Bert and George during a February 1903 performance of their blackface musical comedy *In Dahomey*. Taking readers behind Bert's mask, Phillips highlights the performer's acute awareness of his white audience's deep investment in wielding sociocultural power, within and without the entertainment industry:

> He stares at the contended white faces in the orchestra stalls knowing that he can hold an audience like nobody else in the city. He knows when to go gently with them, and he carefully observes their mood; he knows not to strain the color line for he respects their violence. At other times, when he can sense something close to warmth, he might push and cajole

> a little, and try to show them something that they had not thought of before. . . . He is keen that at the end of the evening, they should all leave safely and without either party having broken the unwritten contract that exists between the Negro performer and his white audience.[17]

Phillips elucidates the tightrope Bert walks between enjoying an empowered position onstage and with one misplaced step or joke becoming a scapegoat for white fears. Debunking pseudoscientific myths about Black natural subservience to whites, Phillips likewise evinces the precarious position that even the most famous (and nimble) Black performers found (and, in many cases, find) themselves in: they must not only countenance the white gaze but also anticipate the mercurial anxieties and desires that inform it.

In this respect, Phillips implies continuity with today's sociocultural and political landscape, in which people of African descent are encouraged to strike an even keel in their public remarks, while they may feel a private sense of rage and disappointment with the often unreasonable expectations of white America. The contemporary comedians Keegan Michael Key and Jordan Peele enacted this dynamic in their recurring skit about former US president Barack Obama and his "anger translator" Luther on their hit Comedy Central series *Key and Peele*. The joke, of course, was that Obama, known for his cool-under-pressure demeanor ("no drama Obama"), was inwardly enraged at the seemingly racially motivated roadblocks to his agenda engineered by the Republicans in control of Congress and likewise supported by their conservative constituents. Peele, playing Obama, and Key, playing Luther, stage this inner conflict and implicitly put the onus on viewers to consider *why* this skit was hilarious. What undue pressures, we had to ask ourselves, did Obama face that he, unlike all other US presidents, needed an "anger translator"? Although Phillips's tone is not comedic, his *Dancing in the Dark* engages in a similar frame-breaking move, whereby readers are encouraged to discern kernels of truth about Black celebrity distinct from the narrative generated by what Rancière describes as "the fictions of the powers that be."[18]

Reimagining Bert's interior thoughts, Phillips likewise turns readers' attention away from the objectification of the stage and toward the complex life of the mind that is routinely ignored in accounts of Black celebrity, both then and now. As Nicole Fleetwood notes, "The racial icon is both an exceptional and a common figure. She or he is exceptional as a symbol of overcoming racial inequality and perceived inferiority; she or he is common, given the American public's familiarity and investment in exhausted notions of race, nation, and (under)achievement."[19] As a famous Black man, Bert is considered exceptional by white audiences ("he can hold an audience like nobody else in the city"), and at the same time these fans are unable to appreciate him beyond "exhausted notions of race." Moreover, for Phillips, Bert is not a tragic figure but instead a groundbreaking one, who is especially adroit at using his stature to push white audiences beyond stereotypes of Black men and women and, however surreptitiously, toward a recognition of their humanity: "He [Bert] understands that one false step and he risks toppling over into the musician's pit and being replaced by Bob Cole or Ernest Hogan or one of the scores of other colored performers who are keen to usurp him without fully understanding that they *do* have the choice of offering these white faces in the orchestra stalls some artistic drollery and a little repose instead of clownish roughness and loud vulgarity."[20] While contemporary appraisals of Williams and his entourage might condemn these figures' repertoire of blackface antics as denigrating and offensive to Black Americans, Phillips recuperates Bert's strategic calculations as acts of artistic agency ("they *do* have the choice"). As Robinson notes, "Aida Overton Walker, George Walker (her husband), and Bert Williams shared a deep resentment towards the dominant representation of blackness in American popular culture and entertainment. Another similarity between these artists was that they all possessed the inventiveness and resolve to appropriate minstrelsy for their own ends."[21] In turn, Phillips's free indirect probing of Bert's interior world disentangles the entertainer from the man and implies that his minstrel act was carefully crafted for distinct political ends.

At the same time, the world beyond the stage continuously threatens the tentative power that Bert establishes on it, as when Bert and Lottie stroll through midtown Manhattan and "hear the word 'n[*****]s' fly from a horse-drawn carriage." Although "neither looks up to investigate what foul mouth has unleashed this missile," Phillips ably describes its polluting aftershocks: "Were they to turn around they would still see the word hurtling around the junction of Fifty-first Street and Broadway, picking up speed here, losing tempo there, as purposefully silent as a bird's flight, yet furiously burning energy deep into the New York night."[22] Even as the couple ignore the harassment, Phillips suggests the chilling pall that it casts over their sense of optimism about an upwardly mobile, liberated future. Moreover, the poignancy of the description and its present-tense action verbs imply that this ephemeral act of "white rage" continues to haunt the contemporary landscape,[23] making it all the more crucial to excavate these experiences and to consider the lessons that they foretell for our own age, in which anti-Black racism remains woven into the fabric of everyday life.

Playing in the archive, Phillips also destabilizes the monologic of dominant narratives to evince the multiple ways of knowing Black cultural history. For instance, he reanimates the repertoire of Bert, George, and Aida, illuminating the frustrations and disappointments (and at times satisfaction) they experienced as they strove to be appreciated as artists, not natural embodiments of the buffoonery and exoticism projected onto people of African descent. As Scheper asserts, "employing critical archival practices that look at, for instance, the interplay of onstage and offstage performances . . . can reveal this aspect of performer's labor: the labor of critique."[24] Additionally, because marginalized theatrical performers were often unsuccessful in their "challenges to the status quo," Scheper encourages critics to appreciate the ways in which the performances themselves and, subsequently, the archive mark these "uneven" attempts at opposing denigrating discourses on and off the stage.[25] Employing the techniques of postmodern fiction, Phillips adopts a similar stance toward both the politics of performance and the curation of afterlives.

In particular, Phillips incorporates scripts that Bert and George enacted, mobilizing these archival documents to the novel's printed page and bookending them with these figures' imagined interior reflections. One such excerpt is from the aforementioned production of *In Dahomey* (1903) and features Bert and George scheming about a bank robbery, which is preceded by Bert speculating about his partner's increasing dissatisfaction with roles that conform to white-supremacist expectations. While this is an especially long passage, it bears full reproduction here as an example of the dexterous ways in which Phillips interlaces materials from the archive and repertoire:

> Some days, Bert feels that their act, although seamless and coherent on the outside, is beginning to fracture internally for George has absolutely no interest in going gently with an audience and learning how to seduce them, and Lord help the man, white or colored, who would dare refer to him with an unpleasant epithet. In fact, an increasingly successful, and confident, George is beginning to act as though he doesn't give a damn about white folks:
>
> *Walker:* I tell you I'm letting you in on this because you're a friend of mine. I could do this alone and let no one in on it. But I want you to share it just because we're good friends. Now after you get into the bank, you fill the satchel with money.
>
> *Williams:* Whose money?
>
> *Walker:* That's the point. We don't know who put the money there, and we don't know why they got it. And they won't know how we got it. All you have to do is fill the satchel. I'll get the satchel—you won't have nothing to bother about—that's 'cause you're a friend of mine, see?
>
> *Williams:* And what do I do with the satchel?
>
> *Walker:* All you got to do is bring it to me at a place where I tell you.
>
> *Williams:* When they come to count up the cash and find it short, then what?
>
> *Walker:* By that time we'll be far, far away—where the birds are singing sweetly and the flowers are in bloom.
>
> *Williams: (With doleful reflection)* And if they catch us they'll put us so far, far away we never hear no birds singin'. And everybody knows you can't smell no flowers through a stone wall.
>
> He listens to the applause for this slow and cautious character. He listens to the applause for George's dapper, city-slick Negro dude. Does the audience understand that his character,

> this Shylock Homestead whose dull-witted antics amuse them, bears no relationship to the real Egbert Austin Williams? Every evening this question worries him, and every evening as he takes his curtain call he tries to ignore it, but he often lies in his bed late into the night trying to calculate where he might force a little more laughter here, or squeeze an inch more room to work with there, and therefore impress them with the overwhelming evidence of his artistry.[26]

Phillips enjoins readers to bear witness to the conflicting impulses at work during this performance: "George is beginning to act as though he doesn't give a damn about white folks," "I could do this alone and let no one in on it," and "Does the audience understand that his character, Shylock Homestead whose dull-witted antics amuse them, bears no relationship to the real Egbert Austin Williams?" Coupled together, this passage's staged lines and interior thoughts underscore these artists' negotiation of pervasive stereotypes about Black male criminality circulating during the decades following the Civil War.

Further reorienting the white hegemonic gaze so that readers imagine this act through Bert's eyes, Phillips evinces the frustration of Black entertainers whose calculated attempts to be appreciated as artists went unappreciated by white audiences who used these stage personae to confirm their deep-seated beliefs in Black inferiority. As Nowatzki argues, "The novel repeatedly juxtaposes the performative, counterfeit nature of Williams's and Walker's stage personae with the white audience's belief that they are simply being themselves."[27] Indeed, Phillips decouples performer from performance, reminding readers of the demeaning tendency in our own time to collapse the difference between Black artists' personae onstage and their multifaceted identities off it. Additionally, Phillips's repeated reference to the audience's applause revivifies the appropriative relationship—what Eric Lott terms "love and theft"—that white audiences pursued with Bert, George, and their colleagues.[28] That is, the novel suggests that audiences were keen to shore up an essentialist, hierarchical racial logic by witnessing anti-Black stereotypes enacted onstage.

When the troupe travels to England, where their performances of *In Dahomey* are so popular that they are invited to Buckingham

Palace, Phillips contraposes press accounts with Bert's embodied response, continuing to defamiliarize dominant narratives in the process. For instance, "*Mostly About People, London,* 1903" imputes animalistic characteristics to Bert ("like an elephant on the broad path ['Bun Avenue'] at the Zoo") and fails to distinguish between the act and the actor: "With his heavy, rocking gait, he [Bert] 'hovers around' like one who has found himself on the stage by taking the wrong passage, and thinks he may as well stay there since no one has interfered with him."[29] Phillips undercuts this objectifying, exoticizing account by returning to Bert's perspective on their travels throughout the country: "Bert especially enjoys Oxford, the center of books and learning."[30] Moreover, he becomes fascinated with John Ogilby's 1670 volume *Africa*, a text that "always enabled Bert to experience the temporary peace of being able to moor himself in some other place."[31] The novel's reimagining of Bert's "quiet" habits underscores the distinction between his erudite proclivities and the dim-witted man he plays onstage, while subverting the authority of the archive to tell us the complete history of Bert Williams and, by extension, Black cultural production more generally. As Diana Taylor ruminates, "Whose memories, whose trauma, 'disappear' if only archival knowledge is valorized and granted permanence?"[32] Interpolating press clippings with Bert's private thoughts, Phillips takes up this question and uses the imaginative landscape of the novel to inscribe often-unacknowledged traumas into the written record.

Further, during Bert and George's restaged *In Dahomey* tour of the United Kingdom, they pose their own questions that continue to haunt us as we encounter these turn-of-the-century celebrities: "As the ship moves slowly in the direction of the United States, Bert stands on deck with his partner. He turns to George and silently revisits the same questions that have plagued him through many lonely evenings. . . . Is the colored performer to be forever condemned to pleasing a white audience with farce, and then attempting to conquer these same people with music and dance? Is the colored American performer to be nothing more than an exuberant, childish fool named Aunt Jemima, Uncle Rufus, or simply Plantation Darky, who must be neither unique nor individual?"[33] Through these uneasy queries about the fine line between perpetuating stereotypes and, to recall Ralph Ellison's phrase, "chang[ing] the joke to slip the yoke," Phillips draws implicit connections with our own era, in which African American entertainers are subjected to distinctly racialized (not to mention gendered) expectations.[34] As the performance theorist Harvey Young observes, an "*idea* of the black body has been and continues to be projected across actual physical bodies"; moreover, "the misrecognition of individuated bodies as 'the black body' creates similar experiences."[35] This homogenization of Blackness has also long been entangled with public performances of stereotypes and caricature, especially since "the blackface minstrel tradition has never left us, not since the early nineteenth century."[36] *Dancing in the Dark*'s emphasis on the interior and emotional landscapes of these Black artists makes readers aware of these oppressive patterns of white control and exploitation, while encouraging us to appreciate figures like Bert and George on their own terms.

Phillips's attention to Du Boisian double consciousness *and* Quashian quiet also allows for a reorientation toward today's Black celebrities, whereby we can discern the constraints placed on their artistic expressions. For example, Phillips imagines Bert contemplating his fame while trying to reconcile the anti-Black stereotypes in which he traffics: "*In Dahomey* is doing well, and he and George continue to collaborate with Mr. Jesse Shipp, with whom they are working hard to sharpen every aspect of the show. Theirs is the first all-Negro production on Broadway—real Broadway—and everybody is talking about it. Bob Cole and Ernest Hogan are jealous, but even *they* are talking. Everybody is talking. Just thirty years of age and he is starring in a musical show on Broadway. What more could he want?"[37] This seemingly existential question is then answered as Bert recalls his and George's early days in San Francisco, when "they were encouraged to impersonate Africans," and their subsequent train journey to New York, when they dreamed of the unbridled freedom that seemed to be on offer to Americans of a paler complexion: "'A colored man like me don't need no ship when I've got this whole wide country to roam free in.' But this was before gold-toothed George was beaten by the rabble, and thereafter began to noisily proclaim what they both already knew to be true, that America wasn't so wide and free after all. For a colored man, that is."[38] Bert is unable to enjoy the fruits of his labor because of the nagging reminders of his subordinate status.

As the novel segues into further memories, Phillips continues to offer rich context for Bert's feelings of disappointment and alienation, despite being the creative pioneer and star of the first Black show on Broadway. Bert recalls a race riot, during which he hides in the theater and George is brutally beaten by a white mob whose recognition of the star only further incites their wrath: "'Walker!' They beat him with fierce blows until he fell over. . . . And a half dozen blocks to the south, Bert hides in his dressing room with the lights out, his makeup already removed, his street clothes hanging neatly from his broad shoulders, ready to leave when America is ready to receive him."[39] Bert's next memory is of meeting an actual man from Dahomey in San Francisco, who, along with his fellow Dahomans, is sent back home after the stage manager deems the impersonators more palatable to the fantastical yearnings of the audience to see "savage" Africans on display: "The man from Dahomey stands in front of Bert and stares in disbelief at this pitiful apparition and he worries about this strange land called America."[40] On the next page and just preceding several pages of the script to *In Dahomey*, Phillips imagines, "Nineteen-year-old Bert stands barefoot with a mottled animal skin draped over one shoulder, and he watches the melancholy men and women of Dahomey prepare for their departure."[41] Through these juxtapositions that both focalize Bert's perspective and, because they are free indirect rather than first person, maintain a narrative distance, Phillips emphasizes the surrogate nature of the minstrel stage. Additionally, he affirms that white audiences preferred to patronize imitations of the savagery they imagined rather than engaging with the humanity (or the artistry) of actual Dahomans or, for that matter, Bert and George.

Continuing to interlace archive and repertoire, Phillips next returns to the script for the Broadway production of *In Dahomey*, "A Negro Musical Comedy," providing the list of the cast members, which includes Bert, George, Aida, and Lottie, as well as the dialogue to act 1, scene 1.[42] In the scene, Dr. Straight (played by Fred Douglas) is trying to sell a gathered crowd "Straightaline," which "straightens knappy or knotty hair," and "Obliticuticus," a skin-bleaching cream that "removes the outer skin and leaves in its place a peachlike complexion that can't be duplicated—even by peaches."[43] Restaging this performance, Phillips bears witness to these artists' strategic forms of social critique. While the script appears to satirize Black desires for "white" hair and skin for comedic effect, the dialogue implicitly puts the lie to biological claims about inherent white supremacy by suggesting that the epidermis is only an outer layer that signifies nothing about what lies beneath its surface.

This excerpted scene from the script of *In Dahomey*, buttressed as it is by Bert's aforementioned recollection of "watch[ing] the melancholy men and women of Dahomey prepare for their departure," accrues more complexity, evincing the ways in which "repertoires trouble and produce the possibility for a new conception of archives as spaces of critique."[44] For example, after Fred Douglas's lines in act 1, scene 1, end, Phillips returns to Bert's inner world: "Strangely enough, the first night that he actually slept in the house on Seventh Avenue, he was sure that he was in Africa. He dreamt of natives with bare feet and painted faces who leapt wildly in frenzied dances."[45] Phillips imagines that Williams was haunted by his staged depiction of Africa, with white primitivist fantasies circulating in popular culture seeping into his consciousness. In fact, "his dreams were an embarrassment that he knew he must never admit to carrying in his head."[46] Transposing the script alongside these passages about Williams's emotional turmoil, Phillips demonstrates his careful research into the lives and careers of his historical subjects, but he does not allow the limitations of the archival record to constrain his representation, especially with regard to the "quiet" (or, in this case, the disquiet) of the mind. As Quashie rightly notes, "The problem here is not expressiveness per se, but that black expressiveness is so tethered to what is public and to a discourse of resistance."[47] In Phillips's portrait of Bert, he is especially concerned with the emotional repertoire that was (often by necessity) withheld from appropriative white audiences and onlookers. Not unlike the imaginative representations of the sporting arena examined in previous chapters, *Dancing in the Dark* invites readers to question the overemphasis on public expression as the basis for understanding Blackness in general and Black celebrity in particular.

Phillips likewise reframes George's public statements, suggesting the epistemological gaps that remain unfilled when we rely solely on the written record. Situating an excerpt from "The Real Coon of the Stage," an article Walker published in *Theatre Maga-*

zine,[48] between narrative passages, Phillips distinguishes between what was publicly asserted and privately expressed and implies that "truth talk," to recall Rancière, is accessible in the interplay between them:

> Hell, I ain't nobody's uncle, and I ain't called Tom, cries his partner. George believes, but Bert wonders why George has chosen not to speak with him about his beliefs.
>
> > All that was expected of a colored performer was singing and dancing and a little storytelling. . . . [white performers] used to make themselves look as ridiculous as they could when portraying a "darky" character. In their "make up" they always had tremendously big red lips and their costumes were frightfully exaggerated. The one fatal result of this to the colored performer was that they imitated the white performers in their make-up as "darkies." Nothing seemed more absurd than to see a colored man making himself ridiculous in order to portray himself.
> >
> > GEORGE WALKER
>
> George moves toward the conclusion of his speech now, taking them through their own history. Farewell, Tambo and Bones, white men with blackened faces acting out their fantasy. . . . George insists that they are performers, they are artists, and he expects them to carry themselves as such, and behave with the dignity that is their calling at this point in their history. George insists that America expects.
>
> Later, when the company has dispersed, Bert resolves to remind his partner that indeed they are performers, but it is the paying audience, and not George's mythical America, that expects.[49]

Employing both this collage method of archival citation and free indirect discourse, Phillips augments understandings of George's evolving outlook, which became increasingly political over the course of his career: "Nothing seemed more absurd than to see a colored man making himself ridiculous in order to portray himself." Also distinguishing between Bert's and George's conceptions of their roles—"George insists that they are performers, they are artists" versus "Bert resolves to remind his partner that indeed they are performers, but it is the paying audience, and not George's mythical America, that expects"—Phillips challenges the tendency to homogenize Black people's outlooks, as well as to assume that one individual speaks for the whole.

"I'd Like to Be a Lady"

Reimagining Aida's and Lottie's perspectives, and placing their thoughts and feelings alongside Bert's and George's, Phillips likewise revivifies them as both complex individuals and innovative artists. As Daphne Brooks observes, "Singers Abbie Mitchell, Lottie Williams, and Hattie McIntosh drew critical attention for their roles in the musical [*In Dahomey*], and the activist actress and choreographer Aida Overton Walker garnered praise from journalists and audiences that often rivaled that of the stars of the show. These women's participation in the company reinforced the belief that theatre could serve as a particularly viable field of opportunity for African American women of the new century."[50] Chude-Sokei adds that Overton Walker "managed to unveil a layer of protofeminist assertion within and against the sexual orthodoxies of both white expectations and black 'womanhood' and pan-Africanism itself."[51] Yet, as Scheper notes, "critics were ill equipped to understand the larger meaning and significance of Overton Walker's career," a point she evinces with a contemporaneous reviewer's critique: "She [Overton Walker] looks like some pretty savage and there is an unconventionality about her movements which suggest[s] the jungle."[52] In addition to these degradations, Aida and Lottie have suffered more cultural neglect than their husbands, who are often forgotten or shunted to the side because of their capitulations to blackface and other derogatory stereotypes. Creatively recuperating Aida and Lottie, Phillips enjoins readers to consider "the simultaneity of oppression" they confronted and the artistry they performed, while drawing through lines with the experiences of today's Black women celebrities.[53]

Through Lottie, Phillips elucidates the particular pressures placed on women to sideline their own aspirations and rely on men for economic support, whereas he portrays Aida as a figure equally undervalued both by her husband and by a white- and male-dominated entertainment industry. As Phillips reimagines Lottie's and Aida's "quiet" thoughts, he also subverts the default focus on Black women's bodies or their public personae. For example, in the early part of the novel, Aida and Lottie are both performers, comfortable confiding in each other about their personal lives. When Lottie tells her friend of her decision to marry Bert, Aida expresses skepticism—"Lottie child, you really want to marry a colored performer? Girl, you scarcely know the man"; but Lottie eschews this concern, and her thoughts immediately jump to her aging appearance: "These days she finds it necessary to apply extra makeup, which both depresses and alarms her. She knows that at her age she ought to be thinking of taking up something other than hoofing and clowning. . . . All young Mr. Williams does is *act* as though he is better than other folks, and this is good enough for her."[54] Justifying Lottie's need to marry Bert by considering her waning ability to capitalize on either her roles onstage or her youthful appearance, Phillips demonstrates the additional, intersectional constraints placed on Lottie and Aida's social mobility. In Aida's final attempt to convince her friend to call off her wedding plans, she lodges her own complaint about the subordinate role she foresees playing in George's life: "All they ever think about is what they need to do to make Williams and Walker even more famous. I mean, do you think that either of them are really going to lose any sleep troubling themselves over us?"[55]

This question is answered later in the novel after a dejected Lottie realizes that Bert, who has taken almost immediately to calling his wife "Mother," avoids any form of intimacy with his new bride, and Aida discovers George's affair with the white actress Eva Tanguay. Here Phillips takes full advantage of poetic license, mining personal and emotional turmoil that is absent in the archives of playbills, press clippings, and photographs. As Rancière argues, "Fiction is a way of changing existing modes of sensory presentations and forms of enunciation; or varying frames, scales and rhythms; and of building new relationships between reality and appearance, the individual and the collective."[56] Accordingly, Phillips makes use of his fictional landscape to draw readers into a reconstructed intimacy between these historical Black women artists, whose success in the entertainment industry nonetheless renders them disempowered in their relationships with their husbands. When an emotionally bruised Aida seeks comfort from Lottie after discovering George's affair, Phillips underscores both women's pain and disappointments:

> Aida tries to speak with Lottie, but the more tight-lipped Lottie becomes, the more Aida opens up until Aida eventually tells her what she realizes her friend probably already knows, George and the wild white girl. She knows about this, doesn't she? Lottie nods slowly, understanding that she will have to confess. . . . Has Lottie ever met the woman with George? Lottie shakes her head and wonders if Aida has forgotten that she has done what Bert wished and retired from the stage. Lottie's theatrical circle is shrinking. . . . She smiles at Aida, whose hurt is both public and private, but she has no advice to offer the poor woman, who, luckily does not appear to be asking for any.[57]

In Phillips's representation, Lottie is increasingly isolated, alienated from her "theatrical circle" and denied her husband's warm affections, while Aida is publicly and privately humiliated by George's indiscretions. There is "no advice to offer," since it is impossible for either of them to avail themselves of the agency necessary to disentangle their futures from Bert and George in an era in which an economically independent Black woman artist was nearly an oxymoronic concept.

Phillips is especially concerned with this conundrum for Aida, whose performances the novel reimagines as layered with implications about Black women's lack of individual and collective agency. For example, Phillips juxtaposes Aida's performance of the song "I'd Like to Be a Lady" from *In Dahomey* with George's guilty thoughts about his affair:

> Ada asks him about Eva Tanguay and George notices that his wife has a crazy glint in her coal black eyes and so he kisses her delicately on the cheek and then ushers her from the deck of the ship and in the direction of their cabin, where he will gently cradle her small breasts as though they were newborn twins for he knows that his Ada is partial to such attention.

> I'd like to be a real lady, yes,
> I'd like to be the genuine,
> I'd like to look a real mansion in the face
> and say to my friends "that's mine,"
> I'd like a blue grass lawn on which to give my pink green tea,
> I'd like an English butler to announce my company,
> I'd like a golden sleeping room
> a maid to bathe me in perfume,
> I'd like to be a real lady.[58]

Revivifying Aida's performance of this song alongside her marital woes, Phillips invites twenty-first-century readers to hear the star's plaintive plea, augmented by the knowledge that neither the white audiences who flocked to see *In Dahomey* nor her husband treated her as "a real lady." A few pages later, Phillips inhabits Bert's perspective on George's indiscretions: "Bert stares at his friend, but he deems it best to say nothing further. George likes to live dangerously, he knows this, but as stubborn as Ada can be, doesn't she at least have a right to some dignity?"[59] Withholding Aida's perspective here and enlisting Bert and George instead as the arbiters of her feelings, Phillips reinforces the systemic disregard for Aida's outlook.

Phillips continues this demonstration of Aida's struggle for agency in his juxtaposition of her public statements and performances, alongside contemporaneous press accounts. For example, Phillips cites Aida's response to a *New York Times* critique of *In Dahomey*:

> It is all too easy for a colored show to offend a white audience, so instead we pretend that we have no such emotions, and we are all guilty of this pretense, all of us. We accept that the remotest suspicion of a love story will condemn us to ridicule, but my husband, Mr. George Walker, he is trying to change this situation and I am right behind him in his efforts. There are ten thousand things we must think of every time we make a step and I am not sure that the public is fully aware of the limitations which other persons have made on us.[60]

Aida publicly offers steadfast support of her husband, while (as we have already observed) Phillips's novel emphasizes the fissures in their marriage, as well as the distinct forms of oppression she faces as a woman, which do not make their way into her editorial. Moreover, citing a review from the *Philadelphia Inquirer*, Phillips exposes the "ten thousand" biases that Aida and other Black performers were conscious of as they took the stage: "Those shaded show girls are led by Aida Walker who used to be Ada Overton. Is the change from 'Ady' to 'I-e-da' meant to mark a musical advance by Williams and Walker from Negro melody to operatic music? Aida is a lively lightweight, impish, sprightly, and coquettish. Her complexion is half-tone and her hair hesitates between Marcel waves and Afric kinks."[61] Next, Phillips reproduces the lines to the song "Kinky *Introduced by Aida Overton Walker*":

> Kinky your skin is kind o' kinky,
> But I love you I do,
> Shady maybe but a perfect lady.
> Ev'ry inch of you
> Kinky, Kinky there's a little dinky hut
> Just build for us two,
> Tarry, marry and it's there I'll carry you my Kinky True.
> True.[62]

As Phillips does with George and Bert, he disentangles Aida the complex individual from her performance of minstrel songs such as "Kinky," revealing an astute artist who was also subject to the tyranny of the white patriarchal gaze, evinced by the aforementioned reviewers' degrading portrait (an "impish" "shady show girl" with "Marcel waves and Afric kinks"). Setting these materials alongside one another, Phillips subverts "the fictions of the powers that be and their translation into historiography."[63]

Additionally, Phillips juxtaposes the archive's delimited portrait with glimpses of Aida's inner world that are otherwise unknowable in a historiographic system that tends to rely on both tangible evidence and the accounts of dominant groups. A few pages after the *Philadelphia Inquirer* piece, Phillips describes an anxious Aida wandering Harlem in search of her unfaithful husband until "she realizes that it is time for her to go home and wait in the privacy of their apartment."[64] Once there, we bear witness to Aida's unspoken contemplation, as "she watches the slow light begin to bleed through the black; then through the blue-black; and then finally flood the sky. A new day."[65] As Quashie notes, "Quiet is not a performance or a withholding; instead, it is an expressiveness that is not necessarily legible, at least not in a world that privileges public expressiveness."[66] In *Dancing in the Dark*, we are given traces of Aida's "quiet" moments offstage as she attempts to reconcile her personal woes. Taken together with her song lyrics and press accounts, these private thoughts present a more complete picture of Aida as a forerunner in the fruitful marriage of Black entertainment and political activism, a victim of infidelity and neglect, and, perhaps most importantly, a multifaceted human being whose public persona was distinct from an inevitably quiet life of the heart and mind.

As Joseph Roach points out, performances within the repertoire may produce a "counter-memory," which makes visible "the disparities between history as it is discursively transmitted and memory as it is publicly enacted by the bodies that bear its consequences."[67] Phillips uses the novel to give readers access to the counter-memories enfolded within the repertoire. For instance, when George is dying from syphilis contracted through his affair with Eva, Aida sings to him, and from Bert's perspective, readers get a sense of both her captivating voice and the devotion she showed to her unfaithful husband. Especially given the lack of recordings of Aida, it is key that Phillips reproduces this description in a context removed from the racialized assumptions that would have informed contemporaneous assessments of her public performances: "I sit downstairs with my wife and listen to Aida, who is upstairs singing gentle lullabies to her fragile George. She sings as though serenading a child, and her sweet notes float through the paper-thin walls and then down through the wooden floors, and while one might have ordinarily regarded this as some kind of disturbance, Mother and I just sit and listen, transfixed by the beauty of Aida's waiflike voice."[68] Filtered through Bert and Lottie, who are "transfixed" by Aida's "sweet notes," Phillips enacts a counter-memory to the minstrel stage. Indeed, freed from what Jennifer Stoever describes as "the racial gaze and its aural counterpart, the listening ear,"[69] Phillips recasts Aida's "waiflike" voice as an artful expression of love, not the commodified sound of entertainment (and objectification) set down in the archives.

Surveying our current media landscape, we can discern that circumstances for Black women artists have evolved considerably, with celebrities like Beyoncé arguably surpassing her husband, Jay-Z (Shawn Carter), in popularity and critical acclaim. As L. Michael Gipson notes of Beyoncé's groundbreaking performance at the Coachella Music and Arts Festival in 2018, "The prevailing attitude on that stage was not anything remotely interested in being 'ladylike' (despite modestly appearing in tight-clad Daisy Dukes and a made-up HBCU sweatshirt), but was instead bold, powerful, unafraid of drifting into coarse and provocative language, and was rich in political statements, Southern and street euphemisms, and feminine strength every bit as brass and braggadocio as any man."[70] In recent years especially, Beyoncé has become a signifier of Black women's empowerment, suggesting a break with the objectification of and subsequent cultural amnesia about figures such as Aida Overton Walker and Lottie Williams. And, of course, there are scores of Black women musicians and entertainers who paved the way for Beyoncé and her numerous talented contemporaries. Nonetheless, Farah Jasmine Griffin cautions that "Beyoncé has been easier for the public to accept because she is an entertainer, a long-accepted role for black women. As a sex symbol, moreover, she does not present a threat to established categories."[71] Even as Beyoncé's music has become more overtly politically conscious, the pressure to sustain a circumscribed role persists. As Maiysha Kai observes, "We don't want Beyoncé to enlighten us, only to entertain us. Hell, some of us don't even trust her to enlighten herself. We want her art, not her agency"; such constraints, whereby "there is always a sacrifice, a devil's deal to be paid," hark back to Aida's career and Phillips's representation of it.[72]

At the same time, I would argue that Beyoncé is aware of this history, perhaps not in its actual specifics but rather in its received racialized and gendered norms, and has assiduously curated her image in order to exercise a level of control to which Aida, Lottie, and other predecessors did not have access. Beyoncé limits what the public knows about her private life, even while offering tantalizing autobiographical tidbits on the eponymous *Beyoncé* (2013), the visual album *Lemonade* (2016), the cowritten Jay-Z and Beyoncé album *Everything Is Love* (2018), the documentary about her Coachella performance, *Homecoming* (2019), and the film and album *Black Is King* (2020), among other releases and performances. Put another way, Beyoncé safeguards her privacy and artistic control in ways that reflect a studied knowledge of the joys and perils of Black celebrity. As the cultural critic Wesley Morris has recently noted of Beyoncé and other innovative contemporary Black artists, "From the start, black people have been at the center of American popular culture—essentially because white people placed them there, through imitation and mockery and fascination. Ever since, the struggle for black artists has been to wrest control of their own culture. . . . So while the power these [twenty-first-century] artists have attained might amount to a breakthrough, the primacy energizing their art is centuries old, . . . amount[ing] to what someone like Beyoncé knows well: homecoming."[73] Beyoncé's art is riveting, for sure, but her negotiation of the role of the famous Black (woman) performer, including its attendant sociocultural and political pressures, connects her to predecessors such as Aida and Lottie. As Samantha Pinto points out, "we continue to inherit and inhabit the political world early black women celebrities created."[74] Further, Beyoncé offers only one example of the heterogeneous group of Black women musicians and artists of all sorts who are flexing and finessing in a media environment that is more inclusive on the one hand and still largely controlled by white men on the other. In revivifying Aida and Lottie for twenty-first-century readers, Phillips thus reminds us of the shifts that have (and have not) occurred in regard to the intersecting discourses of race, gender, sexuality, and class that impinge on contemporary Black women artists' self-expressions, as well as their public reception. Beyoncé and her contemporaries have more control over both their artistic choices and public images and narratives than Aida and Lottie ever did, even while dominant ideologies about Black women as both sexual objects and natural entertainers continue to inform their experiences in the spotlight.

Legacies and Residues

As *Dancing in the Dark* draws to a close, Phillips narrativizes each figure's decline, portraying Black celebrity as an exhausting experience, particularly as mainstream stardom is dependent on a fickle and potentially wrathful white public—a reality that has transmogrified along with shifts in racial and cultural consciousness but has not entirely dissipated. As Ellis Cashmore observes, "White audiences, in warming to the minstrel shows, effectively reduced the suffering and abjection of black people to a series of amusing tableaux. They could enjoy the sight and sounds of African Americans, or their imitators, without actually considering the social experiences of the performers and their peers. This depersonalization or even dehumanization was—maybe still is—characteristic of whites' appreciation of black culture."[75] Correspondingly, the novel's central characters, not unlike the historical figures on which they are based, experience varying degrees of public opprobrium as they fade from the limelight. George Walker dies ignominiously from complications from syphilis, Aida's final years are dogged by depression and alcoholism, Lottie perseveres in her role as a rather dissatisfied housewife, and Bert is finally unable to perform any longer, dying with the knowledge that his artistic contributions may be unrecognized.

Even as the novel's conclusion highlights these setbacks and misfortunes, taken as a whole, *Dancing in the Dark* does not dwell in tragedy. Instead, Phillips consistently fuses archive and repertoire in order to recuperate Bert, George, Aida, and, to a certain extent, Lottie as artists. Toward the end of the novel, Phillips stages one of Aida's last performances from Bert's perspective. Bert observes that "she [Aida] still dances well, if somewhat eccentrically and in bare feet, but he understands that this *style* is her own contribution to the world of dance," even as the audience "is clearly somewhat mystified by what is being presented to them."[76] Bert's observations are coupled with a 1914 *Variety* magazine obituary that reports, "Aida Overton Walker, easily the foremost Afro-American woman stage artist, widow of George Walker of the formerly famous team of Williams and Walker, died Sunday night (Oct. 11) at her home, 107 West 132nd Street, New York. Mrs. Walker had been confined to her bed for about two weeks with an attack of kidney trouble. Her last appearance was at Hammerstein's in *Modern Society Dancers*, August 3rd."[77] Through these varied perspectives, Phillips invites readers into the archive to consider Aida's artistic significance, while he draws implicit connections between the ways in which Black women artists were misunderstood and undervalued both during the early twentieth century and now. Put another way, Aida's impact has been erased not only by the "forgeries of memory" but also by a US public that could not appreciate her "eccentric" choreography because of the social devaluation of Black women writ large.[78]

Phillips's conclusion is similarly devoted to creatively recuperating Bert as a misunderstood artist. Incorporating the program from the Ziegfeld Follies, Bert's final troupe, Phillips evinces the historical breakthrough of being the only Black man in an otherwise all-white cast, even as he notes Bert's anxiety as the most racially hypervisible and personally invisible figure onstage: "Bert found himself onstage and staring out at Mr. Ziegfeld's audience, sometimes singing, sometimes dancing, sometimes telling an anecdote, but always the only tanned player. . . . In 1910 his n[*****] face shocked Ziegfeld's patrons with its elastic elegance while his colored body made them laugh with its alarming, but perfectly choreographed, eccentric grace."[79] Phillips likewise quotes Florenz Ziegfeld from a press clipping in which he praises Williams as "a consummate artist in a sea of banality; technically perfect, timing immaculate, his portrayal of his people the only flaw on his otherwise perfect diamond."[80] This paradoxical portrait, one that Phillips suggests Bert himself internalized, evinces the immense challenge facing Black entertainers as they negotiated the postbellum, pre–Harlem Renaissance cultural landscape.

In addition, Phillips shows that Bert was increasingly dogged by, as Ziegfeld puts it, "his portrayal of his people" as social discourses were shifting in ways that ultimately led to the flowering of the Harlem Renaissance, which likewise ushered in a new sociopolitical rubric, under which the historical Williams, Walker, Overton Walker, and other former Black minstrel troupes did not fare so well. Phillips stages a meeting between Bert and "six finely dressed colored men," who beseech him to play the part of the "new, twentieth-century Negro, as opposed to a low type who is a deliberate travesty of our race."[81] Phillips then provides what he imagines was Bert's artistic outlook (or perhaps justification or both): "I am merely trying to give this low-bred colored man some humanity. My colored man may be interpreted by some as a gin-guzzling, crap-shooting, chicken-stealing, no-good n[*****], but there is more to him than this. He suffers. Our compassion goes out to him. . . . The essence of my performance is that we know and sympathize with this unfortunate creature."[82] In this imagined dialogue, Phillips reframes what may initially appear to be an enactment of anti-Black caricatures, thereby encouraging contemporary readers to consider the multiple and competing forces at play in Bert's performances. In fact, excerpting reviews, Phillips shows that when Bert transitions to film in order to play "an uncorked colored person of cunning and resourcefulness" in *Darktown Jubilee* (1914), white audiences revolted, the performance leaving "a sour taste in the mouth of all who paid money to attend this presentation."[83] In Phillips's portrait, Bert is unable to express himself artistically without the ridicule of whites, Blacks, and sometimes both. In an interview, Phillips remarked that "one of the reasons [he] wrote this novel [*Dancing in the Dark*] now is because of hip hop. . . . At what point do you tell an individual, 'You are letting the side down'? 'You should not do that because your responsibility is not to your art, your responsibility is to your imagined community'? Bert Williams had to tread this line a hundred years ago and deal with all these same debates."[84] Recognizing the contemporary parallels with the sociocultural discourse informing hip hop, Phillips suggests the significance of Bert's (not to mention George's and Aida's) legacy with regard to the pressures of respectability and racial leadership placed on the shoulders of Black celebrities, for which there is no analogous expectation for their white counterparts.

Exceeding the limits of the archive to explore the residue of what was left undocumented, as well as to speculate about what was felt and thought but unexpressed, Phillips concerns himself with defamiliarizing and reframing "the fictions of the powers that be," to recall Rancière.[85] In the final lines of the novel, Bert reconciles that he is only a surrogate for racialized rituals and behaviors over which he has little control; Phillips puts the onus on readers, therefore, to consider our own exploitative treatment of Black performers:

> Others will come after me to entertain you, and they will happily change their name and put on whatever clownish costume

> you wish them to wear, and dance, and sing, and perform in a manner that will amuse you, and you *will* mimic them, and you *will* make them money, but know that at the darkest point of the night, when no eyes are upon them, these people's souls will be heavy, and eventually some among them will say no, and you will see their sadness, and then you will turn from them and choose somebody else to place in the empty room, or nudge onto your empty stage.[86]

Having reoriented the hegemonic gaze so that it is firmly aimed at white consumers of Black culture, past and present, Phillips suggests the contemporary resonances with Bert Williams's experiences in the limelight. As the acclaimed comedian Dave Chappelle bemoaned in an interview, "White people, white artists, are allowed to be individuals. But we always have this greater struggle that we at least have to keep in mind somewhere."[87] Providing a narrative portal to the postbellum stage, Phillips highlights this long-standing struggle for Black artists who unduly bear what James Baldwin termed "the burden of representation."[88] Further, *Dancing in the Dark* encourages readers to search our own souls and ensure that we are not demanding the sacrifice of one's dignity in order to satisfy our longing for a song and dance.

Challenging dominant historiographies that track a progressive timeline from the end of the Civil War to the present, *Dancing in the Dark* likewise underscores the continued sociocultural relevance of Bert Williams, Lottie Williams, George Walker, and Aida Overton Walker. As Scheper notes, both onstage and offstage performances do not end with the deaths of the artists; thus, scholars must mine "not only material traces and object artifacts, but ephemeral artifacts and affective histories, which make up the aftereffects of these performances."[89] Concomitantly, Phillips harnesses fictional tools to sift through varied materials from the archive and repertoire (and the spaces in between), creatively recounting performers, performances, and their afterlives. *Dancing in the Dark* takes readers backstage, as it were, to observe the calculus particularly of Bert and George as they sought to capitalize on the white ravening for blackface minstrel antics, while simultaneously attempting to convince these audiences of their artistry. Aida is similarly recast as an innovative dancer (and singer), who had to negotiate a cultural landscape controlled not only by white-supremacist norms and codes but also by misogynistic forces; through Lottie, Phillips illustrates the challenge to find emotional and psychological solace in a post-theater life restricted almost entirely to a subordinate domestic role. At the same time, Phillips attempts to recover glimpses of these figures' interiority—in other words, to show that their lives were not defined by public expression and reception, especially the whims and anxieties of white people.

In the essay "The Power of History," Don DeLillo avers, "The novel is the dream release, the suspension of reality that history needs to escape its own brutal confinements"; moreover, "Fiction is all about reliving things. It is our second chance."[90] Phillips's *Dancing in the Dark* accords with such a description, refusing the confinements of recorded history and imagining the interior thoughts, fears, desires, and disappointments occluded by the various masks and mise-en-scène of the vaudeville and, later, Broadway stages on which Bert, George, Aida, and Lottie performed. While they could not be publicly candid about their experiences for fear of alienating their audiences, Phillips steps into the breach and avails himself of the "second chance" to tell their story in rich, intimate detail. In so doing, *Dancing in the Dark* provides Rancièrean "truth talk" about the intersecting (and often imperiling) forces of racism and sexism within and without the entertainment industry. In chapters 5 and 6, we will see Phillips's contemporaries Jeffery Renard Allen and Tyehimba Jess engage in similar forms of excavation and reckoning as they mine the archives and reimagine the repertoire in order to make visible the ties that bind famous postbellum, pre–Harlem Renaissance artists and their twenty-first-century descendants.

5
"BLIND TOM, MUSICAL PRODIGY OF THE AGE"
Unrecoverability in Jeffery Renard Allen's Song of the Shank

In a January 1866 article in the Albany, New York, newspaper the *Argus*, an unnamed reporter described a performance by the celebrity pianist Thomas Greene Wiggins (1849–1908), otherwise known as "Blind Tom":

> A wild uncouth figure, angular at all points which should be curved, and curved at all points that should present acute lines—loose-jointed, close-wooled, thick-lipped, sprawl-footed, with forehead almost covered with kinky locks, eyeballs prominent and distended, and an idiotic, staring expression of countenance—in short, a regular specimen of the African in his unadulterated and barbarous condition, before he has been elevated by the influence of social surroundings or Caucasian infusion. Such is Blind Tom as he first strikes the eye and impresses the mind of the observer. . . .
>
> There is no law by which to measure and determine such exhibitions as this. Meanwhile, we only state what we saw in all its astonishing features, and leave our readers to determine for themselves whether the Chinese transmigration theory is correct—whether the soul of some unfortunate defunct musician, misbehaving on earth, has been banished into the awkward and angular body of Blind Tom.[1]

This account—ostensibly one praising "Blind Tom's" ability—reveals an endemic *post*bellum debasement of people of African descent, with the final paragraph suggesting that Tom must be a kind of awful miracle insofar as his musical prowess defies all of the laws of nature that render Blackness (not to mention blindness) inferior. This pervasive racism and ableism likewise led to the pianist's lifelong servitude to the Bethune family, which had similarly enslaved Tom's parents and siblings. As Deirdre O'Connell puts it, "Emancipation failed to deliver Tom from the shackles of slavery, his master's son merely morphing into the role of guardian and manager. Legally adjudged insane, Tom spent much of his life in perpetual motion, performing to packed houses across the continent—the profits of which financed his guardian's [the Bethune family's] extravagant lifestyle."[2] Moreover, as Daphne Brooks notes, "Having left behind no conventional writings of his own and having apparently never quested to 'tell a free story' in the most legible ways that one associates with the slave narrative genre or abolitionist aesthetics, the physically disabled and cognitively challenged Blind Tom remains a conundrum to scholars of nineteenth-century American culture."[3]

In this chapter, I examine Jeffery Renard Allen's novel *Song of the Shank* (2014), which interweaves a host of excavated and imagined accounts of "Blind Tom," imputing complex, embodied meaning to an enigmatic pianist who was "seen at once too much and not at all."[4] Like many of the other works examined in the present book, *Song of the Shank* has been critically acclaimed by reviewers but as of yet understudied by scholars. For example, in a *New York Times* review of the novel, Mitchell S. Jackson effuses, "'Song of the Shank' brilliantly portrays the story of Blind Tom while providing keen insight into the history of Reconstruction. But at its heart, it also reminds us denizens of never-will-be postracial America of one simple but everlasting essential truth: 'Them chains is hard on a man. Hard.'"[5] In a similar endorsement of both the novel's innovative style and subject matter, the *Los Angeles Times*'s Hector Tobar observes that "Allen appears completely uninterested in creating heroes or in using his prodigious language gifts to simply evoke a distant time and place. Instead, 'Song of the Shank' feels like a kind of exercise in deep thought and immersion in Tom's uniquely bizarre experience and the cruel history he was forced to live."[6] In a 2015 issue of the journal *Obsidian: Literature & Arts in the African*

Diaspora devoted to Allen and his oeuvre (and timed to coincide with the publication of *Song of the Shank*), the scholars Thadious Davis, Michael A. Antonucci, and Horace A. Porter offered the first critical snapshots of *Song of the Shank*. Davis explains the significance of mapping and imaginative geography within the novel; Antonucci observes Allen's "attention to the combination of promise and tension that accompanied the pianist [Wiggins], both on and away from the stage"; and Porter considers *Song of the Shank* within the context of the slave and neo-slave narrative traditions.[7] Enriching this critical conversation, this chapter considers the ways in which *Song of the Shank* intervenes in understandings of early Black celebrity, especially through the novel's subversion of conventional historical and archival modes of representation.

Allen's nonlinear structure, parenthetical asides, and the fantastical setting of Edgemere call attention to the novel's constructedness, affirming in the process that "history is always ideologically invested, and its power rests in large part on its methods of crafting only seemingly disinterested stories about the past."[8] Elsewhere, Allen ruminates on the challenge of portraying a figure who was hypervisible as a spectacle but personally invisible: "Who was the actual person, Thomas Greene Wiggins? This person is far harder to know and understand because the reputed firsthand reports about him are informed by the racial prejudices of the time. Added to this, Wiggins himself remained largely silent during his life. He gave no interviews. He dictated no letters, essays or narratives. This silence cost him."[9] In many respects, *Song of the Shank* is a recuperation of this silence in the face of exploitation. For instance, Allen employs free indirect discourse not to narrativize Tom's interiority but instead to illuminate the largely undocumented interior thoughts of those who controlled Tom's life and career. For Allen (unlike for the poet Tyehimba Jess, whom we will see inhabit Tom's perspective in chapter 6), Tom must remain more or less silent, underscoring this paradoxically subjugated and celebritized figure's lack of agency and self-determination and, moreover, the obstacles facing contemporary novelists as they try to stitch together a narrative of a figure who was never able to "own" his story.

Allen also denaturalizes what Jennifer Stoever conceives of as a "sonic color line," whereby aural production and consumption are inextricably entangled with racial stratification.[10] Incorporating archival fragments, *Song of the Shank* especially demonstrates white listeners' failure to reconcile Tom's Black, disabled body with his virtuoso performances, which include original compositions, precise mimicry of all manner of sounds, and renditions of iconic European composers (such as Bach, Beethoven, and Chopin). Additionally, as Perry Hall observes, "A complex 'love-hate' relationship connects mainstream society and African-American culture—in which white America seems to love the melody and rhythm of Black folks' souls while rejecting their despised Black faces. In no area is this complex relationship more evident than in musical tradition[s]."[11] Restaging Tom's performances, Allen exposes this sonic and cultural dissonance (also laid bare in the *Argus* piece), whereby intersecting forms of racism and ableism led audiences to assume that Tom was nothing more than "a 'vacant receptacle' through which a 'higher muse' communicated."[12]

Using a range of perspectives and modes, Allen destabilizes the linear, written record as the arbiter of truth about Tom in particular and the United States' cultural history in general. As Diana Taylor observes, "the dominance of language and writing has come to stand for *meaning* itself. Live, embodied practices not based in linguistic or literary codes, we must assume, have no claims on meaning."[13] Defying the empirical strictures of conventional histories and taking seriously what Taylor refers to as the repertoire of embodied experiences,[14] Allen inhabits the thoughts of a range of figures—Eliza Bethune, Charity Wiggins, Tabbs Gross, Perry Oliver, and others—who played central roles in Tom's life as a celebrity musician in perpetual bondage. Moreover, Jacques Rancière argues that "literature has its own tense and it has its own space: the localized present of the performers who actually took part in that particular assault, retreat or groping march; it has its truth, which is the truth of the anonymous people whose many combined actions have given shape to the event."[15] Allen draws us into his speculative "truth of the anonymous people" in Tom's life, many of whom are not so much unknown as flattened out by dominant narratives. Engaging in creative recuperation while foregrounding its limitations for revivifying a figure so overdetermined in the white imagination, Allen makes the imprint and residue of "Blind Tom's" experiences legible, suggesting the ways in which sonic color lines and white audience's love-hate relationships with Black musicians continue to shape contemporary sociocultural discourse.

"Listen to Them. The One the Many."

Song of the Shank begins after the Civil War and works backward to the antebellum period and then forward again but without marking any substantive change in the racial ideologies informing the characters' thoughts and deeds. The novel's opening and closing sections begin with the same image with slight variation: "Carved Door in Darkness" and "Carved Door in Light."[16] Bookending the novel with these artworks, Allen offers a glimpse of progressive enlightenment, as the second title "in Light" suggests, while the nearly identical closed doors imply that the same barriers or foreclosures remained in place across Tom's lifetime (and in many ways into our own era). Allen portrays the postbellum epoch as an embryonic cultural moment in which Black Americans entered the entertainment industry for the first time, at least potentially, as agents capable of generating their own profit, henceforth changing the theatrical and musical landscape. Yet *Song of the Shank* shows that the immense potential ushered in by the end of the Civil War was unrealized, as the postbellum era both fortified racial and ethnic scaffolding and intensified white America's alternating fetishization and dehumanization of performers like "Blind Tom."

Moreover, instead of relying solely on archival materials or biographies of Tom, Allen uses these as touchstones for elucidating the novel's Rancièrean "truth" about the pianist in particular and nineteenth-century Black celebrity in general, approaching history as "a production as much as an accounting of the past."[17] For example, the book's first narrative section marks the year as 1866 and begins in media res with the free indirect perspective of Eliza Bethune (née Elise Stutzbach) on her guardianship of Tom, without explaining how and why the famous musician is in the care of the former daughter-in-law of the Bethune family that enslaved him. In fact, Eliza did not marry John Bethune, the eldest son of the former Confederate general and Tom's "master," James Bethune, until 1882. John and Eliza were divorced shortly thereafter, and

John suffered a fatal accident in 1884; in 1887, Eliza successfully wrested custody of Tom from General Bethune.[18] Dispensing with this timeline and the details of these legal disputes and transactions, Allen begins the novel by focalizing Eliza's interiority, exposing her impulses to control the celebrity musician she has spirited away from public view:

> She comes out of the house and sees fresh shapes in the grass, a geometrical warning she does not understand. . . . Had she [Eliza] been back in the city, the idea would already have occurred to her that the journalists were to blame, those men of paper determined in their unstoppable quest to unearth the long lost—three years? four?—"Blind Tom"—*Half Man, Half Amazing*—to reproduce the person, return him to public consumption, his name new again, a photograph (ideally) to go along with it, the shutter snapping (a thousand words). . . . Alarm breaks the surface of her body, astonished late afternoon skin, all the muscles waking up. Where is Tom? Someone has stolen him, taken him away from her at last.[19]

In this opening introduction to the famed "Blind Tom," Allen suggests the multiple conflicts at work: on the one hand, Eliza expresses fear about the frenzy of the news media that, not unlike today, refuses to abide by the conventional boundaries of privacy; on the other hand, Allen implies that Tom remains a subjugated commodity even a full year after the end of the Civil War, as he still might be "stolen" from Eliza's care. Moreover, while Tom and Eliza share in daily rituals—"she dries Tom then herself, using the same towel made from Georgia cotton"—Eliza finds that "she doesn't want his ugly touches."[20] Perhaps most strikingly, Allen represents Tom's utter lack of agency or even thought of self-determination, so thoroughly has he been denied the ability to imagine a life free of white control.

Reconstructing Tom's life and career through Eliza's (and others') outlook, Allen underscores the ways in which both his music and his sense of self have been shaped by the views of white audiences:

> He takes her hand in his—the right palm, wet and greasy with fish—and leads her to the piano. (Not the objects themselves but the way to arrive at them.) Sits down, fingers flexing and finding themselves. (Idle hands, the devil's playthings.) *His*

> *notes are so thrilling, and his execution so perfect and so startling as to amuse every listener. The piano itself seems gifted, and sends forth in reverberation, praises, as it were, to Blind Tom. Blind Tom is the temple wherein music dwells.*
>
> He jerks her sideways with his always-perfect timing. Pulls her into his chest, close enough for his hammering heart to break her resistance. Pieces their forms back together in a harsh rhythm. A dance. (What he wants). Tom free and light, enjoying his own movements.[21]

The italicized encomium that Tom recounts as he plays further represents his internalization of media accounts of his art. Eliza's observations, including her parenthetical asides, also highlight Tom's lack of voice in the narrative of his own life—a pattern that has continued into the present as African Americans are routinely "colonized for pleasure and financial gain."[22] In other words, even as Allen reads against the archival grain, he makes it clear that all we know about what Tom "want[ed]" or "enjoy[ed]" was filtered through the vantage point of others. At the same time, these moments of domestic intimacy illuminate Tom's humanity, supplementing the archival record of his "thrilling" performances with imagined testimony about his life beyond the stage.

As the novel transitions to the inner thoughts of Tabbs Gross, a tenacious man who attempts to assume custody of Tom from the Bethune family, Allen continues to braid together what Taylor describes as the archive and the repertoire.[23] Preceding Tabbs's free indirect perspective, Allen inserts an unidentified photograph of a small sailboat making its way across the water, utilizing this artifact as an associative touchstone, not evidence for any one particular narrative. The sailboat is suggestive of mobility but also liminality and vulnerability, as it attempts, not unlike postbellum African Americans like Tabbs (and Tom), to navigate especially choppy waters. Subsequently, Tabbs describes the soaring, frenzied hopes of the newly free as they have made their way to "the City" (reminiscent of New York) and, in some cases, to the island community of Edgemere:

> Tabbs sees the agitation in their faces, faces heavy with an expectation that cannot be put down. So assured, so much purpose, so determined—promised (a plot so wide so long;

> a beast of burden so young so strong), thought capable of, expected to—To your tents, O Israel!—bringing their hands tightly together in prayer to defeat Doubt. . . . Tom's mother speaks at double the speed he recalls her speaking in the South—even he gets stuck in the thick speech of fresh arrivals, those just off the boat as it were, struggles to understand their muddy English, the thick drawn-out syllables, and the way certain words sink beneath sense altogether. Listen to them. The one the many. Here those who were not now are.[24]

Here Allen paints a portrait of "the one the many" that suggests the Reconstruction promise of forty acres and a mule ("a plot so wide so long; a beast of burden so young so strong"), as well as the immense challenges for emancipated people seeking not only to find and restore their often fractured families but also to establish their citizenship rights in a society still wary of their humanity ("Here those who were not now are"). In distinct ways, the experiences of Tabbs and Tom's mother, Charity, thus parallel the small sailboat, both filled with "an expectation that cannot be put down" and vulnerable to a range of imperiling forces.

Inhabiting Tabbs's perspective, Allen also offers new valences on the paradoxes of Black musical celebrity in the postbellum epoch. Instead of showcasing Tom's purportedly natural propensity for entertaining whites—a gross caricature of all Black Americans circulating during the nineteenth century (and arguably still operative today)—Allen uncovers the layers of trauma and struggle that surrounded the pianist's performances. In particular, Tabbs ruminates on the aftermath of chattel slavery that white Americans were ill prepared and categorically uninterested in confronting:

> Wobbly creatures with wasted bodies knocking out of rhythm under sagging skin. One to the next. The hard lines of their hunger sketch a blueprint of possibility against the faded backdrop of recent history. No language for this. Slavery is a puncture—have you ever picked cotton?—the hole (hold) that can never close. The hole that still bleeds cotton, rice, sugarcane, tobacco. How do they lift their feet without becoming undone?
>
> *I would never have believed*
> *That death could have undone so many*

> He starts for the ferry to Edgemere, a long line of bodies following him, bringing their uncertainties and contradictions along. So it is. They lift their faces expectantly toward the heavens. Their eyes seem to look through and beyond everything they see for some visitation of blessing or warning.[25]

Alluding to T. S. Eliot's *The Waste Land* (1922) and his description of the carnage of World War I ("I had not thought death had undone so many"), Allen draws readers back to a much more distinctly American catastrophe and effort toward redemption ("They lift their faces expectantly toward the heavens"). Perhaps most importantly, Allen provides an emotional archive that, though imagined in its particulars, elucidates what Rancière termed earlier "the truth of the anonymous people."[26]

Moreover, Allen's attention to the multiple figures and ways of knowing "Blind Tom" evinces the ways in which history can never be contained within discrete, neutral units, however much the archive gives that allusion with its boxes and catalogues. As Jennifer L. Morgan contends, "We must tell stories, we must engage in the project of mounting counter-histories of slavery and enslavement, and we must navigate the ethics of historical representation. Doing so is at the core of the projects that engage us, and meeting its methodological challenges both impede and propel the work. The archive is a site of violent dispossession, a point of departure, not a conclusion; so to navigate that archive is to foreground the speculative, to juxtapose the record with the imaginary, to leave the questions unanswered."[27] Correspondingly, Allen juxtaposes his speculative free indirect narration with archival and biographical materials, shifting the white gaze while evincing its epistemological limitations. For example, he mines the archives about Tabbs not only to call attention to his attempts to wrest custody away from the Bethune family but also to reimagine Black efforts to use the burgeoning cultural industry to gain an economic and even political foothold in an endemically racist society: "He [Tabbs] will break into the world of the alabasters on his own terms, through the boy. *Blind Tom.* Having worked the details—the mother and Tom together here on Edgemere—in full and determined preparation, Tabbs is ready to take advantage."[28] Tabbs's plot, according to Allen, is not motivated by altruism but instead speaks to the many ways in which postbellum Black Americans were using the entertainment industry (not unlike the burgeoning sports industry documented by his poet contemporaries Kevin Young, Adrian Matejka, and Frank X Walker) to gain a foothold in the "alabaster" economy, which was only provisionally accessible.

Put another way, Tabbs is representative of Black Americans' use of the performance circuit to, as Brooks describes, counter "the condition of alterity" through "specific strateg[ies] of cultural performance."[29] Tabbs muses, "What it will mean to give Blind Tom back to the world, back to the Race, and put the lie once and for all to the vicious claims for the Negro's lack of intellect and refinement, genius and culture—the collateral and collective gains of his personal campaign against the Bethunes."[30] Allen's portrait of Tabbs is in keeping with the historical record, including Tabbs's failed attempt to legally liberate Tom from the Bethune family's custody. As O'Connell reports, "Tabbs Gross must have left the court wondering how much had really changed. Slavery may have been dead but the white power base was alive and kicking. By virtue of his race, he was branded an alien and a traitor while [General] Bethune was welcomed open armed into the fold."[31] While Allen reimagines aspects of Tabbs's encounters with Tom as occurring on Edgemere, he remains true to the official documentation of their relationship: Tom played a key role in Tabbs's plot to "put the lie once and for all" to white supremacy. Perhaps most importantly, Allen uses free indirect discourse to focalize Tabbs's interiority, thereby allowing readers to engage with Tom from a politically conscious Black perspective disentangled from both the love-hate dynamic and sonic color line that informed white responses to the star pianist.

Through Allen's recuperation of Tabbs, he also offers a rich counternarrative to teleological readings of the late nineteenth century, repeatedly highlighting the immense challenges and failures of Reconstruction to facilitate the transformation from enslaved to citizen and the disdain that white Americans (North and South) continued to feel for people of African descent. As Horace A. Porter observes of the novel, "Slavery and its consequences as borne out during the reconstruction period surround many scenes. But Allen zooms up close to the implacably human dimensions of things."[32]

Accordingly, Tabbs recalls watching federal troops roughly herding Black Americans in "the City," and he thinks to himself, "Futures denied. They [the 'brown caravan'] greedily fell (fall) upon every cup of milk offered them, each loaf of bread. Yearning (Life piled on life). They will not—even *now*—settle in his mind, his thoughts. Is it for them that he was here? To build a better day? (The soon-come day without the n[*****])."[33] The tensions teeming in this passage, made more tension-filled by the layering of parenthetical asides, indicate the traumatic aftermath of the Civil War, in which newly freed African Americans were refugees in a nation unprepared and generally uninterested in caring for their needs. Tabbs likewise recalls seeing a "Negro woman" with her "three children of various ages" viciously attacked on a train platform: "From somewhere—Tabbs still hasn't puzzled it complete—a white man runs up to her, lunges, and punches her in the face, reams of blood spilling red to the earth."[34] Such random acts of violence against women and children evince the "white rage" that was fueled by Emancipation,[35] and this incident occurs, of course, in the purportedly more enlightened northern City, not in the land of secession. Allen's parenthetical asides also suggest the constructed nature of Tabbs's reportage, implying the multiple ways to know and interpret the postbellum period and thereby calling into question the concealing character of sweeping narratives of racial progress. In other words, Allen does not portray Tabbs's perspective as authoritative or heroic, particularly in his desire to capitalize on the celebrity of "Blind Tom." Nonetheless, by revivifying a man who is a footnote in the annals of US history, Allen offers an alternative means of understanding the vexing dilemmas facing a people traumatized and abandoned after a war that was, at least in part, fought to liberate them from bondage.

Indeed, Morgan notes that the interventionist work of diasporic writers is crucial in "subvert[ing] the archives that want only to testify to the completion of the slave owners' project,"[36] and Allen's portrait not only of Tabbs but also of Charity Wiggins offers a keen example of this creative resistance to the anti-Black epistemic violence layered into the archive. In particular, Allen emphasizes Charity's suffering over the forced relinquishing of any maternal rights to her son, first to General Bethune, later to his former daughter-in-law Eliza, and, more generally, to an entertainment industry controlled and patronized by whites. O'Connell notes that Charity's "life story has been largely obliterated, leaving only a few fragments from which we can begin to imagine a life scarred by separation."[37] Writing into this void, Allen inhabits Charity's consciousness, portraying her chronic distress over the loss of her beloved Thomas and her hopeful feelings about their reunion on Edgemere after eleven years apart:

> At the far point of their lives, mother and son on the verge of great joy after an existence of great sorrow, granted the means to pick up from where they left off eleven years ago when Thomas was so rudely and wrongly taken from her at Hundred Gates, a moment that her mind holds on to and will hold on to, so help her God, for as long as she lives. *Never forget, never forgive.* Thomas, I am here. Your mother is here. Here we are, together again. (Words she might have even spoken once or twice to him since her arrival here on Edgemere.)[38]

Rather than echoing paternalistic narratives that portray General Bethune as, to quote the judge's decision in the *Gross v. Bethune* trial, "a venerable man . . . of unusual intelligence and kindness of heart,"[39] Allen, via Charity, emphasizes the irreparable trauma that resulted from Bethune's greed ("Never forget, never forgive"). In Allen's parenthetical remark, he also acknowledges his inability to document precisely what Charity thought or felt—"Words she might have even spoken once or twice to him since her arrival here on Edgemere"—especially since her perspective has been so thoroughly erased from the written record.

Allen does not purport, therefore, to know Charity's consciousness but instead suggests what it might have felt like to have a son ripped from one's care and to have no institutional recourse to ensure his safe return. As Kevin Quashie notes, "Love demands a descent into the interior, leaves us filled with vulnerability and ambition and rage that rivals anything the social world can produce."[40] Attending to the fallout from Charity's intense love for her son, feelings absent from the artifacts and media accounts that constitute how we know what we know about "Blind Tom," Allen implies the gaping holes in our knowledge while using the novel to speculate about "details that would answer the questions the archive disavows."[41] Whereas press accounts of "Blind Tom" mostly negate Charity's outlook, *Song of the Shank* portrays Charity in a near-constant state of agony and regret about her loss: "(How many times had she and Little Thomas strolled, hand in hand, in the murmuring shad of the water oak trees?) His voice would flood the evening with stories he couldn't tell fast enough."[42] Even during their Edgemere reunion that Tabbs engineers, Charity is unable to rekindle the former intimacy between herself and Tom: "Tears stanched behind her shut eyelids, she cried all down inside herself that first night and many nights after. (The ache still even though he [Tom] is here). Never the full outpouring of grief because she knew that such letting go would unravel her, turn the spindle of the self until nothing was left."[43] Allen highlights not only Charity's initial trauma but also the pain she must countenance after her son's rebuff of her maternal care decades later: "Thomas was there, on the island [Edgemere], surrounded by all that water. What had happened to the Thomas of old that she can still picture, still feel? *Don't ever touch me like that again.*"[44]

Ultimately, Allen elucidates grief that can be stanched but not overcome, despite Emancipation, the end of the Civil War, and, in this case, a reuniting of mother and child. These are feelings that archival facts about Tom's mother cannot substantiate but that Allen's novel, with its focus on truths, brings to life. In particular, Allen uses free indirect discourse to "descen[d] into the interior" of Charity's mind,[45] as she stood disempowered on the sidelines while her son became one of the era's most famous (and famously exploited) musical performers. Further, Charity becomes representative of the tens of thousands of Black Americans who not only were unable to rekindle their familial ties but were also emancipated without provisions made for their survival. The last time readers encounter Charity, Allen imagines her new, postbellum identity as "Stray. Contraband. Refugee. Free."[46]

"This Body Isn't His (He Doesn't Own It)"

When Allen introduces readers to Tom's onetime manager Perry Oliver, he continues to juxtapose archival materials and free indirect discourse to expose the limitations of traditional historiographic methodologies. For example, he begins this section with a reproduction of a blurry photograph of Tom riding in a man's horse-drawn carriage, and as the "Illustration and Epigraph Credits" page tells us, it is "Blind Tom and Lerche" and "from the *Ladies Home Journal*, September 1898."[47] Albrecht Lerche was Eliza Bethune's lawyer-cum-husband, and the two managed Tom's career after the 1887 trial that granted custody to Eliza.[48] Perry Oliver, on the other hand, was hired by General Bethune to manage Tom in 1858.[49] In other words, Allen's insertion of this image is meant not to provide photographic evidence of Tom and Oliver's relationship but rather to suggest the revolving door of white handlers that sought to reap the profits from the musician's sonic gifts throughout his lifetime. The portrait is of Lerche, but it could easily be of Oliver; and the interior thoughts that follow are representative less of these specific historical figures than of the mind-set of white men (and women) who actively sought out Black musical talent while routinely objectifying the performers themselves.

Plumbing Perry's interior thoughts, Allen calls particular attention to the ways in which the dehumanization of Blacks was thoroughly internalized by many white Americans, implicitly drawing connections between Black entertainment and white exploitation during the nineteenth century and the current era. Juxtaposed with the photograph, for instance, is Perry's ruminations on the behavior of the Bethunes and their guests at their plantation garden party, where Perry first meets Tom: "In this garden setting, all the women exchanged kisses in the European style—Perry Oliver had never been to Europe—while the men seemed to take pride in their provincial accents. A few guests had even brought their n[*****]s to fan them cool."[50] Several pages later, we learn that Perry has set his sights on exploiting Tom as a means of realizing his own socioeconomic mobility: "He [Oliver] was in a state of becoming. In a word, Tom summed up everything he desired."[51]

The contract negotiation that follows further highlights Tom's lack of agency over his life and art, as well as the ways in which entertainment was becoming yet another way to commodify Black people:

> I am prepared to pay you five thousand dollars upon signing of the contract, even should that signing be today.

> General Bethune seemed to study those words carefully. Perry Oliver felt triumphant, knowing fully well that only a fool would turn down five thousand dollars for a blind, crazy n[*****].
>
> You have done an excellent job in laying out your case, General Bethune said. It would be uncouth of me to refuse you. Come to the offices of the newspaper tomorrow. My lawyer will be present. We will sign and notarize whatever documents are necessary to put Tom at your disposal.[52]

Reimagining this exchange, of which there is no archived transcript, Allen supplements how we know what we know about the backroom deals and machinations that ensured Tom would spend his life lining the pockets of white men, whose only labor appeared to have been devising ways to further exploit people of African descent. As Lisa Tomlinson notes, these predatory practices have continued: "Black musical products are bought and sold in the marketplace and most of the economic returns or profits go to white entrepreneurs, other music industry players, and artists. The media (i.e. music magazines, radio shows etc.) and other institutions that disseminate culture are also chiefly owned and controlled by white people and positioned to engage in the economic exploitation of Black music."[53] While Allen's imagined conversation between General Bethune and Perry Oliver is specific to "Blind Tom," Allen's restaging of it reminds us of the long pattern of white control over Black artists that remains stubbornly entrenched well over a century later.

As Allen's nonlinear, polyvocal novel weaves in and out of various characters' consciousnesses, he also demonstrates how endemic notions of Black inferiority were during the late nineteenth century, influencing those who were sympathetic to Black Americans and even Tom's own self-image. To this end, Tom refers to himself and other African Americans as "n[*****s]" and repeats primitivist caricatures imputing animalistic characteristics to Blacks, asking Tabbs, "Does it hurt to sit on your tail?"[54] When asked, "And how does it feel to be a n[*****]?" Tom replies with the assessment of Black Americans he has presumably heard throughout his life: "A n[*****]is a thing of no consequence."[55] In an interview with Jessie

Vail Aufiery, Allen observed, "In some ways he [Tom] is the answer to American history. He doesn't fit into the official narrative."[56] Tom is not a conventional icon of Black exceptionalism but rather a touchstone for explaining nineteenth-century pseudoscientific notions of Black animality and white supremacy—conceptions that the nation has yet to fully redress and that Allen confronts as he breathes new life into this now-obscure star of the stage.

That we have access to Tom almost entirely through other characters and reprinted promotional materials likewise calls attention to the voices and experiences that have been effaced by a chronic reliance on white perspectives to construct knowledge about US history. As previously noted, Allen does not inhabit Tom's persona, implying that, as a blind and probably autistic slave-cum-indentured-servant, Tom's thoughts and feelings were thoroughly disregarded, thereby precluding the possibilities of recuperating his inner world. In other words, Allen's omission of Tom's interiority underscores the pianist's lack of agency and self-possession in a society in which he was never granted the legal right to his self-determination. In the page and a half that most closely approximates Tom's perspective before segueing back into Charity's interior thoughts, Allen poses these questions of ownership: "This body isn't his (he doesn't own it) but moves when he moves"; "He can hear the sound of his own breathing. (Does he own it?)"; "Home. (What else would he call it?)."[57] With the parenthetical asides, Allen elucidates the utter objectification that Tom and, by extension, all enslaved people endured. He does not have control over his own body, including the very life force of breathing; and "home" is a misnomer for the site of his enslavement, but there is no other word to name the place that he dwells but to which he has no claim. Further, while Allen's free indirect discourse probes deeply, if elliptically, into the interior thoughts of other characters, this portrait of Tom evinces what Allen perceives to be the limitations of representing the emotional and psychological landscape of a man so thoroughly denied his selfhood.

"It's not surprising," Rancière avers, "that history just goes on reproducing indefinitely the myth of the great men who make history. History's documents are the fictions, in the future tense, of these great men, as well as the fictions, in the past tense, of those whose job is to show that things did indeed happen in keeping with their illusory mastery of events."[58] Allen dislodges these documented facts from "an illusory mastery of events," reimagining Tom's life from kaleidoscopic perspectives while reframing standard interpretations. Thadious Davis likewise observes that "Allen sees into the past with a sense of imaginative possibilities for rearranging known 'facts' and creating a mosaic of plausible voices."[59] For instance, Allen imagines Tom's ardent affection for Eliza, which does not dissipate once Tabbs removes him from her care and successfully ensconces him on Edgemere with Charity. In fact, Tom pines for Eliza there, refusing to play the piano and resume his touring schedule until he is reunited with her. "I want her [Eliza] now," Tom tells Tabbs.[60] Several pages later, he repeats his demands: "*Bring her to me.*"[61] Tabbs finally relents after Tom has worn him down with his incessant desire to see Eliza:

> Take me to her.
>
> Okay. I'll take you.
>
> Bring me her.
>
> Do you understand? I will take you.
>
> When can we go?
>
> Anytime you want.
>
> Tom lowers his head. You'd better go now, Mr. Tabbs, he says, circling the piano, in his own sphere of separation.[62]

When Tom is finally reunited with Eliza, he expresses warmth and fondness—Tom "holding her at the elbow, hugging her, touching her hair"—absent in the "sphere of separation" that characterized his sojourn to Edgemere with Tabbs and Charity.[63]

This almost romantic reunion of Tom and Eliza also circles back to the novel's first chapter, in which Tom expresses his deep affection for "Miss Eliza" by attempting to carry her over the threshold of their doorstep and "almost drop[ping] her when he is setting her down."[64] In this portrait of Tom's unwavering attachment to Eliza, Allen does not excuse her exploitative transgressions against him or Charity but instead offers a nuanced interpretation of their relationship. Was Tom in love, experiencing Stockholm syndrome, or trying to replace the mother that he was separated from once the Bethune family realized the riches to be made from his talent?

Allen never quite answers these questions, implying that all three possibilities might be at work. In other words, *Song of the Shank* is not purporting to offer the true tale of "Blind Tom" but instead disrupting the process by which "history just goes on reproducing indefinitely the myth of the great men who make history," which discounts the complex, nearly ineffable layers of trauma engendered by enslavement and its aftershocks.

Considering the work of Langston Hughes and Melvin Tolson, Kathy Lou Schultz contends that these poets "write into the voids in official records, making their own histories, highlighting the fact that the construction of the archive—of memory—must constantly be tended."[65] Allen invests in a similar kind of archival tending in regard to "Blind Tom." As Allen notes elsewhere, "the research for *Song of the Shank*, the reading, the watching and the listening—articles, books of fiction and nonfiction, recordings, and movies—eventually would encompass easily a thousand texts in whole or part."[66] Through his unmediated reproduction of handbills and posters, Allen invites contemporary readers into this research process with him, encouraging them to engage with the fetishization and dehumanization inscribed into these archival documents. One such antebellum poster announces, "Blind Tom, Musical Prodigy of the Age: a Plantation Negro Boy hailing from Savannah, a wonderful chattel worth $2,500, with a decidedly African-type face and every mark of idiocy, unlettered, blind and awkward, and cursed with little of human nature, but who yet has the amazing ability to both play and improvise."[67] Yet another poster promotes upcoming shows in London and Paris, billing Tom as "The Marvelous Musical Prodigy, the Negro Boy Pianist."[68] Inserting these archival findings into the middle of the novel, Allen confronts head-on the racist and ableist discourse of the mid- to late nineteenth century. In particular, Tom's "owners" fashioned his image in accordance with both white desires for musical and theatrical entertainment ("The Marvelous Musical Prodigy") *and* the prevailing belief in Black inferiority ("a wonderful chattel worth $2,500"), which was interlaced with degrading rhetoric about nonnormative bodies ("every mark of idiocy, unlettered, blind and awkward"). As Therí Pickens affirms, "disability always exists as part of an intersected identity that includes, at minimum, race, gender, sexuality, class, and gender presentation."[69] "Playing in the archive," Allen highlights these intersections between Blackness and disability, while reminding readers of both Tom's lack of agency in shaping his own narrative and the voices and perspectives absent in historical documents.[70]

Narrativizing the disparities between the ways Tom was marketed and his extraordinary performances, Allen likewise demonstrates the racialization of sound, particularly "how the dominant culture exerts pressure on individual listening practices to conform to the sonic color line's norms."[71] For instance, an audience member queries Tom's aforementioned manager, Perry Oliver: "Does he [Tom] know the fifth chapter of [Plato's] *The Republic*? Why indeed, you say. He does know it. And for the audience's additional pleasure, he will also recite chapters six and seven. So Tom does, reciting one chapter in Greek, the next in Latin, and then the last in French, Tom's voice, the way it holds each person in the audience like a hand gripping a face, a kind of hypnosis."[72] The audience is so bewildered by Tom's prodigious memory and, by extension, his transgression of the sonic color lines that they rush him backstage, where Tom experiences "poking, probing, and prodding, medical fingers sounding his chest, tugging at his nose and ears, tapping his eyes as if testing an eggshell's firmness, prying his teeth apart."[73] On the following page, Allen inserts an archived account of one of Tom's performances from the *Columbus Observer*, in which the reporter compares the pianist's posture to "*an ape clawing his food*" and "*a boar snorting up a well-buried black truffle*" and then dismisses Tom's music as unsophisticated: "*All in all, his music was a conventional affair, uncomplicated in melody, rudimentary in harmony, exact in rhythm and pace, and basic in structure and form.*"[74] Elucidating the "overlapping forms of discrimination that have occurred for both Black and disabled people," Allen shows the ways in which Tom's audiences refused to recognize him not only as an artist but also as a human being.[75] As Michael Antonucci observes, "Casting doubt on his [Tom's] humanity as well as his musical abilities, the passage nearly presages mid-twentieth-century discussions of another pioneering African American pianist, Thelonious Monk. This connection becomes evident, in a 1948 *Down-Beat* feature by George Hoefer: referring to Monk's music as 'weird sounds,' Hoefer writes, '[the pianist's] technique is not the greatest, but his originality in improvisation is that of a genius.'"[76] Treating Tom as a specimen whose alterity, in bell hooks's terms, renders him "more exciting, more intense, and more threatening,"[77] Allen gestures toward an intergenerational experience of being thrust into the limelight ("light burning Tom into fame") only to be subject to further white objectification and abuse.

Juxtaposing the reporter's racist assessment with Tom onstage exceeding the criteria of the white audience's own Western canonical rubric, Allen also questions the reliability of archival accounts of "Blind Tom" and his counterparts. Instead, he offers new ways to engage with Tom's performances by, in Rancière's terms, giving voice to "the localized present of the performers."[78] In this regard, Allen reimagines Tom's 1860 recital at the White House, in which crowds of African Americans gathered to see the first Black man enter the sanctified space not as a slave or a servant but as a performer:

> Doors opening, pouring Negroes out into the afternoon, so many faces brown and beaming bright, cheeks swollen with pride. Oh happy day! Tom puts words into their mouths and movements into their bodies. . . .
>
> Tom, would you like to say a few words to the people?
>
> Yes, Tom says. I am Blind Tom, and so are you.
>
> He sounds just like the Lord.
>
> Praise be.
>
> Tom walks right past President Buchanan, positions himself before the Chickering full grand piano, and starts to play. About the first song, the president's niece is heard to say, I never felt that song as I did just now. About the second song, a prominent senator in attendance will remember *majestic rivers winding over the floodplains*, while his wife will opine, Away flew the notes. Of the many journalists present, one will later sum up the recital this way: Music broke out on Blind Tom like the smallpox.[79]

Fusing archived citations ("Music broke out on Blind Tom like the smallpox") with the imagined repertoire of emotional and embodied responses ("so many faces brown and beaming bright"), Allen reimagines Black onlookers cheering Tom on as President

Buchanan, his family, and other members of the Washington elite are awestruck by his musical acumen. In this way, Allen elucidates the paradoxes of Black celebrity, both then and now, as whites fawn over Tom's music, while ignoring the fact that he is still "owned" by the Bethune family.

Additionally, Allen calls attention to issues of access that remain live in regard to popular Black musicians and their audiences. In the novel, Tom's Black fans are immensely proud of his success, but they are either barred from or sequestered into the balconies of the recital halls in which he performs. Although much has changed in the decades separating "Blind Tom's" concerts from those of contemporary Black musicians, current socioeconomic disparities linked to structural racism mean that white fans have greater access to, for example, hip-hop performances than their Black counterparts do. As Reiland Rabaka points out, "Rap has become so popular among white youth that most rap concerts are no longer convened in African American communities and clubs, but mostly held in posh suburban concert halls and venues."[80] In journeying back to Tom's antebellum White House performance, the first of its kind, we can see the genesis of this phenomenon, whereby whites still control a great deal of Black musical production, including venues, audiences, and, of course, profits.

Likewise indicating the persistence of sonic color lines, Allen draws implicit cultural parallels with today's musical landscape. Perhaps no other recent example is as resonant as the Atlanta artist Lil Nas X's "Old Town Road," a song that laid bare the music industry's racialized criteria for what is categorized as "country" (a genre now firmly associated with, though not quite accurately, rural white America) and "rap" (a genre engendered by and associated with Black Americans). The enterprising Lil Nas X initially had streaming success with his self-release of "Old Town Road" in December 2018 on the app TikTok, classifying the song as "country trap" and thereby ushering it into contention for *Billboard*'s Hot Country Songs after what turned out to be a viral level of downloads and shares. The tune simultaneously charted on *Billboard*'s Hot 100 Singles and Hot R&B/Hip-Hop, indicating its multigenre influences and appeal.

Yet, as Allen demonstrates in the case "Blind Tom," whose performances of classical compositions were in such violation of sonic color lines that, to quote the aforementioned *Argus* reporter, "There is no law by which to measure and determine such exhibitions as this," the music establishment does not respond kindly to perceived transgressions of (racialized) musical genres. Thus, *Billboard* removed "Old Town Road" from its Hot Country Songs chart and defended the deletion by explaining that "while 'Old Town Road' incorporates references to country and cowboy imagery, it does not embrace enough elements of today's country music to chart in its current version."[81] This exclusion did not tamp down enthusiasm for the song or Lil Nas X's ascendancy; he subsequently remixed "Old Town Road" with multiple collaborators—notably the country icon Billy Ray Cyrus—and signed a recording contract with Columbia Records. If anything, the controversy and Lil Nas X's deft reaction to it cemented his fame, with "Old Town Road (remix)" winning the Country Music Association's 2019 Music Event of the Year Award. Recording and performing in a vastly changed sociopolitical climate, Lil Nas X, unlike artist-ancestors such as Tom Wiggins, had the agency and cultural capital to chart his own musical course, including his celebrated pushback against the gatekeepers of country music. Still, the public's expectations for particular artists—expectations that are often at least implicitly based on race (not to mention gender, disability, class, and sexual orientation)—is ongoing. Allen's narrativization of "Blind Tom's" performances and listeners' responses to them sheds helpful light, therefore, on the discursive residue of nineteenth-century sonic color lines in the twenty-first century.

Allen similarly counterposes white responses of fetish and fear with the varied reaction of Black fans, indicating the multiple ways to read "Blind Tom" and, by extension, all Black celebrities. Educing the conflicted feelings of pride, sympathy for his plight, and shame at what Tom's eccentricity onstage means for African Americans as a people, Allen especially highlights "the weight of being regarded as representative of an entire culture."[82] From Tabbs's free indirect perspective, Allen enacts a conversation between two African American men as they debate the famous pianist:

> I would never pay a penny of my hard-earned salary to hear him [Tom], the well-dressed man said. This is the way of these alabasters, to present us in a bestial light.

> You've got it all wrong, his companion said, casual dress, casual bearing. So what if the little blind n[*****] whirls around onstage. He's probably just taking some exercise cause those candlefaces keep him cooped up all the time, under their thumbs.[83]

Staging this conversation, Allen draws us behind what W. E. B. DuBois termed "the veil" to complicate the white media reports that form much of the basis of our knowledge about the reception of "Blind Tom."[84]

Transitioning into the second person, Allen then places contemporary readers in the "quiet" of Tabbs's mind as he recalls hearing Tom for the first time at a segregated postbellum recital hall.[85] Allen thus invites readers to reimagine a "Blind Tom" performance from the perspective of someone who is acutely aware of the oppressive forces that have orchestrated this event and, by extension, the pianist's entire career:

> Listen:
>
> Here is the piano in semidarkness, plates of light, planks of darkness, black keys and white keys. Here is the boy seated at the piano, a Negro like yourself. The boy center stage placed before a packed house, and you quietly wedged inside a custodian's closet in clandestine repose. . . . You are skilled in fine general culture and know how to listen. Shut your eyes to skin and you are forced to admit that the performance is thoroughly in tune with the very best of European art. . . . Ears pressed to air, you, Tabbs, stand for nearly an hour without words and listen, sound rushing in and piling up inside your head in copious abundance. . . . In this nowhere, you, Tabbs, feel yourself more solidly, no longer worrying about the mundane this or that. Something to behold.[86]

Allen illuminates Tabbs's interior thoughts as he sits in "a custodian's closet," transported from concerns about "alabasters" and the feelings of "all eyes watching, *all eyes on me*" to the sublime sounds of Tom's hands flying across the keyboard ("Something to behold").[87] Offering an important supplement to promotional materials and press accounts, Allen makes use of the second person to displace the white hegemonic gaze and situate twenty-first-century readers in the role of a contemporaneous African American listener as he both observes the "packed house" rapt with the spectacle of "Blind Tom" and defamiliarizes the sonic color line ("Shut your eyes to skin") in order to appreciate the beauty of "sound rushing in and piling up inside your head in copious abundance."

"Hysterical Music"

In addition to these varied reimagined accounts of Tom and his performances, the novel's title indicates Allen's commitment to a Rancière-esque "heretical" history that makes possible the "erratic speech" eschewed by hegemonic readings of the past.[88] In particular, the title *Song of the Shank* references anti-Black violence and resistance, as well as the music that propelled Tom to fame. Early on, Allen provides Charity's understanding of the word "shank"—"Where she comes from *stab* is another word for *knife. Slit* another word for *throat. Shank* another word for *dead*"—with linguistic glosses that signify the novel's alternative to (or "another word for" or subversive conception of) the white male master narratives that US archives have historically preserved.[89] Moreover, the title speaks to the elegiac character of Allen's novel, which elucidates what Brian Kelly describes as the "sharp reversal in the possibilities for Black freedom that followed so soon after the slaves' jubilee."[90] *Song of the Shank* climaxes with Eliza, Tom, Tabbs, and Tabbs's young, anonymous companion (referred to as "the boy") on a train journey to, as Tabbs notes, "the South where the soldiers can protect us. Our only guarantee of protection."[91] That the South, at least in theory, offers refuge from the racial terrorism of "the City" underscores the dark and uncomfortable nineteenth-century truths that Allen uncovers for his twenty-first-century readers. Tabbs makes a fatal miscalculation, as federal soldiers stationed in the South during Reconstruction were incapable of stamping out every act of white vigilante violence (of which there were countless numbers). When, almost inevitably, white men harass the foursome, Tom bellows "hysterical music," whereby the men become increasingly incensed, attacking Tabbs, as well as the boy, who "moves the shank in furious desperation at his attackers. A second falls, and a third, and a fourth. Then someone seizes his shank-wielding hand, while another jumps in to afflict damage."[92] In Allen's portrayal, the boy's resistance marks the unending struggle for human rights and racial justice that continued long after Robert E. Lee's surrender in 1865.

Tom's "hysterical music" is his swan song, a final mourning cry for the tremendous losses that the novel tracks from its beginning. Important, too, is that this song is catalyzed by white-supremacist forces but is not orchestrated by them, unlike all of Tom's public performances recorded by his white "owners," fans, and the media. In other words, this is a sound made possible through fiction that is not archived or otherwise accessible in historical records. Jerome de Groot argues that "fictions challenge, 'pervert,' critique, and queer a normative, straightforward, linear, self-proscribing History. They are entities that are interested in mocking and undermining such a way of analysing the past, while suggesting instead a set of very strange templates for a type of understanding that does not neatly fit with perceived notions of the historical."[93] Inviting readers to hear Tom's paralinguistic utterances in response to an attack by white supremacists, *Song of the Shank* challenges the monologic of teleological readings of the postbellum period, imagining instead what the sonic and affective landscape might have been like for this star musician, who, in Allen's words, still "remains beyond the purview of all who seek to tell or claim his story."[94] Absent Tom's perspective, the novel suggests his role as a shapeshifter, a figure on whom others projected their hopes and fears but who never controlled his own image and narrative. Inhabiting the consciousness of Eliza, Charity, Tabbs, and others, Allen also digs these figures out of the dustbin of history and into the contemporary light, where readers might consider the lessons that their experiences foretell for our own age, in which racial injustice, sonic color lines, and white America's love-hate relationship with Black artists persists.

In the two-page coda that ends the novel, Allen's narration jumps to a glimpse of the postbellum white northern perspective on Eliza and Tom, who are sequestered in her apartment at "6 Gracie Square"; showing the deeply entrenched prejudices that the Civil War has done little to erode, the neighbors "considered her [Eliza] barbarous in electing to live with a Negro, even if they were too well bred and polite to tell her so."[95] After a brief sighting of Tom on the balcony, the neighbors recall "hearing piano music, a tune that none of them recognized. Soon thereafter, the music stopped. And no one ever heard it again."[96] They are listening avidly and intently, as their lack of recognition to this new tune reveals, and still the neighbors treat the pair only with "humor and disgust," never inquiring about Tom's health after "the music stopped."[97] Likewise, most Americans will not have "heard" of Tom, nor will they ever have access to his playing since he was a celebrity musician in a prerecording age.

Allen's interest is less in the recorded knowledge of Tom and more in what his story tells us twenty-first-century readers about the complex residue of the mid- to late nineteenth century that progressive narratives of US history have attempted to wipe away. Fiction, as Rancière notes, "frames a new fabric of common experience, a new scenery of the visible and a new dramaturgy of the intelligible."[98] Using the fictional landscape to interpolate and supplement historical records, Allen frames this "new fabric," calling particular attention to the repertoire of thought and feeling. In "Venus in Two Acts" (2008), Saidiya Hartman recalls similar aims for her memoir *Lose Your Mother: A Journey along the Atlantic Slave Route* (2006): "I longed to write a new story, one unfettered by the constraints of the legal documents and exceeding the restatement and transpositions, which comprised my strategy for disordering and transgressing the protocols of the archive and the authority of its statements and which enabled me to augment and intensify its fictions."[99] Exceeding the archive's contents and authority in search of new epistemological truths, Allen retrains the hegemonic gaze away from Tom's spectacularized body and scrutinizes instead the exploitative motivations of the Bethunes and the prejudices of the fans who packed concert halls to see this "Plantation Negro Boy" perform.[100] In the process, *Song of the Shank* reconstructs a Black celebrity past on which a more equitable future may be constructed, imparting to readers the responsibility to listen to the many countervailing voices and alternative ways of knowing that pressure congratulatory narratives of US history. The words of Reverend Wire—Allen's minor but exceedingly memorable character—sum up the conclusions that *Song of the Shank* draws about the postbellum period and its continued resonance: "A people cannot be redeemed by military victory, Wire says, but only by the spiritual and moral rebirth of the individual and the nation."[101] This is precisely the rebirth that Allen implies has never actually occurred and for which his creative recuperation of "Blind Tom" enjoins us twenty-first-century (and perhaps still postbellum) citizens to confront.

In chapter 6, Tyehimba Jess focuses on a similar form of redress, as he utilizes the emotive economy of poetry to reimagine the inner world of "Blind Tom" and his many contemporaries, picking up where Allen leaves off in reminding readers of the parallels between the experiences of the first wave of Black celebrities and those of today's musicians and entertainers of all sorts.

6

"LET THIS BELTING BE OUR UNBINDING"

Reconceptualizing Black Entertainment in Tyehimba Jess's Olio

In a 2013 *Guardian* interview, the social activist and writer Eduardo Galeano averred, "History never really says goodbye. History says, see you later."[1] Tyehimba Jess's Pulitzer Prize–winning 2016 poetry collection *Olio* is congruent with this view of history. Bookending the collection with the name of the Mother Emmanuel African Methodist Episcopal Church in Charleston, South Carolina, which was both famously destroyed by white supremacists in 1822 and at which the massacre of nine parishioners occurred in 2015, Jess signals the relentless assault on Black lives. Affixed to sonnets memorializing the much-admired nineteenth-century troupe the Fisk Jubilee singers, these dates (along with other years and names of churches damaged and destroyed by white terrorists) elegize the Black individuals whose cultural and sociopolitical (not to mention spiritual) work is often erased from white-dominated narratives.[2]

Olio specifically elucidates the paradoxical experiences of African Americans within the entertainment industry, prompting readers to consider, Whose perspectives have been elided from US cultural history, and what kinds of fresh insights emerge when we creatively recuperate them? Saidiya Hartman notes in her own revivification of postbellum African Americans, *Wayward Lives, Beautiful Experiments: Intimate Histories of Social Upheaval* (2019), "Every historian of the multitude, the dispossessed, the subaltern, and the enslaved is forced to grapple with the power and authority of the archive and the limits it sets on what can be known, whose perspective matters, and who is endowed with the gravity and authority of historical actor."[3] Using the poetic page, instead of Hartman's creative nonfiction approach in *Wayward Lives*, Jess similarly reconstructs a history out of scraps of knowledge, which "require[s]" him "to speculate, listen intently, read between the lines, attend to the disorder of mess of the archive, and to honor silence."[4] *Olio*'s lengthy bibliography also demonstrates the extensive archival and biographical research Jess conducted in order to produce this near-encyclopedic collection, which comes in at 235 pages, but his poems are not beholden to his sources. Resonant with Jacques Rancière's assertion that "literature makes history possible as a discourse of truth" with "the invention of a new narrative," Jess uses his findings as a creative springboard, availing himself of both the formal flexibility and emotive economy of poetry in order to reanimate nineteenth- and early-twentieth-century stars of the stage.[5]

In fact, *Olio* builds on Jess's stunning debut collection, *leadbelly* (2005), which similarly showcases the affordances of persona poetry for reimagining Black cultural history. In *leadbelly*, Jess inhabits the perspective of the famed bluesman Huddie Ledbetter (Leadbelly) along with a host of other figures, among them Leadbelly's wives, his parents, fellow musicians, and even his beloved twelve-string guitar, Stella. Moreover, in Jess's series of "leadbelly vs. lomax" poems, he puts the musician and his onetime manager, the ethnomusicologist John Lomax, in richly contentious dialogue. In so doing, Jess offers a necessary alternative to the denigrating narrative of Lomax as a savior and Leadbelly as a savage savant, propagated not only by Lomax himself but also by the mainstream press, such as *Life* magazine's 1937 piece "Bad N***** Makes Good Minstrel." *leadbelly*'s innovative, subversive use of persona (and the contrapuntal) influenced Jess's contemporaries as well. As Frank X Walker previously noted, "Studying Marilyn Nelson's *Carver* and Tyehimba Jess's *Leadbelly* helped me enter the cultural and creative space that first birthed my book *Buffalo Dance: The Journey of York*."[6] Howard Rambsy II likewise observes that *leadbelly* is a "striking contribution to a large assembly of volumes that are shaping the contours of African American poetry," by "exploring the promise of utilizing persona verse and pursuing aspects of creative world building to disrupt or augment historical narratives."[7] In Jess's tour de force *Olio*, he stretches the possibilities of persona and contrapuntal poetry (and their fusion) even further, no doubt broadening his artistic influence but also pivoting toward the complex experiences of the generation of musicians and entertainers that preceded Leadbelly and other famous blues artists.

Before Jess's poems commence, he sets the nineteenth-century stage in ways that signal his "reading against the grain" of official historical records.[8] In the book's front matter, Jess glosses his title as "a) a miscellaneous mixture of heterogeneous elements; hodgepodge b) a miscellaneous collection (as of literary or musical selections) also: the second part of a minstrel show which featured a variety of performance acts and later evolved into vaudeville."[9] Within this "hodgepodge" framework, Jess's collection wends its way into the lives of a wide range of postbellum figures, including "Blind Tom" (Thomas Greene Wiggins), John William "Blind" Boone, Paul Laurence Dunbar, the Fisk Jubilee Singers, Ernest Hogan, Sissieretta Jones, Millie and Christine McKoy, Booker T. Washington, Bert Williams, George Walker, Edmonia Lewis, and Scott Joplin. With all the wit and verve of the lyric poetry that follows, Jess also provides pithy bios for his "Cast of Characters," whom he identifies as the "Owners of This Olio."[10] Following these descriptions, Jess includes an image that further signals his subversion of the white hegemonic gaze through which much of the archival documentation of these figures has been filtered. As with the book's cover, Jess spells out the word "olio" in the shape of an inverted triangle, with an additional "O" and the letters bolded and in all-caps. The additional "O" serves as an elongated mouth, the shape resembling a minstrel mask in which the unnaturally large eyes and mouth are meant to caricature the features of citizens of African descent; moreover, the Black letters against the page's white background recall the sharp contrasts created through burnt cork and white face paint. Jess implies the exploitative gazes that "*these first-generation freed voices*" navigated, as they strove to (as he notes in the poem "Millie McKoy & Christine McKoy Recall Meeting Blind Tom, 1877") make "a way / *out of no way*."[11] At the same time, the image of the eyes and the mouth signifies Jess's recuperation of these voices, who, via his polyvocal persona poetry, will now speak to us rather than being objectified and spoken for.

In a glowing review, Jacob Sunderlin notes, "These characters may be more than a hundred years old, some of them a hundred years dead, but they are alive in *Olio*, and they call out to you."[12] Tom Griffen similarly concludes that "Jess's work is a determined web of strategic resistance and humble persistence. Above all, it is a documentation of hope where each individual plays a crucial role in the plight of the whole."[13] Metta Sáma concludes, "Tyehimba Jess is to be applauded for this archival research work and for daring to attempt as much formal invention as did the brilliant musicians who passed through this life ahead of him."[14] While these and other reviews of *Olio* have offered the collection early and consistent praise, this chapter works to initiate a critical conversation about *Olio*, particularly regarding its intervention in historical accounts of early Black celebrity.

Focusing specifically on *Olio*'s series of lyrical portraits of "Blind Tom" Wiggins, Christine and Millie McKoy (the "two-headed nightingale"), and Sissieretta Jones (the "Black Patti") and with a concluding consideration of the poem "The Bert Williams / George Walker Paradox," I examine Jess's recuperation of these figures' artistry through his own skillful, innovative poetics. Citing, reconfiguring, and enriching archival and biographical materials, *Olio*, I argue, illuminates these artists' experiences in ways that suggest their continued relevance for confronting the long tradition of white ravening for Black culture, especially music, and the simultaneous degradation of its producers. Indeed, as with Caryl Phillips's *Dancing in the Dark* (chapter 4), which recuperates Bert Williams and George Walker, and Jeffery Renard Allen's *Song of the Shank* (chapter 5), which recuperates "Blind Tom," the poems in *Olio* elucidate postbellum artists' negotiation of the sonic color line, whereby "the collusive relationship between sight and sound deliberately interweaves the racial gaze and its aural counterpart, the listening ear."[15]

Portraying "Blind Tom," the McKoy sisters, and Sissieretta Jones, among others, as artists and not simply entertainers naturally predisposed to delight white audiences, Jess's persona poems likewise attend to these figures' active interior lives. As Kevin Quashie points out, "The inner life is not apolitical or without social value, but neither is it determined entirely by publicness. In fact, the interior—dynamic and ravishing—is a stay against the dominance of the social world; it has its own sovereignty."[16] Lyrically moving between archival traces of nineteenth- and early-twentieth-century Black musical performances and the imagined "quiet" of these artists' minds, Jess subverts the tendency to reduce Black celebrities to their public selves. As I indicate in my concluding analysis of Donald Glover / Childish Gambino's acclaimed 2018 music video "This Is America," *Olio* is also not strictly a historical text. Excavating truths, in the Rancièrean sense, about now-obscure Black stars, Jess evinces cultural (and sonic) resonances between the postbellum and contemporary eras, advancing counternarratives (or counterarchives) to dominant ways of engaging with Black cultural production.

"Fetters *Breaking Free*"

In "Owners of This Olio," Jess introduces "Blind Tom" Wiggins (1859–1908) by foregrounding the paradoxes of his legacy and, by extension, those of myriad nineteenth-century figures: "Tom was born [an] autistic slave savant, possessing formidable piano skills. Under the lifelong 'management' of his masters, the Bethunes, Wiggins played $1 million worth of tunes. He's family inheritance, bound from father to son to wife, until his Final Freedom on the other side."[17] Jess's bio note sums up the conventional reading of Tom as a "slave savant" that has dominated popular understandings of the musician and for which his lyrical portraits add considerable depth. For example, the poem "Mark Twain v. Blind Tom" arranges Mark Twain's commentary on Tom published in, the footnote tells us, "letters to the San Francisco *Alta California*, August 1, 1869," alongside the pianist's imagined self-reflections.[18] Whereas for Twain, Tom is an imbecile, unaware of his divine gifts, Jess's Tom persona is an inspired artist whose creative energies are fueled by the sonic landscape into which he is especially attuned:

this dull clod *weighted in my chest*
with impulses and inspirations *—it finds freedom after*
it no more comprehends *hurt. I hear Earth's tremble harsher*
than does the stupid worm *—better than the soil itself. When*

the stirring of the spirit within *land and tree sing to me, I hear*
her *notes*
of the *wildly*
gorgeous captive *blooming inside—a spirit*
whose wings she *shadows across my face,*
fetters *breaking free*[19]

Formally modeling the process by which we may attempt to see and hear the voices excluded by the monologic of traditional historical narratives, Jess neither relies on Twain's letter as a stable form of knowledge about Tom's performances nor dismisses it as irrelevant. Instead, Jess follows the logic of Stephanie Smallwood, who focuses on "the fact the archive is seeking to ignore, marginalize and disavow—the detail it does not want to animate and make narratable."[20] Accordingly, Jess juxtaposes Twain's rather ignominious epistolary report with what he imagines to be Tom's embodied experiences, educing "quiet" truths about what it might have felt like to be Tom, the inspired musician who heard "notes / wildly" and was bursting ("blooming inside") with creative energy.

Unlike the portrait of Tom in *Song of the Shank*, in which the pianist was so disempowered that Allen could only inhabit the interior thoughts of the figures who both loved and controlled him, Jess calls attention to the "sovereignty" of Tom's inner world, as Quashie might put it. In the process, Jess destabilizes contemporaneous descriptions of Tom's music, in which listeners were unable to reconcile the exquisite sounds they heard with the African-descended, blind, and purportedly cognitively disabled man who stood before them. Christopher Krentz observes that Tom's "performances astonished spectators partly because they were produced by someone black and disabled and therefore inferior."[21] Lyrically restaging one of Tom's performances, Jess's "Blind Tom Plays for a Packed House, 1873" troubles Tom's white audiences' reductive interpretation of him as "a freak / of nature . . . / A blind, black vessel of spiritspeak."[22] In Jess's rendition, Tom is instead enthralled by the sounds of the natural landscape, which he transforms into musical "Wonder."

Furthermore, in "General Bethune on Blind Tom," which is part of a crown of persona sonnets, Jess inhabits the first-person perspective of Tom's "owner," who dismisses the pianist as "Blind and crazed, like a blessed-up idiot," and then congratulates himself for allowing him to become an entertainer (and line Bethune's own pockets in the process): "My charity finally got its reward. / Who am I to deny this gift to the world?"[23] Beginning the sonnet "Blind Tom plays on . . ." with this same concluding line, Jess's Tom persona refutes Bethune's caricature with his self-assertion of the divine ("blessed") nature of his music:

> Who am I to deny this world? This gift
> of music storming through me? It howls out
> my fingers when I reach into God's mouth.[24]

Through these contrapuntal arrangements, both within the same poem and across a crown of sonnets, Jess draws attention to a prevailing form of nineteenth-century cultural dissonance in which Black men and women were valued as entertainers even as they remained subject to multiple forms of degradation. Moreover, in Jess's attention to Tom's inspired life of the mind—"we are all one wave of notes in the dark / gospel of the universe"—he undercuts the authority of white perspectives to provide a reliable portrait of historical Black celebrity.[25]

Although Jess does not reference Willa Cather's fictional version of Tom as "Blind d'Arnault, the negro pianist" in *My Ántonia* (1918) here, it similarly illustrates the reification of racialized listening patterns.[26] As Jennifer Stoever notes, "Through the listening ear's surveillance, discipline, and interpretation, certain associations between race and sound come to seem normal, natural, and 'right.'"[27] Cather's first-person narrator, Jim Burden, describes Tom's music in these distinctly racialized terms: "To hear him, to watch him, was to see a Negro enjoying himself as only a Negro can."[28] A few pages later, Jim compares Tom to "some glistening African god of pleasure, full of strong, savage blood."[29] In Jess's lyric revivification, Tom is, by contrast, deeply connected to the natural world but not in the service of stereotypes of people of African descent as closer to the Earth—the primitivist ideologies driving Cather's image of "savage blood" and Twain's comparison of Tom to a "dull clod." Instead, Jess's Tom persona finds "*freedom*" in listening to and reproducing the sounds of the natural world, a space that does not cause the burdensome "*hurt*" of enslavement and indentured servitude.[30]

In addition to Jess's use of persona poetry to imagine the countervailing voices and perspectives that often do not make their way into the archive, he creatively recuperates Tom's musical prowess through his own innovative poetics. Jess indicates this strategy in an illustration by Jessica Lynne Brown that introduces the "Blind Tom" series of poems. Featuring a spare sketch of a man with his back turned to the piano and his hands spread across and depressing some of its keys, the illustration refers to Tom's extraordinary musical dexterity. As Whitney Womack Smith notes, "On the piano he [Tom] could play different songs with his left hand and right hand while singing a third tune, all in different keys, and could play with his back to the instrument."[31] Jess reenacts this virtuosity through the lyric form that is his own instrument. The aforementioned "Millie McKoy & Christine McKoy Recall Meeting Blind Tom, 1877," for example, is a contrapuntal persona sonnet in the distinct but conjoined voices of the McKoy sisters (1851–1912), and the two columns of interlocking (or conjoined) text may be read vertically, horizontally, and diagonally. In this way, Jess not only subverts a linear, monosemous reading of history but also gestures toward the stage feats of Tom and the McKoy twins:

Blind Tom never saw my two bodies	*He could only hear the way we were joined,*
fused at the hips. His ears saw our two	*twinned breaths colored in harmony, our blue*
bright voices blooming from one pulse. Slowly,	*reaching out through darkness, through the void—*

he laid his hands on my face, and then he knew—[32]

Each way of reading these lines educes new meanings. "*Blind Tom never saw my two bodies / fused at the hips. His ears saw our two / bright voices blooming from one pulse. Slowly*" may be read instead as "*Blind Tom never saw my two bodies / He could only hear the way we were joined, / fused at the hips. His ears saw our two.*" These lines may also be read diagonally, moving from left to right, "*Blind Tom never saw my two bodies / twinned breaths colored in harmony, our blue / bright voices blooming from one pulse. Slowly*"; or from right to left, *He could only hear the way we were joined, / fused at the hips. His ears saw our two / reaching out through his darkness, through the void—.*"

Alternatively, one might begin with the concluding line of the poem and read the poem's four centered lines linearly or nonlinearly, creating yet other ways of imagining an encounter between Tom and the McKoy sisters:

> he laid his hands on my face, and then he knew—
> our bodies' betrayals have made us a way
> to cause wonder at a god both kind and cruel—
> to show this world the gut meaning of grace.

Refracted through the imagined lens of the McKoy sisters, Tom is no longer the "stupid worm" that Twain observes but a magnanimous musician who appreciates the "gut meaning of grace." Much in the way that Tom and Christine and Millie McKoy displayed their mastery of music and performance onstage, Jess honors these artist-ancestors by crafting polyvocal persona sonnets with myriad interpretive possibilities layered into them. At the same time, the intricacies of Jess's stanzaic structure call attention to his arrangement of these figures' personae for his own poetic purposes, thereby reminding readers of the subjective intentions informing all historical accounts (archival and imaginative).

Jess's final Tom poem, the sonnet "Blind Tom: One Body, Two Graves; Brooklyn/Georgia," further affirms the affordances of creative recuperation both for offering multiple ways to know, see, and even hear US history and for paying homage to the artists of the prerecording age. In this sonnet, Jess inhabits the posthumous persona of the famed pianist as he continues to struggle toward self-determination in the afterlife, for the Bethune family never ceased its proprietary pursuit of Tom's body. As Jess notes in the footnote, "Blind Tom was buried first in Brooklyn's Evergreen Cemetery, and then allegedly moved by the Bethune family to Columbus, GA. However, records in Brooklyn indicate the body was never moved. There are headstones in both states for Blind Tom."[33] While O'Connell and other historians have documented this macabre tale, Jess reimagines this history from Tom's perspective and with the innovative artistry that characterized the musician's oeuvre. Beginning and ending this sonnet with essentially the same line—"*Here I lie, Blind Tom: Piano Man. I'm free*" and "*Here I lie, Blind Tom: Piano Man. Free*"—the poem may be read vertically from the first line to the last and in reverse order, horizontally from left to right and right to left, diagonally, and, ultimately, in any imaginable combination that readers devise.[34] The second half of the sonnet reads, for example,

rooted deep in black muscle memory
that's set slaves almost free, that carved its name *scrawling across each heart, the music's brunt*
ringing like a bell, like an open wound
thick as thunder through city summer air— *shimmering all over the country's soul—*
from mouths that bend flattened dreams into tune—
I'm nowhere at all, but sing everywhere— *I dance inside each holla and whole note—*
Let me introduce to those who ain't heard me:
Here I am, Blind Tom: Piano Man. Free.[35]

New truths emerge from each configuration of lines, as Jess pays his final homage to the virtuosity for which Tom, "billed as the 'Eighth Wonder of the World,'" was known.[36] Building a polysemous reading experience into the structure of the stanza, Jess emphasizes the importance of expanding the linear (not to mention monologic) frame typically used to construct narratives of US history. He models instead a creative mode of "playing in the archive" and seeking truths rather than relying on the purported objectivity of archival facts.[37]

The sonnet's first and final lines—"*Here I lie, Blind Tom: Piano Man. I'm free*" and "*Here I lie, Blind Tom: Piano Man. Free*"—also underscore the tensions between captivity and emancipation that were voiced through the sonic utterances of Tom, the McKoy sisters, and the other "*almost free*" Americans of African descent. The poem's Tom persona identifies him as a "Piano Man," implying his liberation from the life of manual labor thrust on the majority of postbellum African Americans, and at the same time, he is only "free" now that he is lying in his grave(s), with ownership of his corpse still being contested by members of the Bethune family. Formally, Jess makes this struggle clear by centering every other line of the poem so that a full eight-line poem reads down the middle, while the other lines are arranged contrapuntally as "Brooklyn" (left column) versus "Georgia" (right column). In other words, the whereabouts of Tom's physical remains may still be contested, but Jess makes use of this final, elegiac sonnet to set Tom's spirit free, "*shimmering all over the country's soul.*" Furthermore, Jess invites readers to hear Tom "*sing*[*ing*] *everywhere*," his legacy still reverberating in the promise of the liberty "*bell*" and the reality of "*open wound*[*s*]" and "*flattened dreams.*"

"A legible and linear narrative," Marisa J. Fuentes notes, "cannot sufficiently account for the palimpsest of material and meaning embedded in the lives of people shaped by the intimacies and ubiquity of violence."[38] Devising a self-reflexive poetics to match these palimpsestic commitments, Jess recuperates the persona of "Blind Tom" linearly, nonlinearly, from left to right, from right to left, and diagonally, as well as through the lens of his counterparts (Millie and Christine McKoy), those who tried to control him (the Bethunes), and those who recognized his sublime gift but not his humanity (Twain). Jess's sonneteering pyrotechnics are similarly inspired by Tom's own mastery of the keyboard, thereby paying tribute to his neglected artistry, while demonstrating the potential of the persona poem, the sonnet, and the contrapuntal to draw readers into these multifarious, interior ways of engaging nineteenth-century history and its continued reverberations.

"Here—This Is Our Story I Want You to Hear"

Jess likewise invites readers to engage with the imagined backstage and offstage testimony of the McKoy sisters—often referred to as the "Carolina Twins" and the "two-headed nightingale"—not as gawkers seeking voyeuristic pleasure but instead as active listeners. As Fuentes further insists, "Our responsibility to these vulnerable historical subjects is to acknowledge and actively resist the perpetuation of their subjugation and commodification in our own discourse and historical practices."[39] In Jess's McKoy twins series, readers are encouraged to approach the past through the first-person and, appropriately in this case, collective perspective of "vulnerable historical subjects." The poems are preceded by Jessica Lynne Brown's sketch of a butterfly, with its symmetrical wings suggesting the graceful beauty of these conjoined women, who during their lifetime were treated as "freaks" as part of P. T. Barnum's American Museum and similar such sideshow circuits. In this regard, an 1869 promotional broadside for one of the McKoys' performances in Boston announces them as "FREAK OF NATURE / EVEN SEEN ON EARTH / since the creation of our first parents."[40] By contrast, Jess introduces Christine and Millie by describing the complex scope of these sisters' experiences: "The Creator consigned the McKoys with the grace and grit to be conjoined twins. To be born into slavery. To be regularly inspected by physicians to verify their combined condition; to be leased to traveling freak tours at the age of two. When kidnapped to England at the age of three, their owner took their mother there as receipt to retrieve them back—and away from British liberty. Upon emancipation, they famously traveled the world until they bought their old plantation."[41] Rather than pity Christine and Millie's "combined condition," Jess celebrates their "grace and grit" while exposing the numerous traumas that the white power structure inflicted on them. He also suggests the ways in which the sisters capitalized on the spectacularity projected onto them, underscoring the active role they played in their own celebrity—a lesson for today's entertainment landscape, in which the skill and creativity of Black musicians is often underappreciated because of a racially essentialist view of the inextricability of "blackness, the body, rhythm, and sexuality."[42]

Unlike Tom, whose life experiences were filtered entirely through the perspective of others, the McKoy sisters published a promotional autobiography, *The History and Medical Description of the Two-Headed Girl, Told in "Their Own Peculiar Way" by "One of Them,"* which first appeared in 1869 and was subsequently reprinted under slightly altered titles.[43] Passages from a later edition reproduced in Linda Frost's *Conjoined Twins in Black and White: The Lives of Millie-Christine McKoy and Daisy and Violet Hilton* (2009)—a text that Jess cites in his bibliography—precede each of Jess's McKoy sisters persona poems. For instance, the page following Brown's sketch features a quote from the autobiography's introduction that emphasizes the McKoy sisters' exceptional appearance but absent the denigration to which they were routinely subjected: "We are, indeed, a strange people, justly regarded both by scientific and ordinary eyes as the greatest natural curiosities the world has ever had sent upon its surface."[44] Building this dialogic framework into the reading experience, whereby lyric lines respond to and enrich this archival document, Jess both resists the monologic of conventional historical narratives and insists on the utility of multiple perspectives as a means of uncovering what was privately felt versus publicly said and performed versus concealed from the exploitation of the white hegemonic gaze. As Ellen Samuels avers, "Leaving aside the vexed status of truth in even the most reliable of autobiographies, there is very little historical or textual evidence to support treating the *History* [*The History and Medical Description of the Two-Headed Girl*] as a piece authored by the McKoy twins rather than by their managers and former owners."[45] As Jess interpolates passages from the autobiography with his own persona poetry, he similarly implies that there are other, "quiet" truths to uncover and chronicle that were not inscribed into this promotional volume.

Jess's meticulously crafted sonnets (the lines of which are meant to resemble the distinct but interlocking bodies of the McKoy sisters) also draw awareness to the constructed nature of his and, by extension, all historical representations. In the collection's appendix, Jess provides an explanation for the McKoy sonnets that elucidates what Rancière might term the poet's "heretical" approach to history, which questions "the procedures of meaning by which a historicity is defined."[46] "Syncopated sonnets," Jess explains, "sometimes sing in circles to allow recitation that'll roll interstitial, antigravitational, and diagonal, with voices splitting to each side but joining in the middle. . . . Our dear McKoy sisters syncopate regularly with such sonnets."[47] Jess does not subscribe to a tidy timeline of racial progress; rather, he evinces a recursive, palimpsestic approach to the past that reaches beyond "the fictions of the archive."[48]

Titled simply "Millie and Christine McKoy," the section's first contrapuntal sonnet visually mirrors the shape of a butterfly (or conjoined twins) and opens with the sisters musing about the unique timbre and rhythm of their repertoire, while conveying their self-consciousness as artists: "*We've mended two songs into one dark skin / We ride the wake of each other's rhythms*."[49] With the following lines' poignant images of "bleeding soprano into contralto" and "beating our hearts' syncopated tempo," Jess invites us to reimagine what it would have been like to witness the mellifluous sounds of the "two-headed nightingale."[50] The innovative reading strategies that Jess layers into his persona poems also parallel the purportedly exquisite harmonies and duets performed by Christine and Millie, which, given the prerecording age in which they rose to fame, only survive in textual memory. As Laura Engel rightly notes, "Performance does not vanish; it lingers across bodies, gestures, voices, and texts in ways that connect the past to the present."[51] Accordingly, Jess's intricately crafted sonnet, which can be read vertically, horizontally, diagonally, linearly, and nonlinearly, restages these nineteenth-century musicians' sonic mastery with his own artistry.

Continuing to place readers in the position of active listeners, Jess's "Millie-Christine's Love Story" also elucidates, recalling Quashie, the twins' "quiet" creativity:

Here—this is the story I want you to hear—
our own duet. Listen to how we're bound.   *in unison. Listen to the grace we have*
—one body crooning two notes. By God, we're
like sympathetic strings. Each sung sound   *ringing within me and my other half;*
airborne, shook and shimmering through my head,
with Christine's voice at my side. I have sung   *with Millie's embracing contrapuntal,*
in a way very few could comprehend—
with souls ablaze. This is how I know love—   *so you can see my life is brimmed. It's full.*[52]

In many respects, this is a poem of Black and disabled pride, which begins with an imperative call to readers to internalize this version of the narrative, rather than the voyeuristic ones circulating in popular culture: "Here—this is our story I want you to hear—." Rendering the twins' lifetime together as a "love story," Jess likewise imagines the sisters' affection for each other and their singing ("By God, we're / like sympathetic strings"), refusing the relentless focus on their bodies while indicating the gaps in the archive when it comes to the interiority of Black cultural figures. As Quashie notes, "Love is an ethic, a responsibility to and of the self. And in its self-centeredness, it is not apolitical but neither is it driven by the terms set by political or social discourse."[53] Matching the sisters' duets with "shimmering" alliteration and slant rhyme, Jess celebrates a state that "very few could comprehend"—one that is not dictated by the white hegemonic social order but affirms instead that "love is the practice and the prize."[54]

Also crucial is that the currency of Jess's poems is the written word, removing the possibility of the visual voyeurism that Christine and Millie experienced during their performances. For example, in "Millie-Christine: On Display," a contrapuntal sonnet in which the twins' outlooks are distinctly rendered in two parallel columns while they also share eight centered lines of text, Jess bears witness to their individualized and combined experience as objects of prurient fascination who nonetheless see themselves as blessed:

We've been probed, prodded, and roughly examined—   *from backbone to backbone, from hip to hip*
our wondrous oneness exists. We're conjoined.
and we've lists of doctors who understand   *our miracle is real. Hear and see this:*
We're not frauds, but born of providence:
God mended two souls into one dark skin.[55]

Emphasizing "two souls" and not the unique anatomical features that linked the two sisters, the sketches that readers may outline in our heads are informed by a sympathetic artist (Jess) and not the freak-show promoters or unscrupulous doctors, who "probed, prodded, and roughly examined" Millie-Christine. The final line's revision of W. E. B. Du Bois's iconic description of the double consciousness that Black Americans experience—"two souls, two thoughts, two unreconciled strivings; two warring ideals in one dark body, whose dogged strength alone keeps it from being torn asunder"—further reframes Millie-Christine's "mended two souls into one dark skin" as a condition of joy and providence.[56]

The final McKoy sisters poem, "McKoy Twins: Syncopated Star / *step right up* . . . ," is a salient example of Jess's multimodal strategies that allow him to braid traces of the archive and the repertoire, to recall Diana Taylor's helpful phrasing.[57] In addition to the visual and lyrical dialogues made possible by Jess's contrapuntal persona poetry, "McKoy Twins: Syncopated Star" is a legal-sized, double-sided perforated gatefold page, with one side featuring this section's five contrapuntal sonnets arranged to mirror the shape of the butterfly (or the conjoined twins' bodies) that opened the section. On the other side, Jess mimics a carnival barker's call to "*step right up*" and witness "*a double dose of darkie*," who will "*astound and amaze as they attract your gaze*."[58] This racist rhetoric is inextricably bound to the lyricism of the syncopated persona sonnets;

however, the poetry also stands in productive counterpoint to the denigrating voyeurism advocated by the anonymous barker. Readers may in fact be "astound[ed] and amaze[d]" by what they gaze upon, but it is not the bodies of Millie and Christine that transfix. Again, it is the mastery of Jess's sonnet handiwork, which facilitates the reading of all five of his McKoy sonnets in horizontal, vertical, and diagonal arrangement.

For Rancière, history constitutes "the exploration of the multiple paths at the unforeseen intersections by which one may apprehend the forms of experience of the visible and the utterable."[59] Jess is similarly skeptical of traditional historiographic methods and the dominant, exclusionary narratives that they produce, and his innovative poetics adumbrate "multiple paths" and "unforeseen intersections" relevant to the legacy of Millie and Christine. Regarding the formal affordances of poetry for elucidating such multiplicity, Jess's contemporary Bettina Judd offers the following: "Poetry, with its weighted language dependent on rhythm, cadence, and tone, has the capacity to signify multiple meanings at once and, conveyed appropriately, has the capacity to reveal the complexities of the *context* of its utterance."[60] Through Jess's syncopated contrapuntal persona poetry, readers are able to engage with not only the postbellum context of Millie and Christine's fame but also the multidimensionality of their emotional lives. We bear witness to the pain of exploitation ("*We sing straight from America's barbwired heart*") coupled with the joy that Millie and Christine derived from both each other and their extraordinary music: "*with souls ablaze. This is how I know love—so you can see my life is brimmed. It's full—.*"[61]

"We Thrall Her Miss Jones"

As with the McKoy twins and "Blind Tom," Jess introduces Sissieretta Jones (1868–1933) with an illustration by Jessica Lynne Brown, whereby Jones stands open-mouthed, with an outline of a spotlight making it clear that she is the star of the show. A crowded auditorium also stands before her, demonstrating the wide appeal that this now-obscure soprano opera star once had. Leading her own troupe, performing in the most prestigious of cultural spaces, and generally succeeding in a musical arena that was dominated by people of European descent, Jones was an exceptional figure. According to the biographer Maureen D. Lee, Jones "sang before four presidents," and "at one time she was the highest-paid African American female performer."[62] Nevertheless, Jones's accomplishments, as well as the personal identity that lay behind the moniker of "Black Patti," have not been well represented, especially across the twentieth century and into our own era. In Michael Cooper's 2018 "overlooked" obituary for the *New York Times*, he notes that Sissieretta Jones "forged an unconventional path to singing opera, becoming the first African-American woman to headline a concert on the main stage of Carnegie Hall, in 1893. She sang at the White House, toured the nation and the world, and, in a performance at Madison Square Garden, was conducted by the composer Antonin Dvorak. But there were color lines she never managed to break, like the one that kept the nation's major opera companies segregated, denying her the chance to perform in fully staged operas."[63] In addition to this racial barrier, an obstacle for Jess and others attempting to recuperate her legacy is that there are no known recordings of Jones, and "she left no diary or cache of letters, making it impossible to know her private thoughts and feelings."[64] As with "Blind Tom" and Christine and Millie McKoy, Jess can only attempt to recapture Jones's musical mastery through his own lyrical dexterity.

Jess's pithy bio in his aforementioned "Cast of Characters" likewise affirms the recuperative work that *Olio* performs on Sissieretta Jones's behalf: "They dubbed her 'Black Patti.' We thrall her Miss Jones. Hailing from Providence, the first Black Diva to croon in Carnegie. Led a worldwide tour of her eponymous Troubadours from 1896–1916."[65] Inhabiting Jones's persona and thereby allowing her to write back against the labels "they" (white-dominated media outlets and concertgoers) affixed, Jess attempts to restore Jones's original artistry. Implying the through lines between the racialized and gendered treatment of Jones and similar responses to Black musicians and artists today, Jess also transgresses the prevailing sonic color line, which reinforced (and in many respects continues to do so) the notion that people of African descent were naturally endowed with the gift of song but only on a vernacular, intuitive level. Contemporaneous press accounts documenting Jones's career reveal white audiences' inability to appreciate Jones as an opera singer without inflecting their appraisals with racist assumptions. For example, a *New York Herald* review of an 1890 Jones performance at Madison Square Garden quotes one of the members of the Italian prima donna Adrelina Patti's entourage: "This colored woman [Jones] is certainly a very good natural singer, and while I should hardly feel like comparing her voice with Mme. Patti's, I find her negro dialect much better, as shown in her rendering of the 'Suwanee River.'"[66] After an 1892 performance in Pittsburgh, a local reporter praised Jones but in similarly derogatory terms: "This sable diva sings intelligently, wholly without affectation and with sound musical feeling. . . . Though [her voice] does not ring with passion, it shakes the heart, not your ears, with the pathetic warmth that marks all negro singing."[67] In addition to these reductive reactions, the moniker "Black Patti" diminished Jones's achievements by situating her in the shadow of Adelina Patti. Working within and against these representational constraints, Jess probes the song behind the song, as well as the *quiet* of Jones's otherwise-inaccessible interior thoughts.

In the process, Jess affirms the necessity of consulting a wide range of sources and modes in order to recuperate the complexities of Black cultural history signified by an underappreciated artist such as Sissieretta Jones. As Taylor argues, "The relationship between the archive and the repertoire, as I see it, is certainly not sequential. . . . Nor is it true versus false, mediated versus unmediated, primordial versus modern. Nor is it a binary."[68] Accordingly, Jess places Jones's imagined first-person perspective on her career and her artistry more generally alongside fictionalized 1935 Works Progress Administration interviews with Eva Shoe, who "used to work for Black Patti."[69] Staging this dialogic, multimodal encounter between an invented archive and repertoire, Jess both speculates about Jones's life beyond the stage and indicates the ways in which all historical representations (whether based on preserved documents or sprung from the imagination) are curated to support subjective interpretations.

In Jess's creation of Shoe's WPA interviews, he is also careful to exclude white hegemonic perspectives—the aforementioned "they"—and instead showcases the testimony of a Black woman fellow artist alongside Jones's own accounts. Shoe notes that "black folks used to line up for blocks to see all of us. The mighty Black Patti Revue. Each one of them crowed waitin to see her belt it out the way white folks would do—even better."[70] Shoe likewise suggests that Jones was "caught up in the truth she was workin out of each note. She wanted to resurrect all the church she could muster out of those opera stories. She wanted to muscle arias out all those spirituals."[71] Absent her own testimony but wishing to creatively recuperate some semblance of Jones's truth, the prose-poem "My Name Is Sissieretta Jones" explicitly subverts the "Black Patti" appellation: "Once word got out about the way I sing, the world wanted to bleed all the sass out my name. To scratch the gift my mother gave me and shove a would-be white diva in my spotlight. . . . But the darkened sense inside my name won't be silenced."[72] In Jess's portrait, Jones rejects being named a Black cognate for a white diva, which reduces her to mere imitation, a derivative of the white opera singer.

Moreover, Rancière observes that "artistic practices are 'ways of doing and making' that intervene in the general distribution of ways of doing and making as well as in the relationships they maintain to modes of being and forms of visibility."[73] Utilizing poetic license to disrupt traditional "ways of doing and making," Jess plumbs Jones's inner world, where resides the memory of her mother as well as an almost ineffable feeling of diasporic haunting and yearning: "Every night, in the dark offstage, I hear my mother's voice in my head, her backyard hum, the sea in her distance with the weather of storm. She'd look out and see the thrall of water heave its back to the sky. I'd look out to the darkness and hear my true name."[74] In a private moment out of the spotlight, this Jones persona considers a seascape replete with her mother's "backyard hum" and an unarticulated but deeply affective connection to an African homeland, represented by the "thrall of water" and the "true name" that may never be recovered. Analyzing the work of one of Jess's contemporaries, Natasha Trethewey, Quashie avers, "This is the achievement of the poem—to use form to tell a story quietly, which is to tell it with the expressive complexity of the inner life."[75] After beginning "My Name Is Sissieretta Jones" with a correction to what Jess perceives as a public misnaming that diminished Jones's artistry, he then "tell[s] a story quietly," elucidating the dynamic inner life that Jones and, by extension, all Black women celebrities possess, even as they are often reduced to their public personae.

"Even in the worst circumstances of domination," as bell hooks notes, "the ability to manipulate one's gaze in the face of structures of domination that would contain it, opens up the possibility of agency."[76] This is the transgressive reorientation that Jess facilitates with the poem "Sissieretta Jones, Carnegie Hall, 1902: *O patria mia*" in particular. Through a series of anaphoric statements, the Jones persona compares herself to the enslaved Ethiopian princess (the eponymous operatic character Aida) and invites readers to hear "O patria mia" (Oh, my homeland) as a song about the liberation of African Americans, including Jones herself. The poem thus commences with "Aida, buried in the darkness / of her fate. Aida, singing."[77] The "darkness" here takes on multiple meanings, but perhaps most importantly Jess represents Jones as a self-possessed opera singer who delivers a stunning performance that (temporarily at least) negates the dominance wielded by the elite white audience at Carnegie Hall. In other words, here Jones is not the spectacularized "Black Patti" but the incisive interpreter of one of the most iconic operas.

It is not possible to hear a recording of Jones sing "O patria mia," but the lyrical rhythm that Jess constructs through anaphora and poignant imagery gives readers a sense of the soaring heights to which she ascended. Indeed, the following lengthy passage exemplifies the work of artistic homage in which Jess is engaged:

I stand solo in this country
of concert. I am multitudes
of broken chains. I am Aida
with war on her lips.
I am Aida against drowning
in all that summons her alive.
I bear the crescendo
of ocean inside me.
I carry its bones inside
my attack. I am a wave
reaching beyond this shore.

Let this belting be our
unbinding. Let o bring
the sound of all our wanting.
Let *patria* speak the names
of all my fathers.
Let the curtain rise
to show the face that is
known. Let the country
be mine. Let the country
be mine. Let this country
be mine.[78]

Here Jones is not simply singing "O patria mia" as it was composed for Italian audiences. Instead, she conveys through this song of homeland the historical displacement and dispossession that African Americans have endured and cries out for her nation to recognize the "broken chains" of "all [her] "fathers" and, ultimately, to be hers. While this is a poetic reenactment of a historical performance, Jess likewise implies that the emphatic call to "Let this belting be our / unbinding" has still not been fully heard and heeded. He thus encourages readers to engage with this long-forgotten opera singer not only in a historical sense but also in relation to the resonances that her rendition of this song has in the contemporary Black Lives Matter era.

Inhabiting Jones's perspective, Jess also defamiliarizes the racialization of sound, showing the expectations that white audiences had for Jones that did not apply to her counterparts of European descent. Writing about the antebellum opera star Elizabeth Greenfield (dubbed "the Black Swan"), Stoever observes that "the sonic color line not only regulated 'black' sound but also deemed certain sounds publicly expressive of whiteness."[79] This color line and its aural consequences held sway long after the Civil War as is clear in the documented responses to Jones's performances, and her moniker (the Black Patti) is a prime example of the continued enforcement of "Black" and "white" artistic expressions. In this regard, immediately following "Sissieretta Jones, Carnegie Hall," Jess segues to Eva Shoe, who remarks that "even when [Jones] did belt out some opera born outside of this country's peculiar history, she'd still have to come right back down and weave her way out of the cakewalk of blackface and jim crow. Every evening, she'd waltz all proper out of the spotlight—and then let the okie doke shuffle and that coontalk grin take over the stage. You know—the circus they was all comin to see."[80] Juxtaposing the crescendoed conclusion of "Sissieretta Jones, Carnegie Hall"—"Let the country / be mine. Let the country / be mine. Let this country / be mine"—with Shoe's rueful remarks about the minstrel act that Jones was required to participate in, Jess evinces the ramifications of the sonic color line, as well as the double standard that Black performers faced in a white-controlled culture industry, whereby their primary role was that of entertainer, not artist.

In an interview with Adam Fitzgerald, Jess noted that he wanted *Olio* to facilitate "a real conversation with the 19th and 21st centur[ies]," and these portraits of Sissieretta Jones do just that.[81] Although it would be satisfying to believe that the racialized expectations Jones endured have shifted with time and circumstance, Black celebrities continue to negotiate a cultural minefield that their white counterparts mostly jettison. In this regard, Miles White notes that "African American minstrelsy formed the bedrock of virtually all subsequent African American stage and theatrical performance—from vaudeville and musicals to stand-up comedy and film."[82] John Strausbaugh likewise identifies parallels between nineteenth-century minstrelsy and twenty-first-century hip hop: "In both eras, the performers could easily say that they were merely living up to the expectations of their predominantly, though not entirely, White audiences."[83] Current Black musicians, including women singers, exercise more agency and control than perhaps ever before, but there remain significant parallels between today's Black celebrity landscape and the one that Jess's creative recuperation of Jones and others brings to light. As Nicole R. Fleetwood reminds us, "The concept of hypervisibility has particular resonance in contemporary popular culture and mass entertainment where the black body as commodity fetish has a heightened salience," and the fetishization of these commodified bodies conceals "power relations and historical contexts that produce systems of inequality and the consumption of difference."[84] Encouraging readers to engage with these power imbalances from the perspective of historical

Black artists, *Olio*'s Jones section concludes with Eva Shoe reflecting on her crash course in how to navigate white-dominated cultural spaces: "That's what I learned from the great Sissieretta Jones. How to know where the mask begins and you end."[85] Distinguishing between the performance and the artist, the public persona and the private interior, these are the lessons that we must take from Jess's portraits of Jones (and Shoe) as we reengage with our own sociocultural landscape, in which Black musicians predominate but are still subjected to racial hypervisibility and depersonalization.

"That's the Role I Play"

These racialized expectations are poignantly realized in another innovative contrapuntal, "Bert Williams / George Walker Paradox," which links *Olio* with Phillips's novel *Dancing in the Dark* (chapter 4), affirming the contemporary interest in revisiting these postbellum, pre–Harlem Renaissance stars of the stage. Illuminating what Rancière terms a "new narrative," in this case about Bert Williams (1874–1922) and George Walker (1873–1911), Jess augments *Dancing in the Dark*'s recuperative work by both fusing archive and repertoire and underscoring the significance of these figures for considering today's intersection of race, gender, and celebrity. As with the aforementioned "McKoy Twins: Syncopated Star," "Bert Williams / George Walker Paradox" is a legal-sized, double-sided, perforated gatefold page with an accompanying explanation and instructions in the collection's appendix: "Bert and George step out in the minstrel box with paradox. These verbal contortionists correlate and syncopate to emancipate themselves from two-dimensional postulates of blackface fate. 'Jonah Man' Bert sings 'Nobody' while George is the straight man dancing onstage. They call themselves 'Two Real Coons' after seeing so many corked up white buffoons—they peddle the genuine article 'cause they know it'll sell (or so they snicker). They turn their backsides to Witmark's *Minstrel Guide* to hawk their hustle in this 'syncopated ghazal,' singing line by line, forward, backward, or on the diagonal."[86] The excerpt from *The Witmark Amateur Minstrel Guide and Burnt Cork Encyclopedia* on the "backside" of the gatefold instructs readers about "How to Black Up," reminding them of the historical investment in minstrelsy: "No form of entertainment is so replete with comedy, nor gives such universal satisfaction when well represented"; further, "Minstrelsy is the most popular form of entertainment and is always selected as a vehicle to present the talent of the club, college, school, or association."[87] Citing this historical text, Jess allows the unabashed celebration of blackface—and the institutionalized anti-Black racism that it conveys—to speak for itself, much as he did in "Mark Twain v. Blind Tom."

Jess also "play[s] in the archive" with his syncopated ghazal that unfolds on the page's other side. Specifically, "Bert Williams / George Walker Paradox" is arranged as two lengthy columns, which, as Jess notes in the appendix, may be read "line by line, forward, backward, or on the diagonal." The left-columned opening couplet—"Sing like me, Jonah in the charcoal hold of the whale— / be smiling till the crowd starts to cry; this nobody"—may be read on its own or paired with the Walker couplet to the right: "Doing justice to my Juba jig. See how I dance? / just might be playing you for a fool. You see, this face." Or we might begin with "You see, this face just might be playing you for a fool. / Doing justice to my Juba jig. See how I dance?" and segue seamlessly to "this nobody be smiling till the crowd starts to cry: / Sing like me, Jonah in the charcoal hold of the whale."[88] We can likewise start with the right column's last couplet and segue to the right column's first couplet:

reflecting on how every live soul holds a dream. We're
wise to the dark's risks. I'll shine the crowd. I'll have each face
Doing justice to my Juba jig. See how I dance?
Just might be playing you for a fool. You see, this face

Or we could move from the right column's last couplet to the left column's first couplet:

reflecting on how every live soul holds a dream. We're
wise to the dark's risks. I'll shine the crowd. I'll have each face
Sing like me, Jonah in the charcoal hold of the whale—
be smiling till the crowd starts to cry: this nobody

These examples only skim the surface of the reading patterns made possible by this multimodal poem, evincing the importance of interpreting Williams and Walker's performances beyond what the archive reports about the supposed all-American pleasure of "blacking up."

Moreover, Jess emphasizes the carefully constructed roles that Williams and Walker designed for themselves, which may have been misunderstood by their predominantly white audiences. As the Williams persona puts it, "That's the role I play, / crooning while coon songs paint my strife," to which Walker echoes, "That's my mask, not my face / making folk double-take what they see."[89] In some respects, this is the most doubly conscious (in the Du Boisian sense) poem in the collection, as the Williams and Walker personae's two columns of black ink on the long white page (buttressed by an encyclopedia on minstrelsy no less) represent public and private resistance to denigrating stereotypes of people of African descent. At the same time, Jess complicates that doubling by choreographing a wide range of interpretative possibilities, thereby both moving beyond the delimited frame of the white gaze and implying further modes of understanding that have not been fully reckoned with in narratives of historical—and, for that matter, contemporary—Black fame. Aptly represented by the merging of syncopation (rhythmic dissonance imported by enslaved Africans) with the ghazal (an Arabic lament), Jess's multifarious poetics thereby unravel the false binaries between archive and repertoire, artist and entertainer, and, perhaps most germane for Williams and Walker, "race traitor" versus "race man."

Jess's both/and approach allows for a recuperation of all of the paradoxes (hence the title) that Williams and Walker, not to mention "Blind Tom," the McKoy sisters, and Sissieretta Jones, among others, represent. For Jess, it seems, Black cultural history must acknowledge the many ways to see, know, and hear, while recognizing that all accounts of the past (including his own) are constructed to advance particular perspectives. Jess's poetics especially accord with Taylor's description of the episodic mode of embodied practices: "The episodic modality expresses itself as a cacophony of voices, not as a monologue. The simultaneity of reactions and perspectives complicates any preferred interpretation. Unlike tragedy, the episodic structure works against the bracketing of a clear beginning and end, cause and effect, before or after. The beginning can be as arbitrary as the end is tentative. The ongoingness and continual juxtaposition of elements keeps the framework open and flexible."[90] Multivoiced, syncopated, and palimpsestic, Jess works within a similar poetic framework, in which a chorus of historical figures riff off one another in a decisively antihierarchical, antiteleological manner. In the collection's appendix, readers are likewise invited to take part in this unfolding narrative of Black celebrity history by ripping out "The Bert Williams / George Walker Paradox" and creating a cylinder, a Möbius strip, or a torus, experiencing the poem anew in all its tactile, kinesthetic possibilities.

Subverting a sweeping narrative of the nation's progressive march forward, *Olio* readers must confront the complex ways in which the promises and failures of the postbellum epoch are still sewn into the sociocultural fabric of life in the United States, particularly playing out in the entertainment industry, in which sonic color lines persist and the line between self-expression and capitulation to racial stereotypes and other forms of white exploitation often remains quite thin.[91] Further, in the same way that minstrelsy, even in its African American form, was often understood through one-dimensional stereotypes, Jess's creative recuperation reminds us that the figures onstage are always more complicated—and even paradoxical—than the public might recognize at first blush. In mining some of the interior thoughts that Williams and Walker shielded from public view, Jess underscores the importance of disentangling individuals from caricatured ideas about Blackness and Black bodies. As the Walker persona notes, "Believe the human / being buried 'neath the ash," and as Walker queries his partner as much as us as readers, "Have you seen their faces? / beyond the skin."[92]

The Afterlives of *Olio*'s Cast of Characters

Reanimating these long-neglected stars of the stage, Jess reconceptualizes what Rancière referred to earlier as "modes of being and forms of visibility," recuperating Bert Williams, George Walker, "Blind Tom," Millie and Christine McKoy, and Sissieretta Jones, among so many others, from the margins of history in order to appreciate them as innovative artists who laid the groundwork for his own riveting poetry. Interlacing materials from the archive and the repertoire, Jess both exposes how these figures were represented during their lifetimes and speculates about the emotions, creative impulses, and intellectual inspirations that are unaccounted for in historical documents and collections of artifacts. As Quashie argues, "Nearly all of what has been written about blackness assumes that black culture is, or should be, identified by a resistant expressiveness—a response to racial oppression, a speaking back to the dominant ideology, a correction of the willful errors of racist history. What else, then, can be said of race as a public discourse? Perhaps nothing; perhaps what is left is to explore other ways of thinking about black culture, not ones that ignore racism or aim to supplant the importance of a discourse of resistance, but ones that help expand how we read what black culture means."[93] Rather than an empirical methodology, Jess reimagines paradoxical feelings associated with being in the spotlight, illuminating a wider range of "what black culture means" than the hypervisibility of racialized, gendered, and disabled bodies, as well as public performances.

Jess is especially committed to extending the legacy of the artists he honors, while affirming the ways in which "the past shadows the present."[94] For example, reflecting on the collection's opening and closing references to the white terrorist attacks on the Mother Emmanuel AME Church in Charleston, Jess laments, "I hadn't planned for history to be so cruelly present when I started writing about the long-dead artists in *Olio*. But it seems that history caught up with me, as it does all of us, in the most telling of ways. My intellect tells me I shouldn't be surprised by now. My soul can't help but tremble for the lessons history keeps teaching me. I'm facing the river to see the ripples across my reflection. And still I sing."[95]

Olio sifts through harrowing and artistically momentous traces of the past and "sing[s]" "the lessons history keeps teaching." In this regard, Rancière contends that literature "deploy[s] a new regime of appropriateness between the significance of words and the visibility of things; on showing the world of prosaic reality as an immense fabric of signs that bear, as written, the history of a time, a civilization or a society."[96] Illuminating the multifarious textures of the postbellum, pre–Harlem Renaissance era, Jess's *Olio* defamiliarizes dominant "regime[s] of appropriateness" that continue to structure how we know what we know about US culture. Moreover, while conventional histories are often monologic and famously written by the victors, the polyvocal, multimodal literature penned by Jess and his contemporaries—Caryl Phillips, Jeffery Renard Allen, Frank X Walker, Adrian Matejka, and Kevin Young, among others—*re*presents the past from the perspective of figures who occupied the limelight but were nonetheless unable to consistently control their own popular images and narratives. Even as more than a century has passed, how much has really shifted with regard to the white desire to consume and subordinate, overdetermine and undervalue today's Black athletes, musicians, and entertainers of all sorts? In other words, in what ways do the inequitable terms inscribed into the Black cultural industry that *Olio* revisits continue to hold sway, and what new epistemological and affective pathways can art trace that are elided in archival records and the histories that draw from them?

I was thinking through these rather live questions when on May 5, 2018, Donald Glover (aka Childish Gambino) dropped his music video "This Is America," crowned almost immediately as one of the cultural flashpoints of the Black Lives Matter era and setting the internet ablaze with interpretative analyses of its densely layered imagery and allusions. Well before this video was certified platinum, Glover was an acclaimed singer, actor, and creator of the hit FX series *Atlanta*, so he was well suited to choreograph and launch an astute performance of the perils of Black life in general and Black celebrity in particular. And that he did. Throughout the video, the bare-chested Glover/Gambino's sensual dance moves captivate viewers, while acts of violence—an assassination, mass murder of a Black choir, the suicide of a young man, and young people running from police, among others—occur in the background and on the sidelines.[97] The viewer is placed, therefore, in the position of needing to pay attention to (and mostly likely failing to, at least the first time around) these variably entertaining and horrific actions all at once. As such, Glover/Gambino enjoins us to consider what we are missing as we delight in the spectacular distractions in the foreground and put out of sight and out of mind the violence around the edges. In fact, this metacommentary about the consumption of Black culture and the simultaneous disregard for Black life is precisely the paradox that the writers discussed in *Black Celebrity* illustrate in eloquent, often gutting terms.

While Glover/Gambino does not specifically cite Bert Williams, George Walker, or for that matter "Blind Tom," Sissieretta Jones, and the McKoy twins, his grinning, gyrating body alludes to freak and minstrel shows. As Clinton Yates succinctly puts it, "Watching him [Glover] dance the Jim Crow dance is jarring and familiar, which is both equally bizarre and, again, frightening—the real scope of the black experience in this country. It replays over and over again on television, movies, the internet and, yes, music videos. Glover/Gambino is not exploiting as much as he's reminding us how well-woven all of it is into our consciousness."[98] Collapsing timelines and disrupting the illusion of substantive racial progress, Glover/Gambino encourages white viewers in particular to consider our expectations of Black citizens, who, as Glover/Gambino's lyrics indicate, are treated as "barcode[s]" to be purchased and then easily dispensed with when we tire of what they are "whippin' up."[99] This impulse to consume and dehumanize with impunity is one that Jess, too, illuminates in his lyric revivifications of "Blind Tom," Christine and Millie McKoy, Sissieretta Jones, Bert Williams, and George Walker, among others. By the conclusion of "This Is America," Glover/Gambino has placed himself firmly in the role of the persecuted, running for his life down a dark hallway. As the camera zooms in on his terror-stricken face, Glover/Gambino reminds his twenty-first-century audience that in the United States no person of African descent (whether a star or an ordinary citizen) is entirely free from white hegemonic forces and their predatory tendencies. This transhistorical lesson in racial hypervisibility and depersonalization is one that all of the creative recuperations in this book, including *Olio*, impart.

At the same time, Glover/Gambino—unlike the Black celebrities who graced the stage, the boxing ring, or the racetrack in the decades following the Civil War—was able to use his public platform to artistically expose white America's hypocrisy without being culturally blacklisted. His fame soared, in fact. Issuing a stunningly artful challenge to viewers and listeners to reflect on their own implicit biases and exploitative behavior, "This Is America" exemplifies a contemporary form of racial truth-telling that has the potential to lead to reparative justice. In this respect, "This Is America" is another kind of *creative recuperation*, whereby

Glover/Gambino self-reflexively conjures the ghosts of minstrelsy to imply the extension of that tradition today, while showing that popular culture and race (and gender) inequities are not mutually exclusive but instead have long been inextricably bound up. "Loving black culture," the cultural critic Wesley Morris observes, "has never meant loving black people, too. Loving black culture risks loving the life out of it."[100] As Glover/Gambino and Jess—along with Jeffery Renard Allen, Caryl Phillips, Frank X Walker, Adrian Matejka, and Kevin Young—demonstrate, art offers perhaps our most poignant vehicle for grappling with these uncomfortable truths and deciding what we, in turn, might do to transform them.

NOTES

Introduction

1. James Weldon Johnson, *Black Manhattan* (New York: Knopf, 1930), 59–60.

2. Ibid., 65–66.

3. Ibid., 63.

4. Ibid., 98.

5. Dave Zirin, "Kurt Busch, Ray Rice and How Sports Disseminates the Burdens of Racism," *Nation*, November 11, 2014, https://www.thenation.com/article/kurt-busch-ray-rice-and-how-sports-disseminates-burdens-racism/. Johnson "faced harassment and persecution for most of his life. He was forced into exile in 1913 on the trumped-up charge of transporting a white woman across state lines for prostitution."

6. Abby L. Ferber, "The Construction of Black Masculinity: White Supremacy Now and Then," *Journal of Sport and Social Issues* 31, no. 1 (2007): 21–22.

7. Howard Bryant, *The Heritage: Black Athletes, a Divided America, and the Politics of Patriotism* (Boston: Beacon, 2018), 184, 185.

8. Robin DiAngelo, *White Fragility: Why It's So Hard for White People to Talk about Racism* (Boston: Beacon, 2018), 31.

9. Philip Drake and Andy Miah, "The Cultural Politics of Celebrity," *Cultural Politics* 6, no. 1 (2010): 52.

10. Michele Wallace, *Dark Designs and Visual Culture* (Durham, NC: Duke University Press, 2004), 321.

11. Ken McLeod, "The Construction of Masculinity in African American Music and Sports," *American Music* 27, no. 2 (2009): 220.

12. Nicole R. Fleetwood, *On Racial Icons: Blackness and the Public Imagination* (New Brunswick, NJ: Rutgers University Press, 2015), 10.

13. Sarah J. Jackson, *Black Celebrity, Racial Politics, and the Press: Framing Dissent* (New York: Routledge, 2014), 169.

14. Ellis Cashmore, *The Black Culture Industry* (London: Routledge, 1997), 179.

15. Samantha Pinto, *Infamous Bodies: Early Black Women's Celebrity and the Afterlives of Rights* (Durham, NC: Duke University Press, 2020), 12.

16. Kevin Quashie, *The Sovereignty of Quiet: Beyond Resistance in Black Culture* (New Brunswick, NJ: Rutgers University Press, 2012), 6, 8.

17. W. E. B. Du Bois, *The Souls of Black Folk* (1903; repr., New York: Barnes and Noble, 2003), 689.

18. Quashie, *Sovereignty of Quiet*, 133.

19. Toni Morrison, "The Site of Memory," in *The Norton Anthology of African American Literature*, 3rd ed., ed. Henry Louis Gates Jr. and Valerie Smith, vol. 2 (New York: Norton, 1987), 1074.

20. Ibid., 1075.

21. Regine Eckardt, *The Semantics of Free Indirect Discourse: How Texts Allow Us to Mind-Read and Eavesdrop* (Leiden: Brill, 2015), 2.

22. Howard Rambsy II, "Catching Holy Ghosts: The Diverse Manifestations of Black Persona Poetry," *African American Review* 42, nos. 3–4 (2008): 550.

23. Howard Rambsy II, "Persona Poems: A Major Trend in Black Poetry," *Cultural Front: A Notebook on Literary Art, Digital Humanities, and Emerging Ideas*, January 3, 2012, http://www.culturalfront.org/2012/01/persona-poems-major-trend-in-black.html.

24. Howard Rambsy II, *Bad Men: Creative Touchstones of Black Writers* (Charlottesville: University of Virginia Press, 2020), 25.

25. Ryan Sharp, "In the Shadow of the Archive: *The Big Smoke* and Black American Persona Poetry," *African American Review* 52, no. 4 (2019): 373.

26. See my interpretation of Tyehimba Jess's *leadbelly* (2005) in my book *The Blues Muse: Race, Gender, and Musical Celebrity in American Poetry* (Tuscaloosa: University of Alabama Press, 2018).

27. Rambsy, *Bad Men*, 40.

28. Tyehimba Jess, "Ethnographer John Lomax Speaks of His Vocation," in *leadbelly* (Seattle: Wave Books, 2005), 66.

29. Ibid.

30. See, for example, Marilyn Nelson's *Carver: A Life in Poems* (2001), Ai's *Dread* (2003) and *The Collected Poems of Ai* (2013), Rita Dove's *Sonata Mulattica* (2009), Natasha Trethewey's *Bellocq's Ophelia* (2002) and *Thrall* (2012), Patricia Smith's *Blood Dazzler* (2008) and *Incendiary Art* (2017), Thylias Moss's *Slave Moth: A Narrative in Verse* (2006), Evie Shockley's *the new black* (2011), Vievee Francis's *Blue-Tail Fly* (2006), Bettina Judd's *patient* (2014), Morgan Parker's *There Are More Beautiful Things than Beyoncé* (2017), Chet'la Sebree's *Mistress* (2019), and Honorée Jeffers's *The Age of Phillis* (2020). This is nowhere near an exhaustive list of all the recent collections by African American women featuring persona poetry.

31. See Annette Debo, "Ophelia Speaks: Resurrecting Still Lives in Natasha Trethewey's *Bellocq's Ophelia*," *African American Review* 42, no. 2 (2008): 201–214.

32. Natasha Trethewey, "Disclosure," in *Bellocq's Ophelia* (Minneapolis: Graywolf, 2002), 44.

33. Patricia Smith, "34," in *Blood Dazzler* (Minneapolis: Coffee House, 2008), 54–56.

34. Rambsy, *Bad Men*, 47.

35. Ibid., 29.

36. Frank X Walker, "Memory, Research, Imagination, and the Mining of Historical Poetry," in *Furious Flower: Seeding the Future of African American Poetry*, ed. Joanne V. Gabbin and Lauren K. Alleyne (Evanston, IL: Northwestern University Press, 2020), 407.

37. Tyehimba Jess, "The Three-Dimensional World of Tyehimba Jess," interview by E. Ethelbert Miller, *Writing Life*, Howard County Poetry and Literature Society, June 13, 2017, https://www.youtube.com/watch?v=phYEo6UXHU8.

38. Jacques Rancière, *The Names of History: On the Poetics of Knowledge*, trans. Hassan Melehy (Minneapolis: University of Minnesota Press, 1994), 98, 92.

39. Jacques Rancière, *The Politics of Literature*, trans. Julie Rose (Malden, MA: Polity, 2011), 15.

40. John Brooks, "The Heretical History of Robin Coste Lewis's *The Voyage of the Sable Venus*," *African American Review* 52, no. 3 (2019): 241.

41. Jacques Rancière, *Dissensus: On Politics and Aesthetics*, ed. and trans. Steven Corcoran (London: Continuum, 2010), 38–39.

42. Michel-Rolph Trouillot, *Silencing the Past: Power and the Production of History* (Boston: Beacon, 1995), 153.

43. Michel Foucault's *The Archaeology of Knowledge and the Discourse on Language*, trans. A. M. Sheridan Smith (New York: Pantheon Books, 1972), and Jacques Derrida's *Archive Fever: A Freudian Impression*, trans. Eric Prenowitz (Chicago: University of Chicago Press, 1995), are landmark texts in contemporary discussions of "the archive" as an institution imbricated in hegemonic power structures. See also Saidiya Hartman's *Scenes of Subjection: Terror, Slavery, and Self-Making in Nineteenth-Century America* (1997; repr., Oxford: Oxford University Press, 2007), Diana Taylor's *The Archive and the Repertoire: Performing Cultural Memory in the Americas* (Durham, NC: Duke University Press, 2003), Ann Cvetkovich's *An Archive of Feelings: Trauma, Sexuality, and Lesbian Public Cultures* (Durham, NC: Duke University Press, 2003), Jeanne Scheper's *Moving Performances: Divas, Iconicity, and Remembering the Modern Stage* (New Brunswick, NJ: Rutgers University Press, 2016), Marisa J. Fuentes's *Dispossessed Lives: Enslaved Women, Violence, and the Archive* (Philadelphia: University of Pennsylvania Press, 2016), and Wendy W. Walters's *Archives of the Black Atlantic: Reading between Literature and History* (New York: Routledge, 2013), all of which I draw on in the present book to elucidate the role that contemporary African American novelists and poets play in recuperating the interior lives of some of the first Black celebrity athletes and artists.

44. Terry Cook and Joan Schwartz, "Archives, Records, and Power: The Making of Modern Memory," *Archival Science* 2 (2002): 13. It is also worth noting that in a 2016 article, "'The Archive' Is Not an Archives: On Acknowledging the Intellectual Contributions of Archival Studies" (*Reconstruction: Studies in Contemporary Culture* 16, no. 1 [2016], https://escholarship.org/uc/

item/7bn4v1fk), Michelle Caswell argues that humanities scholars have been reframing the concept of "the archive" without consulting the robust scholarship of archivists themselves. To remedy this rift, Caswell advises, "Humanities scholars can begin to demonstrate respect for archival studies by reading its literature, engaging its scholars in dialogue, and co-teaching seminars with archival studies scholars." In the present book, I draw on scholarship by historians, cultural theorists, and archivists alike, attempting to bridge some of the gaps that Caswell identifies.

45. Irma McClaurin, "The Black Feminist Archive," University of Massachusetts, 2017, http://irmamcclaurin.com/works/black-feminist-archive/.

46. Saidiya Hartman, "Venus in Two Acts," *Small Axe* 26 (2008): 11.

47. Ibid., 12. It should also be noted that in Saidiya Hartman's recent *Wayward Lives, Beautiful Experiments: Intimate Histories of Social Upheaval* (New York: Norton, 2019), she takes up the challenge of reimagining the interior lives of an array of late-nineteenth- and early-twentieth-century Black Americans, exceeding the limitations of the archive to glimpse unrecorded lived experiences.

48. Fuentes, *Dispossessed Lives*, 146.

49. D. Taylor, *Archive and the Repertoire*, 19.

50. Ibid., 173.

51. Ibid., 26.

52. Eduardo Bonilla-Silva, *Racism without Racists: Color-Blind Racism and Racial Inequality in Contemporary America*, 3rd ed. (Lanham, MD: Rowman and Littlefield, 2010), 3. As Thomas J. Sugrue similarly observes, "As the belief in color blindness gained traction in the last third of the twentieth century, a new set of explanations emerged to explain the persistence of racial separation and inequality. Racial segregation no longer carried the force of law; it was no longer the product of irrational prejudice. Rather racial inequality was a natural consequence of race-neutral market forces" (*Not Even Past: Barack Obama and the Burden of Race* [Princeton, NJ: Princeton University Press, 2010], 111). This post-civil-rights rhetoric of colorblindness was likewise bolstered by scientific evidence that disproved genetic foundations for racial difference. In *The History of White People* (New York: Norton, 2010), Nell Irvin Painter describes a marked shift in racial discourse that occurred in the mid-1990s, when scientists mapping the human genome refuted any genetic support for conceptions of race. Painter cites President Bill Clinton's remarks in 2000 that look toward a future devoid of racial distinctions: "In genetic terms all human beings, regardless of race, are more than 99.9 percent the same. What that means is that modern science has confirmed what we first learned from the ancient faiths. The most important fact of life on this earth is our common humanity" (qtd. in Painter, *History of White People*, 391–392). As the idea of race as a construction and not a biological fact became well accepted, so too did the willful elision of the vestiges of slavery and Jim Crow.

53. Carol Anderson, *White Rage: The Unspoken Truth of Our Racial Divide* (New York: Bloomsbury, 2016), 4.

54. For an overview of the neo-slave narrative genre, see Bernard Bell's *The Afro-American Novel and Its Tradition* (Amherst: University of Massachusetts

Press, 1987); Ashraf Rushdy, *Neo-Slave Narratives: Studies in the Social Logic of a Literary Form* (New York: Oxford University Press, 1999); and Madhu Dubey's "Neo-Slave Narratives," in *A Companion to African American Literature*, ed. Gene Andrew Garrett (Malden, MA: Wiley-Blackwell, 2010), 332–346.

55. Douglas A. Blackmon, *Slavery by Another Name: The Re-enslavement of Black People in America from the Civil War to World War II* (New York: Doubleday, 2008), 394. Eric Foner argues, "Issues central to the Reconstruction era—the relationship between political and economic democracy, for example, and the proper role of the federal government in defining and protecting the rights of all citizens—remain as controversial today as they were after the Civil War" (*Forever Free: The Story of Emancipation and Reconstruction* [New York: Vintage, 2005], 237). Moreover, Keenga-Yamahtta Taylor's *From #BlackLivesMatter to Black Liberation* (Chicago: Haymarket Books, 2016) discusses the postbellum passage of the Black Codes as setting the stage for "modern policing" (109). See also Michelle Alexander's *The New Jim Crow: Mass Incarceration in the Age of Colorblindness* (New York: New Press, 2010), in which she convincingly makes the case that "we have not ended racial caste in America; we have merely redesigned it" (2).

56. Andreá N. Williams, "Postbellum, Pre-Harlem Black Writing before the Renaissance," *A Companion to the Harlem Renaissance*, ed. Cherene Sherrard-Johnson (Malden, MA: Wiley-Blackwell, 2015), 36.

57. Ibid.

58. James Smethurst, *African American Roots of Modernism: Reconstruction to the Harlem Renaissance* (Chapel Hill: University of North Carolina Press, 2011), 7.

59. Barbara McCaskill and Caroline Gehard, introduction to *Post-Bellum, Pre-Harlem: African American Literature and Culture, 1877–1919*, ed. McCaskill and Gehard (New York: New York University Press, 2006), 3. McCaskill and Gebhard adopt the dates set forth by the novelist Charles Chesnutt's 1931 essay "Post-Bellum, Pre-Harlem," the period in which his fiction garnered critical acclaim and admiration as a breakthrough moment for Black writers: "At the time when I first broke into print seriously, no American colored writer had ever secured critical recognition except Paul Laurence Dunbar, who had won his laurels as a poet" (*Charles W. Chesnutt: Essays and Speeches*, ed. Joseph R. McElrath Jr., Robert C. Leitz III, and Jesse S. Crisler [Stanford, CA: Stanford University Press, 1999], 544). As the essay concludes, Chesnutt notes the marked shift in attitudes toward Black writers with the ascendancy of Harlem as a cultural mecca: "The development of Harlem, with its large colored population in all shades . . . its aspirations and demands for equality—without which any people would merit only contempt—presented a new field for literary exploration which of recent years has been cultivated assiduously" (547).

60. Daphne Brooks, *Bodies in Dissent: Spectacular Performances of Race and Freedom, 1850–1910* (Durham, NC: Duke University Press, 2006), 6.

61. Ibid., 4.

62. Kip Lornell, *From Jubilee to Hip Hop: Readings in African American Music* (New York: Prentice Hall, 2010), ix.

63. Greg Tate, introduction to *Everything but the Burden: What White People Are Taking from Black Culture*, ed. Tate (New York: Broadway Books, 2003), 14.

64. Imani Perry, *Prophets of the Hood: Politics and Poetics in Hip Hop* (Durham, NC: Duke University Press, 2004), 27–28.

65. D. Brooks, *Bodies in Dissent*, 5.

66. Patrick B. Miller, "Sport and the Paradoxes of Racial Reform," in *Race and Sport: The Struggle for Equality On and Off the Field*, ed. Charles K. Ross (Jackson: University Press of Mississippi, 2004), 170.

67. Drew D. Brown, "The Portrayal of Black Masculinity in the NFL: Critical Race Theory and the Images of Black Males," in *Black Athletic Sporting Experiences in the United States: Critical Race Theory*, ed. Billy J. Hawkins, Joseph N. Cooper, and Alikah R. Carter-Francique (New York: Palgrave Macmillan, 2017), 217.

68. David Remnick, "The Racial Demagoguery of Trump's Assaults on Colin Kaepernick and Steph Curry," *New Yorker*, September 23, 2017, https://www.newyorker.com/news/daily-comment/the-racial-demagoguery-of-trumps-assaults-on-colin-kaepernick-and-steph-curry.

69. Intisar Seraaj and Christina Zdanowicz, "From Jersey Burnings to Players Being Uninvited, Backlash to the #TakeAKnee Protest Grows," *CNN.com*, September 27, 2017, https://www.cnn.com/2017/09/25/us/anthem-protests-burning-nfl-jerseys-trnd/index.html.

70. NFL, "Roger Goodell's Statement on National Anthem Policy," May 23, 2018, http://www.nfl.com/news/story/0ap3000000933962/article/roger-goodells-statement-on-national-anthem-policy. Despite the NFL's official policy stating that players on the field who do not stand for the national anthem will be fined, no player has been fined for violating the policy (Tadd Haislop, "What Is the NFL's National Anthem Protest Policy? Here Are the Rules for Kneeling in 2020," *Sporting News*, September 20, 2020, https://www.sportingnews.com/us/nfl/news/nfl-national-anthem-policy-2020-kneeling-protests/1088fwivdxvqu1d8nnbiw5dw3z).

71. Ken Belson, "N.F.L. Settlement with Kaepernick and Reid Is Said to Be Much Less than $10 Million," *New York Times*, March 21, 2019, https://www.nytimes.com/2019/03/21/sports/colin-kaepernick-nfl-settlement.html.

72. In a press conference with Goodell, Jay-Z opined, "I think we've moved past kneeling and I think it is time to go into actionable items"—a statement that did not sit well with Kaepernick and other players who have risked their careers for reforms that have yet to be enacted (Chuck Schilken, "Colin Kaepernick Appears to Take a Shot at Jay-Z with Tweet," *Los Angeles Times*, August 19 2019, https://www.latimes.com/sports/story/2019-08-19/colin-kaepernick-jay-z-eric-reid-protests). For distinct reactions to Jay-Z's partnership with the NFL, see Cameron's Wolfe, "Stills Criticizes Jay-Z: He's Never Been on a Knee," *ESPN.com*, August 19, 2019, https://www.espn.com/nfl/story/_/id/27421748/stills-criticizes-jay-z-never-knee.

73. Michael Eric Dyson, "Famous Athletes Have Always Led the Way," *New York Times*, October 22, 2017, https://www.nytimes.com/2017/10/21/opinion/sunday/famous-athletes-have-always-led-the-way.html.

74. Julian Lucas, "Beyond Genealogy: On the Wealth of Stories That Family Novels Leave Behind," *New York Times Book Review*, September 3, 2017, 18.

75. Lynn Abbott and Doug Seroff, *Ragged but Right: Black Traveling Shows, "Coon Songs," and the Dark Pathway to Blues and Jazz* (Jackson: University Press of Mississippi, 2007), 7.

76. John Keene, "Cold," in *Counternarratives* (New York: New Directions, 2015), 259.

77. Ibid., 249.

78. Ibid., 250.

79. Ibid., 252.

80. Ibid., 250, 252.

81. Quashie, *Sovereignty of Quiet*, 24.

82. Jelani Cobb, *The Devil and Dave Chappelle and Other Essays* (New York: Thunder's Mouth, 2007), 90.

83. Ibid., 252.

84. Constance Bailey, "Fight the Power: African American Humor as a Discourse of Resistance," *Western Journal of Black Studies* 36, no. 4 (2012): 254.

85. John Keene, "Upending the Archive," interview by Alex McElroy, *Guernica*, April 15, 2016, https://www.guernicamag.com/upending-the-archive/.

86. Kevin Young, *To Repel Ghosts: The Remix from the Original Masters* (New York: Knopf, 2005), 71.

87. Here I refer to what Imani Perry described earlier as a love and suspicion of Blackness. Perry Hall likewise observes, "America seems to love the melody and rhythm of Black folks' souls while rejecting their despised Black faces" ("African-American Music: Dynamics of Appropriation and Innovation," in *Borrowed Power: Essays on Cultural Appropriation*, ed. Bruce Ziff and Pratima V. Rao [New Brunswick, NJ: Rutgers University Press, 1997], 31).

88. Scheper, *Moving Performances*, 13.

89. Jennifer Stoever, *The Sonic Color Line: Race and the Cultural Politics of Listening* (New York: New York University Press, 2016), 14.

90. Rancière, *Dissensus*, 39.

91. Ibid., 139.

92. Tim Armstrong, *The Logic of Slavery: Debt, Technology, and Pain in American Literature* (Cambridge: Cambridge University Press, 2012), 166–167.

93. After the Civil War, there were three court battles over custody (and the profits) of Tom Wiggins: "Three trials concerning Wiggins's custody occurred between 1865 and 1886. Each trial revolved around three central issues: Wiggins's legal status (i.e., slave or free Black), his mental state (i.e., competent or incompetent), and his potential as income earner for the appointed guardian. Custody . . . in the first two trials was granted to Bethune, with whom Wiggins toured extensively not only in the United States but also in Europe and Canada. Wiggins's 1866 concerts in London alone cleared $100,000 for his managers. Wiggins continued to tour after his custody was granted to Bethune's estranged daughter-in-law, Eliza Stutzbach [Bethune Lerche]" (Stephanie Jensen-Moulton, "Finding Autism in the Compositions of a 19th-Century Prodigy: Reconsidering 'Blind Tom' Wiggins," in *Sounding Off: Theorizing Disability in Music*, ed. Neil Lerner and Joseph Straus [New York: Routledge, 2006], 200).

1. "My Black Body Thrown Free"

1. Gerald Early, "The Black Intellectual and the Sport of Prizefighting," in *The Culture of Bruising: Essays on Prizefighting, Literature, and Modern American Culture* (New York: Ecco, 1994), 10.

2. As Geoffrey C. Ward notes, "Only white men were meant to reign over the heavyweights. John L. Sullivan—the first heavyweight champion of the gloved era and the man most responsible for transforming the fight game from an illicit backroom pastime into a major American sport—had said so. . . . 'I will not fight a negro. I never have and never shall'" (*Unforgivable Blackness: The Rise and Fall of Jack Johnson* [New York: Vintage, 2006], 15).

3. Ibid., 4.

4. As Howard Rambsy II details, Young initially struggled to find a publisher for the lengthy *To Repel Ghosts.* He created "an alternative condensed version" and then "secured a deal to publish his original version of the manuscript with Zoland Books." When Young signed with Knopf in 2005, he also availed himself of an opportunity to publish the alternative manuscript, *To Repel Ghosts: The Remix from the Original Masters* (*Bad Men*, 34). It is this "remixed" version of the collection that is widely circulated.

5. Stefanie Wortman, "What the Ghost Wants: Kevin Young's Ekphrasis," *Post45: Contemporaries* 211 (April 3, 2012), http://post45.org/2012/04/what-the-ghost-wants-kevin-youngs-ekphrasis/.

6. Rick Benjamin, "Mixed-Up Medium: Kevin Young's Turn-of-the-Century American Triptych," in *American Poets in the Twenty-First Century: The New Poetics*, ed. Claudia Rankine and Lisa Sewell (Middletown, CT: Wesleyan University Press, 2007), 193.

7. Rambsy, *Bad Men*, 35.

8. See Rutter, *Blues Muse.*

9. Fred Hoffman, "The Defining Years: Notes on Five Key Works," in *Basquiat*, ed. Marc Mayer (London: Merrell, 2005), 141.

10. D. Taylor, *Archive and the Repertoire*, 19.

11. Rancière, *Names of History*, 14.

12. Quashie, *Sovereignty of Quiet*, 24.

13. Fleetwood *On Racial Icons*, 8.

14. K. Young, *To Repel Ghosts*, 3.

15. Ibid.

16. Denzil Batchelor, *Jack Johnson and His Times* (1956; repr., North Pomfret, VT: Trafalgar Square, 1990), 41.

17. K. Young, *To Repel Ghosts*, 43.

18. Du Bois, *Souls of Black Folk*, 3.

19. Quashie, *Sovereignty of Quiet*, 6.

20. K. Young, *To Repel Ghosts*, 44.

21. Ibid.

22. Jamal L. Ratchford, "The LeBron James Decision in the Age of Obama," in *From Jack Johnson to LeBron James: Sports, Media, and the Color Line*, ed. Chris Lamb (Lincoln: University of Nebraska Press, 2016), 592.

23. Rancière, *Dissensus*, 140.

24. K. Young, *To Repel Ghosts*, 45.
25. Ibid., 47.
26. Ibid.
27. Ferber, "Construction of Black Masculinity," 19.
28. Jimmy Sanderson, "Weighing In on the Coaching Decision: Discussing Sports and Race Online," in *From Jack Johnson to LeBron James: Sports, Media, and the Color Line*, ed. Chris Lamb (Lincoln: University of Nebraska Press, 2016), 556.
29. Des Bieler, "LeBron James Turns 'Shut Up and Dribble' Insult into Title of Showtime Series," *Washington Post*, August 7, 2018, https://www.washingtonpost.com/news/early-lead/wp/2018/08/07/lebron-james-turns-shut-up-and-dribble-insult-into-title-of-showtime-series/.
30. K. Young, *To Repel Ghosts*, 48, 49.
31. Davie Zirin, *What's My Name, Fool? Sports and Resistance in the United States* (Chicago: Haymarket Books, 2005), 55.
32. K. Young, *To Repel Ghosts*, 50.
33. Ibid., 51.
34. Benjamin, "Mixed-Up Medium," 198.
35. K. Young, *To Repel Ghosts*, 55.
36. Ibid.
37. Christina Sharpe, *In the Wake: On Blackness and Being* (Durham, NC: Duke University Press, 2016), 13.
38. K. Young, *To Repel Ghosts*, 71.
39. G. Ward, *Unforgivable Blackness*, 447.
40. K. Young, *To Repel Ghosts*, 72.
41. Natasha Trethewey, "Natasha Trethewey," interview by Chard deNiord, in *I Would Lie to You If I Could: Interviews with American Poets* (Pittsburgh: University of Pittsburgh Press, 2018), 24–25.
42. D. Taylor, *Archive and the Repertoire*, 20.
43. K. Young, *To Repel Ghosts*, 73.
44. Ibid., 41.
45. Ibid., 75.
46. Ibid.
47. Ibid., 76.
48. Huddie Ledbetter (Leadbelly), "Titanic," in *The Leadbelly Songbook*, ed. Moses Asch and Alan Lomax (San Francisco: Oak, 1971).
49. K. Young, *To Repel Ghosts*, 76.
50. Ibid., 75.
51. David J. Leonard, *Playing While White: Privilege and Power On and Off the Field* (Seattle: University of Washington Press, 2017), 3.
52. K. Young, *To Repel Ghosts*, 87.
53. For more analysis of Basquiat's unique style, see Mayer, *Basquiat*.
54. Anthony O. Edmonds, "Joe Louis, Boxing, and American Culture," in *Out of the Shadows: A Biographical History of African American Athletes*, ed. David K. Wiggins (Fayetteville: University of Arkansas Press, 2006), 134.
55. Miller, "Sport and the Paradoxes of Racial Reform," 163.

56. K. Young, *To Repel Ghosts*, 88.

57. Ibid.

58. Ibid., 296.

59. Marlene Manoff, "Theories of the Archive from Across the Disciplines," *Libraries and the Academy* 4, no. 1 (2004): 12.

60. K. Young, *To Repel Ghosts*, 90.

61. Ibid., 89, 91.

62. See, for example, Baseball-Reference.com, which has archived many Black baseball statistics. Yet, as Leslie Heaphy notes, "Due to a lack of news coverage, teams failing to report all their results, and papers unable to afford to send reporters to follow Negro League clubs, the career achievements of players and teams are incomplete, perhaps permanently. . . . Even harder to accumulate than league statistics," she continues, are the records of barnstorming contests, which were "a vital part of the life of Negro League players" (*The Negro Leagues, 1869–1960* [Jefferson, NC: McFarland, 2003], 140).

63. K. Young, *To Repel Ghosts*, 92.

64. Ibid., 51.

65. Jennifer L. Morgan, "Accounting for 'The Most Excruciating Torment': Gender, Slavery, and Trans-Atlantic Passages," *History of the Present* 6, no. 2 (2016): 186–187.

66. Vievee Francis, "Beyond Description: Ekphrasis and the Expanding Lens," *Callaloo* 34, no. 3 (2011): 709.

67. Early, "Black Intellectual and the Sport of Prizefighting," 269.

68. Ibid.

69. K. Young, *To Repel Ghosts*, 93.

70. Early, "Black Intellectual and the Sport of Prizefighting," 272.

71. Ibid., 274.

72. K. Young, *To Repel Ghosts*, 93.

73. Ratchford, "LeBron James Decision in the Age of Obama," 592.

74. Ibid., 593.

75. bell hooks, *Black Looks: Race and Representation* (Boston: South End, 1992), 131.

76. K. Young, *To Repel Ghosts*, 94.

77. Chris Lamb, introduction to *From Jack Johnson to LeBron James: Sports, Media, and the Color Line*, ed. Lamb (Lincoln: University of Nebraska Press, 2016), 5.

78. K. Young, *To Repel Ghosts*, 95.

79. Early, "Black Intellectual and the Sport of Prizefighting," 272.

80. K. Young, *To Repel Ghosts*, 96.

81. Ibid.

82. Michael-Shawn Dugar, "NFL's New Anthem Policy Makes One Thing Clear: It Doesn't Care about Black People," *Athletic*, May 25, 2018, https://theathletic.com/368148/2018/05/25/nfls-new-anthem-policy-makes-one-thing-clear-it-doesnt-care-about-black-people/.

83. D. Taylor, *Archive and the Repertoire*, 29.

84. Ibid., 30.

85. K. Young, *To Repel Ghosts*, 97.

86. As noted in the introduction, Colin Kaepernick reached a multimillion-dollar settlement in 2019 in a joint case with his teammate Eric Reid that accused the thirty-two NFL teams of colluding to exclude them from the sport.

87. Rancière, *Politics of Literature*, 43.

2. *"More of a Man than You"*

1. Jack Johnson, *Jack Johnson—In the Ring and Out* (1927; repr., New York: Citadel, 1992), 21.

2. Adrian Matejka, "Adrian Matejka on *The Big Smoke*," interview, *The Cloudy House: The Poetics of Building a Project Book*, September 15, 2014, http://www.thecloudyhouse.com/2014/09/15/adrian-matejka-on-the-big-smoke/.

3. Sharp, "In the Shadow of the Archive," 381.

4. Rambsy, *Bad Men*, 54.

5. D. Taylor, *Archive and the Repertoire*, 20.

6. Adrian Matejka, *The Big Smoke* (New York: Penguin, 2013), 105.

7. Ibid., 104.

8. Quashie, *Sovereignty of Quiet*, 6.

9. Rancière, *Politics of Literature*, 14.

10. Michael Kimmel, "Masculinity as Homophobia: Fear, Shame, and Silence in the Construction of Gender Identity," in *Race, Class, and Gender in the United States*, 10th ed., ed. Paula S. Rothenberg with Soniya Munshi (New York: Worth, 2016), 63.

11. Matejka, *Big Smoke*, 5, 89.

12. Louis A. Moore, *I Fight for a Living: Boxing and the Battle for Black Manhood, 1880–1915* (Urbana: University of Illinois Press, 2017), 10.

13. Michael F. Higginbotham, *Ghosts of Jim Crow: Ending Racism in Post-racial America* (New York: New York University Press, 2013), 73.

14. Henry Louis Gates Jr. and Cornel West, *The African American Century: How Black Americans Have Shaped Our Country* (New York: Free Press, 2000), 16.

15. Theresa Runstedtler, *Jack Johnson, Rebel Sojourner: Boxing in the Shadow of the Global Color Line* (Berkeley: University of California Press, 2012), 15.

16. Matejka, *Big Smoke*, 3–4.

17. Ibid., 4.

18. Ibid., 5.

19. Runstedtler, *Jack Johnson, Rebel Sojourner*, 260.

20. This is the title of Rhoden's 2006 book *Forty Million Dollar Slaves: The Rise, Fall, and Redemption of the Black Athlete* (New York: Three Rivers, 2006), in which he argues that Black players may dominate particular sports—namely, football and basketball—but lack institutional power within them.

21. Matejka, *Big Smoke*, 11.

22. Ibid.

23. Ibid.

24. Kimmel, "Masculinity as Homophobia," 63.

25. Matejka, *Big Smoke*, 22.
26. G. Ward, *Unforgivable Blackness*, 139.
27. Matejka, *Big Smoke*, 103.
28. Ibid., 38.
29. D. Taylor, *Archive and the Repertoire*, 19.
30. Matejka, *Big Smoke*, 70.
31. Ibid.
32. Sharp, "In the Shadow of the Archive," 381.
33. Walters, *Archives of the Black Atlantic*, 4.
34. John Eligon and Brandon K. Thorp, "Missed in Coverage about Jack Johnson, the Racism around Him," *New York Times*, May 24, 2018, https://www.nytimes.com/2018/05/24/sports/jack-johnson-racism.html.
35. Rambsy, *Bad Men*, 49.
36. Matejka, *Big Smoke*, 105.
37. Ibid., 61.
38. Ibid.
39. Rancière, *Politics of Literature*, 187.
40. Jack Johnson, *Jack Johnson*, 232–233.
41. Matejka, *Big Smoke*, 30.
42. Ibid., 31.
43. Ibid., 37.
44. Ibid., 34.
45. Ibid.
46. Sharp, "In the Shadow of the Archive," 377.
47. Patricia Hill Collins, *Black Sexual Politics: African Americans, Gender, and the New Racism* (New York: Routledge, 2004), 193.
48. Zirin, "Kurt Busch, Ray Rice."
49. Michael Rosenberg, "Colin Kaepernick Can Be an Activist AND a Football Player," *Sports Illustrated*, August 15, 2017, https://www.si.com/nfl/2017/08/15/colin-kaepernick-national-anthem-protests-charlottesville.
50. Matejka, *Big Smoke*, 44.
51. Ibid.
52. Ibid., 52.
53. W. E. B. Du Bois, "The Prize Fighter," *Crisis* 8 (May 1914): 181.
54. Ratchford, "LeBron James Decision in the Age of Obama," 588.
55. Quoted ibid.
56. Matejka, *Big Smoke*, 24.
57. Jack Johnson, *Jack Johnson*, 58.
58. Matejka, *Big Smoke*, 24–25.
59. Du Bois, *Souls of Black Folk*, 3.
60. Quashie, *Sovereignty of Quiet*, 108.
61. Richard Dyer, *White: Essays on Race and Culture* (New York: Routledge, 1997), 39.
62. Matejka, *Big Smoke*, 68.
63. Ibid.
64. Ibid., 68–69.

65. Quashie, *Sovereignty of Quiet*, 122.
66. G. Ward, *Unforgivable Blackness*, 175.
67. Matejka, *Big Smoke*, 66.
68. Ibid., 90.
69. Ibid., 91.
70. Jack Johnson, *Jack Johnson*, 80.
71. Rancière, *Politics of Literature*, 14.
72. Matejka, *Big Smoke*, 97.
73. Ibid.
74. Quashie, *Sovereignty of Quiet*, 24.
75. Jack Johnson, *Jack Johnson*, 79.
76. Ferber, "Construction of Black Masculinity," 20.
77. John Hoberman, *Darwin's Athletes: How Sport Has Damaged Black America and Preserved the Myth of Race* (Boston: Houghton Mifflin, 1997), xviii.
78. D. Taylor, *Archive and the Repertoire*, 19.
79. Ken McLeod, *We Are the Champions: The Politics of Sports and Popular Music* (Burlington, VT: Ashgate, 2011), 153.
80. Matejka, *Big Smoke*, 75.
81. Leonard, *Playing While White*, 84.
82. Yuval Taylor and Jake Austen, *Darkest America: Black Minstrelsy from Slavery to Hip-Hop* (New York: Norton, 2012), 203, 204.
83. Matejka, *Big Smoke*, 82.
84. Ibid., 86.
85. Ibid., 87.
86. Tad Dorgan, "Tad Shows How Johnson Kidded with Sparring Partners When Training for the Big Go," *Chicago American Sports*, July 8, 1910.
87. Matejka, *Big Smoke*, 101.
88. Ibid.
89. Anne Anlin Cheng, *Second Skin: Josephine Baker and the Modern Surface* (New York: Oxford University Press, 2011), 171.
90. Saidiya Hartman, "Intimate History, Radical Narrative," *Black Perspectives*, May 22, 2020, https://www.aaihs.org/intimate-history-radical-narrative/.
91. Ferber, "Construction of Black Masculinity," 12.
92. Fleetwood, *On Racial Icons*, 110.
93. Hoberman, *Darwin's Athletes*, xvii.
94. Rancière, *Politics of Literature*, 182.
95. Serena Williams, "Serena Williams Sits Down with Common to Talk about Race and Identity," *Undefeated*, December 19, 2016, https://theundefeated.com/features/serena-williams-sits-down-with-common-to-talk-about-race-and-identity/.
96. Leonard, *Playing While White*, 179.

3. *"The Sting of Race and Sport"*

1. David K. Wiggins, *Glory Bound: Black Athletes in White America* (Syracuse, NY: Syracuse University Press, 1997), xv.

2. Pellom McDaniels III, *The Prince of Jockeys: The Life of Isaac Burns Murphy* (Lexington: University Press of Kentucky, 2013), 10–11.

3. Ben Carrington, *Race, Sports and Politics: The Sporting Black Diaspora* (London: Sage, 2010), 2.

4. Rambsy, "Catching Holy Ghosts," 549.

5. Affrilachian Poets, "Welcome," August 8, 2017. The Affrilachian Poets' website is no longer live, but the description of their origin and vision is now included on the Berea College library website page devoted to this poetry collective: https://libraryguides.berea.edu/c.php?g=816791.

6. Frank X Walker, "Conscious Narratives: Exploring Historical Poetry with Frank X Walker, by JoAnn LoVerde-Dropp," *Poetry Matters*, June 30, 2014, https://readwritepoetry.blogspot.com/2014/06/an-interview-with-frank-x-walker.html.

7. Frank X Walker, introduction to *Isaac Murphy: I Dedicate This Ride* (Lexington, KY: Old Cove, 2010), 1.

8. Euan McKirdy, "Racial Slur Painted on LeBron's House: 'It's Tough Being Black in America,'" *CNN.com*, June 1, 2017, http://www.cnn.com/2017/05/31/sport/lebron-james-racist-graffiti-incident/index.html.

9. Hanif Abdurraqib, *They Can't Kill Us till They Kill Us* (Columbus, OH: Two Dollar Radio, 2017), 235.

10. D. Taylor, *Archive and the Repertoire*, 19.

11. Rancière, *Names of History*, 44.

12. D. Taylor, *Archive and the Repertoire*, 19.

13. Quashie, *Sovereignty of Quiet*, 24.

14. Ibid., 35.

15. Walker, *Isaac Murphy*, 3.

16. Russell T. Wigginton, *The Strange Career of the Black Athlete: African Americans and Sports* (Westport, CT: Praeger, 2006), 5.

17. Walker, *Isaac Murphy*, 3.

18. Ibid., 4.

19. Ibid.

20. Rancière, *Names of History*, 20.

21. Walker, *Isaac Murphy*, 7.

22. Ibid., 9.

23. Katherine Mooney, *Race Horse Men: How Slavery and Freedom Were Made at the Racetrack* (Cambridge, MA: Harvard University Press, 2014), 196.

24. Walker, *Isaac Murphy*, 13.

25. D. Taylor, *Archive and the Repertoire*, 19.

26. Quashie, *Sovereignty of Quiet*, 6.

27. Walker, *Isaac Murphy*, 13.

28. Krystal Beamon and Chris Messer, "Professional Sports Experiences as Contested Racial Terrain," *Journal of African American Studies* 18, no. 2 (2014): 182.

29. Blackmon, *Slavery by Another Name*, 9.

30. Walker, *Isaac Murphy*, 26.

31. Daina Ramey Berry and Kali Nicole Gross, *A Black Women's History of the United States* (Boston: Beacon, 2020), 77.

32. Angela Y. Davis, "Reflections on the Black Woman's Role in the Community of Slaves," *Massachusetts Review* 13, nos. 1–2 (Winter–Spring 1972): 90.

33. Walker, *Isaac Murphy*, 28.

34. Carrington, *Race, Sport and Politics*, 20.

35. Walker, *Isaac Murphy*, 50.

36. Ferber, "Construction of Black Masculinity," 22.

37. Walker, "Conscious Narratives."

38. Walker, *Isaac Murphy*, 50.

39. Paul Laurence Dunbar, "We Wear the Mask," in *The Norton Anthology of African American Literature*, 3rd ed., ed. Henry Louis Gates Jr. and Valerie A. Smith, vol. 1 (New York: Norton, 2014), 906.

40. Rhoden, *Forty Million Dollar Slaves*, 66.

41. Quashie, *Sovereignty of Quiet*, 17.

42. Ann Cvetkovich, *Depression: A Public Feeling* (Durham, NC: Duke University Press, 2012), 122.

43. D. Taylor, *Archive and the Repertoire*, 32.

44. Walker, *Isaac Murphy*, 49.

45. Kareem Abdul-Jabbar, "Don't Understand the Protests? What You're Seeing Is People Pushed to the Edge," *Los Angeles Times*, May 30, 2020, https://www.latimes.com/opinion/story/2020-05-30/dont-understand-the-protests-what-youre-seeing-is-people-pushed-to-the-edge.

46. As noted in chapter 1, W. E. B. Du Bois, in *The Souls of Black Folk*, describes the Black experience of internalizing the white gaze as "double consciousness": "two-ness,—an American, a Negro; two souls; two thoughts, two unreconciled strivings; two warring ideals in one dark body" (9). Quashie's focus on "quiet" provides an alternative framework for examining Black life that centralizes interiority, rather than, as Du Bois does, the oppressive function of the white gaze or the emphasis on "black expressiveness and resistance" (Quashie, *Sovereignty of Quiet*, 9).

47. In addition to James's aforementioned *Shut Up and Dribble* series, the title of which rebuked the conservative calls for NBA players to remain politically neutral, the LeBron James Family Foundation announced its funding for the I Promise School in the player's hometown of Akron, Ohio. I Promise "specifically targets low-performing students, identifying a pool of at-risk children and then hosting a lottery to decide who gets in" (Mike McShane, "Three Questions about LeBron James' I Promise School," *Forbes*, August 6, 2018, https://www.forbes.com/sites/mikemcshane/2018/08/06/three-questions-about-lebron-james-i-promise-school/#121f91bab97a).

48. Walker, *Isaac Murphy*, 36.

49. See Evelyn Brooks Higginbotham, *Righteous Discontent: The Women's Movement in the Black Baptist Church, 1880–1920* (Cambridge, MA: Harvard University Press, 1994), for a comprehensive overview of the development and deployment of the politics of respectability during the late nineteenth and early twentieth centuries.

50. Walker, *Isaac Murphy*, 36.

51. Ibid., 38.

52. Kwame Anthony Appiah, "Racial Identities," in *Ways of Reading: An Anthology for Writers*, ed. David Bartholomae, Anthony Petrosky, and Stacey Waite (New York: Bedford/St. Martin's, 2014), 59.

53. Hartman, *Scenes of Subjection*, 11.

54. Walker, *Isaac Murphy*, 58.

55. Walters, *Archives of the Black Atlantic*, 5.

56. Mooney, *Race Horse Men*, 203.

57. Walker, *Isaac Murphy*, 55.

58. Rhoden, *Forty Million Dollar Slaves*, 68.

59. It should be noted that in recent years, Latin American jockeys have dominated horse racing. As Paul von Hippel notes, "In 2016, Hispanic jockeys started more races and won more money than jockeys from all other groups combined. In recent Triple Crown races, 60 to 70 percent of starters have had Hispanic last names" ("The Rise, Fall and Rise of Hispanic Jockeys in America," *Thoroughbred Racing Commentary*, September 4, 2017, https://www.thoroughbredracing.com/articles/rise-fall-and-rise-hispanic-jockeys-america/).

60. Barbara Welter, "The Cult of True Womanhood: 1820–1860," *American Quarterly* 18, no. 2 (1966): 152.

61. Hazel Carby, *Reconstructing Womanhood: The Emergence of the Afro-American Woman Novelist* (Oxford: Oxford University Press, 1987), 32.

62. Walker, *Isaac Murphy*, 24.

63. Ibid., 42.

64. Ibid., 60.

65. McDaniels, *Prince of Jockeys*, 364.

66. Rancière, *Names of History*, 20.

67. Walker, "Memory," 408.

68. Wigginton, *Strange Career of the Black Athlete*, 6.

69. Katherine Mooney, "How African-Americans Disappeared from the Race Track," *Smithsonian Magazine*, May 5, 2017, https://www.smithsonianmag.com/history/how-african-americans-disappeared-kentucky-derby-180963159/.

70. Walker, *Isaac Murphy*, 62.

71. McDaniels, *Prince of Jockeys*, 417.

72. Walker, *Isaac Murphy*, 62.

73. D. Taylor, *Archive and the Repertoire*, 32.

74. Rancière, *Names of History*, 20.

75. Drew D. Brown, "The Portrayal of Black Masculinity in the NFL: Critical Race Theory and the Images of Black Males," in *Black Athletic Sporting Experiences in the United States: Critical Race Theory*, ed. Billy J. Hawkins, Joseph N. Cooper, and Alikah R. Carter-Francique (New York: Palgrave Macmillan, 2017), 218, 230.

76. Ibid., 226.

77. McDaniels, *Prince of Jockeys*, 44.

78. Michael Eric Dyson, *Tears We Cannot Stop: A Sermon to White America* (New York: St. Martin's, 2017), 117.

79. D. Taylor, *Archive and the Repertoire*, 29.

80. Michael Bennett with Dave Zirin, *Things That Make White People Uncomfortable* (Chicago: Haymarket Books, 2018), xix–xx.

81. Walker, *Isaac Murphy*, 66.

82. Ibid., 3.

4. *"The Overwhelming Evidence of His Artistry"*

1. Rancière, *Politics of Literature*, 75.

2. Karen Sotiropoulos, *Staging Race: Black Performers in Turn of the Century America* (Cambridge, MA: Harvard University Press, 2006), 4.

3. Louis Chude-Sokei, *The Last "Darky": Bert Williams, Black-on-Black Minstrelsy, and the African Diaspora* (Durham, NC: Duke University Press, 2006): 1, 20.

4. Ibid., 1, 1–2.

5. Ibid., 7.

6. Caryl Phillips, *Dancing in the Dark* (New York: Vintage, 2005), 3.

7. Caryl Phillips, "*Dancing in the Dark*: Caryl Phillips in Conversation with John McLeod," in *Conversations with Caryl Philips*, ed. Renée T. Schatteman (Jackson: University Press of Mississippi, 2009), 144.

8. To distinguish between the historical figures and the novel's fictional representations, the rest of the chapter will refer to Bert Williams, Lottie Williams, George Walker, and Aida Overton Walker by their first names. The spelling of Aida's name also varies, depending on the period in her life that Phillips represents. She was born Ada Wilmon Overton, changing her name to Ada Overton Walker after marrying George in 1899. In 1903, she changed the spelling of her first name to Aida to accord with the "name of the Haitian loa (spirit) of fertility, rainbows, and snakes" (Constance Valis Hill, *Tap Dancing America: A Cultural History* [New York: Oxford University Press, 2010], 38).

9. Stephanie Smallwood, "The Politics of the Archive and History's Accountability to the Enslaved," *History of the Present* 6, no. 2 (Fall 2016): 126.

10. Scheper, *Moving Performances*, 13.

11. Kathie Birat, "Artistic Performance and the Crossing of Boundaries in Caryl Phillips's *Dancing in the Dark*," *Commonwealth* 37, no. 1 (Spring 2014): 53.

12. Robert Nowatzki, "'Blackin' Up Is Us Doin' White Folks Doin' Us': Blackface Minstrelsy and Racial Performance in Contemporary American Fiction and Film," *Literature Interpretation Theory* 18, no. 2 (2007): 117. See also Abigail Ward, "Performing Race in Caryl Phillips's *Dancing in the Dark*," in *Postmodern Literature and Race*, ed. Len Platt and Sarah Upstone (Cambridge: Cambridge University Press, 2015), 98–112.

13. Shauna M. Morgan Kirlew, "For the 'Dark Star': Reading Womanism and Black Womanhood in the Novels of Caryl Phillips," *Ariel: A Review of International English Literature* 48, nos. 3–4 (2017): 51–52.

14. Taylor and Austin, *Darkest America*, 127.

15. Morrison, "Site of Memory," 1075.

16. Quashie, *Sovereignty of Quiet*, 72.

17. Phillips, *Dancing in the Dark*, 10.

18. Rancière, *Politics of Literature*, 75.

19. Fleetwood, *On Racial Icons*, 10.

20. Phillips, *Dancing in the Dark*, 10.

21. Cedric J. Robinson, *Forgeries of Memory and Meaning: Blacks and the Regimes of Race in American Theater and Film before World War II* (Chapel Hill: University of North Carolina Press, 2007), 158.

22. Phillips, *Dancing in the Dark*, 17.

23. Anderson, *White Rage*, 4.

24. Scheper, *Moving Performances*, 6.

25. Ibid.

26. Phillips, *Dancing in the Dark*, 11–12.

27. Nowatzki, "Blackin' Up," 126.

28. Eric Lott's oft-cited *Love and Theft: Blackface Minstrelsy and the American Working Class* (1993; repr., New York: Oxford University Press, 2013) shows how racialized cultural dissonances, whereby white men were both intensely attracted to Black culture and actively propagated the myth of Black inferiority, were enacted through nineteenth-century minstrelsy.

29. Phillips, *Dancing in the Dark*, 98.

30. Ibid.

31. Ibid., 101.

32. D. Taylor, *Archive and the Repertoire*, 193.

33. Phillips, *Dancing in the Dark*, 100–101.

34. I refer here to Ellison's 1958 essay "Change the Joke and Slip the Yoke," in which he argues that the African American utilizes comic masks to subvert "the image created to usurp his identity. Sometimes it is for the sheer joy of the joke; sometimes it is to challenge those who presume, across the psychological distance created by race manners, to know his identity" (in *The Norton Anthology of African American Literature*, 3rd ed., ed. Henry Louis Gates Jr. and Valerie A. Smith, vol. 2 [New York: Norton, 2014], 284–285).

35. Harvey Young, *Embodying Black Experience: Stillness, Critical Memory, and the Black Body* (Ann Arbor: University of Michigan Press, 2010), 6.

36. Stephen Johnson, "Introduction: The Persistence of Blackface and the Minstrel Tradition," in *Burnt Cork: Traditions and Legacies of Blackface Minstrelsy*, ed. Johnson (Amherst: University of Massachusetts Press, 2012), 20.

37. Phillips, *Dancing in the Dark*, 66.

38. Ibid., 66, 67.

39. Ibid., 68.

40. Ibid., 69.

41. Ibid., 70.

42. Ibid.

43. Ibid., 73, 74.

44. Scheper, *Moving Performances*, 9.

45. Phillips, *Dancing in the Dark*, 75.

46. Ibid.

47. Quashie, *Sovereignty of Quiet*, 22–23.

48. In Daphne Brooks's cultural history of these same figures and their contemporaries, *Bodies in Dissent: Spectacular Performances of Race and Freedom, 1850–1910* (2006), she provides an illuminating account of the political stakes of Walker's *Theatre Magazine* article. Quoting Walker's denunciation of

white men performing in blackface—"Nothing about these white men's actions was natural and therefore nothing was as interesting as if black performers had been dancing and singing their own songs in their own way"—Brooks notes that Walker "repeats the moment of observation and appropriation in order to reject the 'counterfeit' act and to clear a space for bold, colorful, and, what he here calls, 'natural' black performance" (*Bodies in Dissent*, 217).

49. Phillips, *Dancing in the Dark*, 119–120.

50. D. Brooks, *Bodies in Dissent*, 219.

51. Chude-Sokei, *Last "Darky,"* 10.

52. Scheper, *Moving Performances*, 3.

53. Barbara Smith, "Some Home Truths on the Contemporary Black Feminist Movement," in *Words of Fire: An Anthology of African-American Feminist Thought*, ed. Beverly Guy-Sheftall (New York: New Press, 1995), 260.

54. Phillips, *Dancing in the Dark*, 37.

55. Ibid., 39.

56. Rancière, *Dissensus*, 141.

57. Phillips, *Dancing in the Dark*, 125.

58. Ibid., 103.

59. Ibid., 107.

60. Ibid., 118.

61. Ibid.

62. Ibid., 119–120.

63. Rancière, *Politics of Literature*, 75.

64. Phillips, *Dancing in the Dark*, 125.

65. Ibid., 126.

66. Quashie, *Sovereignty of Quiet*, 45.

67. Joseph Roach, *Cities of the Dead: Circum-Atlantic Performance* (New York: Columbia University Press, 1996), 26.

68. Phillips, *Dancing in the Dark*, 149.

69. Stoever, *Sonic Color Line*, 79.

70. L. Michael Gipson, "Interlude E: From Destiny's Child to Coachella: On Embracing Then Resisting Others' Respectability Politics," in *The Lemonade Reader*, ed. Kinitra D. Brooks and Kameelah L. Martin (New York: Routledge, 2019), 153.

71. Farah Jasmine Griffin, "At Last? Michelle Obama, Beyoncé, Race and History," *Daedalus* 140, no. 1 (2011): 141.

72. Maiysha Kai, "Interlude A: What Do We Want from Beyoncé?," in Brooks and Martin, *Lemonade Reader*, 6.

73. Wesley Morris, "African-American Art That's Shaping the 21st Century," *New York Times*, March 29, 2020, AR-5.

74. Pinto, *Infamous Bodies*, 206.

75. Cashmore, *Black Culture Industry*, 37.

76. Phillips, *Dancing in the Dark*, 182.

77. Ibid., 185.

78. Robinson, *Forgeries of Memory and Meaning*, xiv.

79. Phillips, *Dancing in the Dark*, 174.

80. Ibid., 176.

81. Ibid., 180.

82. Ibid., 180–181.

83. Ibid., 192.

84. Phillips, "Conversation with John McLeod," 145.

85. Rancière, *Politics of Literature*, 75.

86. Phillips, *Dancing in the Dark*, 209.

87. Dave Chappelle, "Heaven, Hell, Dave Chappelle," interview by Kevin Powell, *Esquire*, May 1, 2006, https://classic.esquire.com/article/2006/5/1/heaven-hell-dave-chappelle.

88. James Baldwin, "Sidney Poitier," *Look*, July 1968, 56.

89. Scheper, *Moving Performances*, 8.

90. Don DeLillo, "The Power of History," *New York Times Book Review*, September 7, 1997, https://archive.nytimes.com/www.nytimes.com/library/books/090797article3.html.

5. *"Blind Tom, Musical Prodigy of the Age"*

1. Quoted in Mildred Stock, "The Story of Blind Tom," draft ms., Box 3, Mildred Stock Research Collection, sc MG 177, Schomburg Center for Research in Black Culture, Manuscripts, Archives and Rare Books Division, New York Public Library, New York, 1, 4.

2. Deirdre O'Connell, *The Ballad of Blind Tom, Slave Pianist* (New York: Overlook, 1993), 10. Stephanie Jensen-Moulton helpfully outlines the court battles over custody (and, ultimately, the earnings) of Tom Wiggins: "Three trials concerning Wiggins's custody occurred between 1865 and 1886. Each trial revolved around three central issues: Wiggins's legal status (i.e., slave or free Black), his mental state (i.e., competent or incompetent), and his potential as income earner for the appointed guardian. Custody . . . in the first two trials was granted to Bethune, with whom Wiggins toured extensively not only in the United States but also in Europe and Canada. Wiggins's 1866 concerts in London alone cleared $100,000 for his managers. Wiggins continued to tour after his custody was granted to Bethune's estranged daughter-in-law, Eliza Stutzbach [Bethune Lerche]" ("Finding Autism," 200).

3. Daphne Brooks, "'Puzzling the Intervals': Blind Tom and the Poetics of the Sonic Slave Narrative," in *The Oxford Handbook of the African American Slave Narrative*, ed. John Ernest (New York: Oxford University Press, 2014), 392. There is some debate about Tom's mental state, and I am electing here to follow disability studies scholars in recognizing him as cognitively disabled while acknowledging the ways in which "race undoubtedly factored into assessments of his cognitive abilities" (Whitney Womack Smith, "'Blind Tom' Abroad: Race, Disability, and Transatlantic Representations of Thomas Wiggins," *Journal of Transatlantic Studies* 14, no. 2 [2016]: 167). Jensen-Moulton, who admits that she "can only conjecture that he [Tom] was an autistic savant" ("Finding Autism," 201), further observes, "Contemporary accounts universally acknowledge his [Tom's] blindness, but his cognitive disability is either disputed or difficult to quantify; secondary sources colored by racism, political bias, or

desire for financial gain further cloud the issue" (200). Indeed, as Susan Wendell notes, the practice of labeling individuals as "disabled" has long "involve[d] the unequal exercise of power" (*The Rejected Body: Feminist Philosophical Reflections on Disability* [New York: Routledge, 1996], 23). Lennard J. Davis affirms that "the 'problem' is not the person with disabilities; the problem is the way that normalcy is constructed to create the 'problem' of the disabled person" ("Constructing Normalcy: The Bell Curve, the Novel, and the Invention of the Disabled Body in the Nineteenth Century," in *The Disability Studies Reader*, 2nd ed., ed. Davis [New York: Routledge, 2017], 3). Moreover, recognizing disability as a social category has, as Simi Linton notes, the affordance of "enrich[ing] the discussion of the intersections of the axes of class, race, gender and sexual orientation, and disability" (*Claiming Disability: Knowledge and Identity* [New York: New York University Press, 1998], 32). Without doubt, Tom Wiggins experienced the acuteness of these intersections "as a slave, as a disabled musician, and as an entertainer whose (stolen) livelihood rested in part on meeting the prejudicial demands of a 'freak show' circuit shaped by P. T. Barnum and others" (D. Brooks, "Puzzling the Intervals," 394).

4. Anne Anlin Cheng, "Shine: On Race, Glamour, and the Modern," *PMLA* 126, no. 4 (2011): 1023.

5. Mitchell S. Jackson, "Command Performance," *New York Times*, June 19, 2014, https://www.nytimes.com/2014/06/22/books/review/song-of-the-shank-by-jeffery-renard-allen.html.

6. Hector Tobar, "Review: 'Song of the Shank' Gives Poetic Voice to a Unique American Musician," *Los Angeles Times*, July 11, 2014, https://www.latimes.com/books/jacketcopy/la-ca-jc-jeffery-renard-allen-20140713-story.html.

7. Thadious Davis, "Mapping the Son(g)'s Echo: *Song of the Shank* by Jeffery Renard Allen," *Obsidian* 40, nos. 1–2 (Spring 2015): 249–264; Michael Antonucci, "From a Hidden Seam in the Blackness": Jeffery Renard Allen's *Song of the Shank*," *Obsidian* 40, nos. 1–2 (Spring 2015): 228; Horace A. Porter, "Inventing Truth: Facts, Fiction and Slavery in *Song of the Shank*," *Obsidian* 40, nos. 1–2 (Spring 2015): 235–248.

8. Smallwood, "Politics of the Archive," 126.

9. Jefferey Renard Allen, "Silence: On the History of Hearing and Seeing Blind Tom," *Black Scholar* 45, no. 1 (Spring 2015): 45.

10. Stoever, *Sonic Color Line*, 14.

11. Hall, "African-American Music," 31. Lott's *Love and Theft* explores a similar form of nineteenth-century cultural dissonance, whereby white men were both intensely attracted to Black culture and actively propagated the myth of Black inferiority.

12. W. Smith, "'Blind Tom' Abroad," 172.

13. D. Taylor, *Archive and the Repertoire*, 25.

14. Ibid., 19.

15. Rancière, *Politics of Literature*, 74.

16. Jefferey Renard Allen, *Song of the Shank* (Minneapolis: Graywolf, 2014), 4, 542.

17. Fuentes, *Dispossessed Lives*, 12.

18. O'Connell, *Ballad of Blind Tom*, 211–213, 223.
19. Allen, *Song of the Shank*, 5.
20. Ibid., 16, 93.
21. Ibid., 78–79.
22. Miles White, *From Jim Crow to Jay-Z: Race, Rap, and the Performance of Masculinity* (Urbana: University of Illinois Press, 2011), 5.
23. D. Taylor, *Archive and the Repertoire*, 19.
24. Allen, *Song of the Shank*, 101.
25. Ibid., 107.
26. Rancière, *Politics of Literature*, 74.
27. Morgan, "Most Excruciating Torment," 186–187.
28. Allen, *Song of the Shank*, 109.
29. D. Brooks, *Bodies in Dissent*, 4.
30. Allen, *Song of the Shank*, 415.
31. O'Connell, *Ballad of Blind Tom*, 155.
32. Porter, "Inventing Truth," 239.
33. Allen, *Song of the Shank*, 428.
34. Ibid., 430.
35. Anderson, *White Rage*, 4.
36. Morgan, "Most Excruciating Torment," 201.
37. O'Connell, *Ballad of Blind Tom*, 19.
38. Allen, *Song of the Shank*, 111.
39. Quoted in O'Connell, *Ballad of Blind Tom*, 154.
40. Quashie, *Sovereignty of Quiet*, 102.
41. Smallwood, "Politics of the Archive," 119.
42. Allen, *Song of the Shank*, 115.
43. Ibid., 124–125.
44. Ibid., 500.
45. Quashie, *Sovereignty of Quiet*, 102.
46. Ibid., 501.
47. Ibid., 569.
48. O'Connell, *Ballad of Blind Tom*, 245–246.
49. Ibid., 74.
50. Allen, *Song of the Shank*, 219.
51. Ibid., 230.
52. Ibid., 251.
53. Lisa Tomlinson, "The Ongoing Economic Exploitation of Black Music," *Huffington Post*, January 8, 2016, https://www.huffingtonpost.ca/dr-lisa-tomlinson/black-music-exploitation_b_8934870.html.
54. Allen, *Song of the Shank*, 418.
55. Ibid., 321.
56. Jeffery Renard Allen, "An Interview with Jeffery Renard Allen, Author of *Song of the Shank*," interview by Jessie Vail Aufiery, *Literary Review*, 2017, http://www.theliteraryreview.org/interview/an-interview-with-jeffery-renard-allen-author-of-song-of-the-shank/.
57. Allen, *Song of the Shank*, 159, 160, 160.

58. Rancière, *Politics of Literature*, 74.
59. T. Davis, "Mapping the Son(g)'s Echo," 254.
60. Allen, *Song of the Shank*, 396.
61. Ibid., 414.
62. Ibid., 421.
63. Ibid., 549.
64. Ibid., 9.
65. Kathy Lou Schultz, "To Save and Destroy: Melvin B. Tolson, Langston Hughes, and Theories of the Archive," *Contemporary Literature* 51, no. 1 (2011): 119.
66. Jeffery Renard Allen, "Reading the Blind and Blacking the Beyond: African American Fiction and Influence-Theory in the Twenty-First Century," *Obsidian* 40, nos. 1–2 (Spring 2015): 269.
67. Allen, *Song of the Shank*, 334.
68. Ibid., 342.
69. Therí A. Pickens, "Blue Blackness, Black Blueness: Making Sense of Blackness and Disability," *African American Review* 50, no. 2 (Summer 2017): 95.
70. Scheper, *Moving Performances*, 13.
71. Stoever, *Sonic Color Line*, 7.
72. Allen, *Song of the Shank*, 352.
73. Ibid., 353.
74. Ibid., 354.
75. Sami Schalk, "Interpreting Disability Metaphor and Race in Octavia Butler's *The Evening and the Morning and the Night*," *African American Review* 50, no. 2 (Summer 2017): 141.
76. Antonucci, "From a Hidden Seam in the Blackness," 230.
77. hooks, *Black Looks*, 370.
78. Rancière, *Politics of Literature*, 74.
79. Allen, *Song of the Shank*, 357.
80. Reiland Rabaka, *The Hip Hop Movement: From R&B and the Civil Rights Movement to Rap and the Hip Hop Generation* (Lanham, MD: Lexington Books, 2013), 317.
81. Quoted in Elias Leight, "Lil Nas X's 'Old Town Road' Was a Country Hit. Then Country Changed Its Mind," *Rolling Stone*, March 26, 2019, https://www.rollingstone.com/music/music-features/lil-nas-x-old-town-road-810844/.
82. John Yau, *The Passionate Spectator: Essays on Art and Poetry* (Ann Arbor: University of Michigan Press, 2006), 92.
83. Allen, *Song of the Shank*, 449.
84. Du Bois, *Souls of Black Folk*, 3.
85. Quashie, *Sovereignty of Quiet*, 6.
86. Allen, *Song of the Shank*, 451–452.
87. Ibid., 451.
88. Rancière, *Names of History*, 98, 88.
89. Allen, *Song of the Shank*, 145.
90. Brian Kelly, "Jubilee and the Limits of African American Freedom after Emancipation," *Race & Class* 57, no. 3 (2016): 64.

91. Allen, *Song of the Shank*, 555.
92. Ibid., 560, 562.
93. Jerome de Groot, *Remaking History: The Past in Contemporary Historical Fictions* (New York: Routledge, 2016), 2.
94. Allen, "Silence," 50.
95. Allen, *Song of the Shank*, 565.
96. Ibid., 566.
97. Ibid., 565.
98. Rancière, *Dissensus*, 141.
99. Hartman, "Venus in Two Acts," 9.
100. Allen, *Song of the Shank*, 334.
101. Ibid., 516.

6. *"Let This Belting Be Our Unbinding"*

1. Eduardo Galeano, "My Greatest Fear Is That We Are All Suffering from Amnesia," interview by Gary Younge, *Guardian*, July 23, 2013, https://www.theguardian.com/books/2013/jul/23/eduardo-galeano-children-days-interview.
2. Tyehimba Jess, *Olio* (Seattle: Wave Books, 2016), 7, 203.
3. Hartman, *Wayward Lives*, xiii.
4. Ibid., 34.
5. Rancière, *Names of History*, 51.
6. Walker, "Memory," 407.
7. Rambsy, *Bad Men*, 45.
8. Fuentes, *Dispossessed Lives*, 78.
9. Jess, *Olio*, i.
10. Ibid., 1.
11. Ibid., 3, 20.
12. Jacob Sunderlin, "'The Gut Meaning of Grace': Tyehimba Jess's *Olio*," *Kenyon Review*, accessed January 20, 2020, https://kenyonreview.org/reviews/olio-by-tyehimba-jess-738439/.
13. Tom Griffen, "It's All in the Wind: A Review of *Olio* by Tyehimba Jess," *Tupelo Quarterly*, November 28, 2016, http://www.tupeloquarterly.com/its-all-in-the-wind-a-review-of-olio-by-tyehimba-jess/.
14. Metta Sáma, "*Olio* by Tyehimba Jess (review)," *Prairie Schooner* 90, no. 3 (Fall 2016): 169.
15. Stoever, *Sonic Color Line*, 79.
16. Quashie, *Sovereignty of Quiet*, 6.
17. Jess, *Olio*, 2.
18. Ibid., 18.
19. Ibid.
20. Smallwood, "Politics of the Archive," 125.
21. Christopher Krentz, "A 'Vacant Receptacle'? Blind Tom, Cognitive Difference, and Pedagogy," *PMLA* 120, no. 2 (2005): 553.
22. Jess, *Olio*, 19.
23. Ibid., 26.
24. Ibid.

25. Ibid., 27.
26. Willa Cather, *My Ántonia* (1918; repr., New York: Quality Paperback Book Club, 1995), 206.
27. Stoever, *Sonic Color Line*, 7–8.
28. Cather, *My Ántonia*, 215.
29. Ibid., 217.
30. Jess, *Olio*, 18.
31. W. Smith, "'Blind Tom' Abroad," 166.
32. Jess, *Olio*, 20.
33. Ibid., 28.
34. Ibid.
35. Ibid.
36. W. Smith, "'Blind Tom' Abroad," 166.
37. Scheper, *Moving Performances*, 12.
38. Fuentes, *Dispossessed Lives*, 6.
39. Ibid., 12.
40. Quoted in Joanne Martell, *Millie-Christine: Fearfully and Wonderfully Made* (Winston-Salem, NC: John F. Blair, 2000), 128.
41. Jess, *Olio*, 2.
42. Noel McLaughlin, quoted in Nicole R. Fleetwood, "Hip-Hop Fashion, Masculine Anxiety, and the Discourse of Americana," in *Black Cultural Traffic: Crossroads in Global Performance and Popular Culture*, ed. Harry J. Elam Jr. and Kennell Jackson (Ann Arbor: University of Michigan Press, 2005), 328.
43. Millie and Christine McKoy's autobiography seems to have functioned chiefly as a promotional vehicle, with several editions and revised titles published over their long performing career. As Linda Frost points out, "at least five versions of the McKoys' show history were produced during their lifetimes." The version that Frost reprints was a later version, "appearing sometime between 1902 and 1912 and published by Hennegan & Co. in Cincinnati." Frost further notes, "While much of the text in these different versions remains largely consistent, the title and other smaller details are altered in later versions" (*Conjoined Twins in Black and White: The Lives of Millie-Christine McKoy and Daisy and Violent Hilton* [Madison: University of Wisconsin Press, 2008], 16).
44. Jess, *Olio*, 39.
45. Ellen Samuels, "Examining Millie and Christine McKoy: Where Enslavement and Enfreakment Meet," *Signs* 37, no. 1 (2011): 60.
46. Rancière, *Names of History*, 98.
47. Jess, *Olio*, 221.
48. Sharpe, *In the Wake*, 13.
49. Jess, *Olio*, 41.
50. Ibid., 53.
51. Laura Engel, *Women, Performance, and the Material Memory: The Archival Tourist, 1780–1915* (New York: Palgrave Macmillan, 2019), 59.
52. Jess, *Olio*, 53.
53. Quashie, *Sovereignty of Quiet*, 102.
54. Ibid.

55. Jess, *Olio*, 45.
56. Du Bois, *Souls of Black Folk*, 9.
57. D. Taylor, *Archive and the Repertoire*, 22.
58. Jess, *Olio*, 60.
59. Rancière, *Names of History*, 103.
60. Bettina Judd, "Sapphire as Praxis: Toward a Methodology of Anger," *Feminist Studies* 45, no. 1 (Spring 2019): 183.
61. Jess, *Olio*, 60.
62. Maureen D. Lee, *Sissieretta Jones: "The Greatest Singer of Her Race," 1868–1933* (Columbia: University of South Carolina Press, 2012), 2.
63. Michael Cooper, "Overlooked No More: Sissieretta Jones, a Soprano Who Shattered Racial Barriers," *New York Times*, April 15, 2018, https://www.nytimes.com/2018/08/15/obituaries/sissieretta-jones-overlooked.html.
64. Lee, *Sissieretta Jones*, 2.
65. Jess, *Olio*, 2.
66. Quoted in Lee, *Sissieretta Jones*, 35.
67. Quoted ibid., 46.
68. D. Taylor, *Archive and the Repertoire*, 22.
69. Jess, *Olio*, 155.
70. Ibid.
71. Ibid.
72. Ibid., 156.
73. Jacques Rancière, *The Politics of Aesthetics: The Distribution of the Sensible*, trans. Gabriel Rockhill (London: Bloomsbury, 2004), 8.
74. Jess, *Olio*, 156.
75. Quashie, *Sovereignty of Quiet*, 108.
76. bell hooks, *Reel to Real: Race, Sex, and Class at the Movies* (New York: Routledge, 1996), 198.
77. Jess, *Olio*, 158.
78. Ibid., 159–160.
79. Stoever, *Sonic Color Line*, 78.
80. Jess, *Olio*, 161.
81. Tyehimba Jess, "Tyehimba Jess on Excavating Popular Music through Poetry: Exploring the Sustenance of Song and Historical Clapbacks," interview by Adam Fitzgerald, *Lit Hub*, May 5, 2016, http://lithub.com/tyehimba-jess-on-excavating-popular-music-through-poetry/.
82. White, *From Jim Crow to Jay-Z*, 12.
83. John Strausbaugh, *Black like You: Blackface, Whiteface, Insult and Imitation in American Popular Culture* (New York: Penguin, 2006), 321.
84. Nicole R. Fleetwood, *Troubling Vision: Performance, Visibility, and Blackness* (Chicago: University of Chicago Press, 2011), 111.
85. Jess, *Olio*, 165.
86. Ibid., 215.
87. Ibid., 130.
88. Ibid.
89. Ibid.

90. D. Taylor, *Archive and the Repertoire*, 276.

91. Sound studies scholars point out that the sonic realm remains as thoroughly racialized today as it was during the nineteenth century. In addition to Stoever, Erich Nunn identifies "a critical juncture between actual interracial musical and cultural forms, on the one hand, and racialized structures of feeling on the other. . . . Like Jim Crow segregation in general," Nunn continues, "it has taken enormous energy to maintain the separation of musical forms along racial lines" (*Sounding the Color Line: Music and Race in the Southern Imagination* [Athens: University of Georgia Press, 2015], 6).

92. Jess, *Olio*, 130.

93. Quashie, *Sovereignty of Quiet*, 133.

94. H. Young, *Embodying Black Experience*, 6.

95. Tyehimba Jess, "Flames of History / Rivers of Song," Poetry Foundation, April 30, 2018, https://www.poetryfoundation.org/harriet/2018/04/flames-of-history-rivers-of-song.

96. Rancière, *Politics of Literature*, 15.

97. Donald Glover (Childish Gambino), "This Is America," RCA, May 5, 2018, http://smarturl.it/TcIgA.

98. Clinton Yates, "Childish Gambino's 'This Is America' Video Is a Beautiful Nightmare," *Undefeated*, May 8, 2018, https://theundefeated.com/features/childish-gambinos-this-is-america-video-is-a-beautiful-nightmare/.

99. Glover, "This Is America."

100. Wesley Morris, "American Popular Music," *New York Times Magazine*, August 18, 2019, 66.

BIBLIOGRAPHY

Abbott, Lynn, and Doug Seroff. *Ragged but Right: Black Traveling Shows, "Coon Songs," and the Dark Pathway to Blues and Jazz*. Jackson: University Press of Mississippi, 2007.

Abdul-Jabbar, Kareem. "Don't Understand the Protests? What You're Seeing Is People Pushed to the Edge." *Los Angeles Times*, May 30, 2020. https://www.latimes.com/opinion/story/2020-05-30/dont-understand-the-protests-what-youre-seeing-is-people-pushed-to-the-edge.

Abdurraqib, Hanif. *They Can't Kill Us till They Kill Us*. Columbus, OH: Two Dollar Radio, 2017.

Affrilachian Poets. "Welcome." August 8, 2017. Available at https://libraryguides.berea.edu/c.php?g=816791.

Alexander, Michelle. *The New Jim Crow: Mass Incarceration in the Age of Colorblindness*. New York: New Press, 2010.

Allen, Jeffery Renard. "An Interview with Jeffery Renard Allen, Author of *Song of the Shank*." Interview by Jessie Vail Aufiery. *Literary Review*, 2017. http://www.theliteraryreview.org/interview/an-interview-with-jeffery-renard-allen-author-of-song-of-the-shank/.

———. "Reading the Blind and Blacking the Beyond: African American Fiction and Influence-Theory in the Twenty-First Century." *Obsidian* 40, nos. 1–2 (Spring 2015): 265–274.

———. "Silence: On the History of Hearing and Seeing Blind Tom." *Black Scholar* 45, no. 1 (Spring 2015): 44–50. http://dx.doi.org/10.1080/00064246.2014.997603.

———. *Song of the Shank*. Minneapolis: Graywolf, 2014.

Anderson, Carol. *White Rage: The Unspoken Truth of Our Racial Divide*. New York: Bloomsbury, 2016.

Antonucci, Michael. "'From a Hidden Seam in the Blackness': Jeffery Renard Allen's *Song of the Shank*." *Obsidian* 40, nos. 1–2 (Spring 2015): 227–234.

Appiah, Kwame Anthony. "Racial Identities." In *Ways of Reading: An Anthology for Writers*, edited by David Bartholomae, Anthony Petrosky, and Stacey Waite, 42–65. New York: Bedford/St. Martin's, 2014.

Armstrong, Tim. *The Logic of Slavery: Debt, Technology, and Pain in American Literature*. New York: Cambridge University Press, 2012.

Bailey, Constance. "Fight the Power: African American Humor as a Discourse of Resistance." *Western Journal of Black Studies* 36, no. 4 (2012): 253–263.

Baldwin, James. "Sidney Poitier." *Look*, July 1968, 50–58.

Batchelor, Denzil. *Jack Johnson and His Times*. 1956. Reprint, North Pomfret, VT: Trafalgar Square, 1990.

Beamon, Krystal, and Chris Messer. "Professional Sports Experiences as Contested Racial Terrain." *Journal of African American Studies* 18, no. 2 (2014): 181–191.

Bell, Bernard. *The Afro-American Novel and Its Tradition*. Amherst: University of Massachusetts Press, 1987.

Belson, Ken. "N.F.L. Settlement with Kaepernick and Reid Is Said to Be Much Less than $10 Million." *New York Times*, March 21, 2019. https://www.nytimes.com/2019/03/21/sports/colin-kaepernick-nfl-settlement.html.

Benjamin, Rick. "Mixed-Up Medium: Kevin Young's Turn-of-the-Century American Triptych." In *American Poets in the Twenty-First Century: The New Poetics*, edited by Claudia Rankine and Lisa Sewell, 193–209. Middleton, CT: Wesleyan University Press, 2007.

Bennett, Michael, with Dave Zirin. *Things That Make White People Feel Uncomfortable*. Chicago: Haymarket Books, 2018.

Berry, Daina Ramey, and Kali Nicole Gross. *A Black Women's History of the United States*. Boston: Beacon, 2020.

Bieler, Des. "LeBron James Turns 'Shut Up and Dribble' Insult into Title of Showtime Series." *Washington Post*, August 7, 2018. https://www.washingtonpost.com/news/early-lead/wp/2018/08/07/lebron-james-turns-shut-up-and-dribble-insult-into-title-of-showtime-series/.

Birat, Kathie. "Artistic Performance and the Crossing of Boundaries in Caryl Phillips's *Dancing in the Dark*." *Commonwealth* 37, no. 1 (Spring 2014): 45–55.

Blackmon, Douglas A. *Slavery by Another Name: The Re-enslavement of Black People in America from the Civil War to World War II*. New York: Doubleday, 2008.

Bonilla-Silva, Eduardo. *Racism without Racists: Color-Blind Racism and Racial Inequality in Contemporary America*. 3rd ed. Lanham, MD: Rowman and Littlefield, 2010.

Brooks, Daphne. *Bodies in Dissent: Spectacular Performances of Race and Freedom, 1850–1910*. Durham, NC: Duke University Press, 2006.

———. "Puzzling the Intervals: Blind Tom and the Poetics of the Sonic Slave Narrative." In *The Oxford Handbook of the African American Slave Narrative*, edited by John Ernest, 391–414. New York: Oxford University Press, 2014.

Brooks, John. "The Heretical History of Robin Coste Lewis's *The Voyage of the Sable Venus*." *African American Review* 52, no. 3 (2019): 239–253.

Brown, Drew D. "The Portrayal of Black Masculinity in the NFL: Critical Race Theory and the Images of Black Males." In *Black Athletic Sporting Experiences in the United States: Critical Race Theory*, edited by Billy J. Hawkins, Joseph N. Cooper, and Alikah R. Carter-Francique, 217–246. New York: Palgrave Macmillan, 2017.

Bryant, Howard. *The Heritage: Black Athletes, a Divided America, and the Politics of Patriotism*. Boston: Beacon, 2018.

Carby, Hazel. *Reconstructing Womanhood: The Emergence of the Afro-American Woman Novelist*. Oxford: Oxford University Press, 1987.

Carrington, Ben. *Race, Sports and Politics: The Sporting Black Diaspora*. London: Sage, 2010.

Cashmore, Ellis. *The Black Culture Industry*. New York: Routledge, 1997.

Caswell, Michelle. "'The Archive' Is Not an Archives: On Acknowledging the Intellectual Contributions of Archival Studies." *Reconstruction: Studies in Contemporary Culture* 16, no. 1 (2016). https://escholarship.org/uc/item/7bn4v1fk.

Cather, Willa. *My Ántonia*. 1918. Reprint, New York: Quality Paperback Book Club, 1995.

Chappelle, Dave. "Heaven, Hell, Dave Chappelle." Interview by Kevin Powell. *Esquire*, May 1, 2006. https://classic.esquire.com/article/2006/5/1/heaven-hell-dave-chappelle.

Cheng, Anne Anlin. *Second Skin: Josephine Baker and the Modern Surface*. Oxford: Oxford University Press, 2011.

———. "Shine: On Race, Glamour, and the Modern." *PMLA* 126, no. 4 (2011): 1022–1041.

Chesnutt, Charles. "Post-Bellum, Pre-Harlem." In *Charles W. Chesnutt: Essays and Speeches*, edited by Joseph R. McElrath Jr., Robert C. Leitz III, and Jesse S. Crisler, 543–549. Stanford, CA: Stanford University Press, 1999.

Chude-Sokei, Louis. *The Last "Darky": Bert Williams, Black-on-Black Minstrelsy, and the African Diaspora*. Durham, NC: Duke University Press, 2006.

Cobb, Jelani. *The Devil and Dave Chappelle and Other Essays*. New York: Thunder's Mouth, 2007.

Collins, Patricia Hill. *Black Sexual Politics: African Americans, Gender, and the New Racism*. New York: Routledge, 2004.

Cook, Terry, and Joan Schwartz. "Archives, Records, and Power: The Making of Modern Memory." *Archival Science* 2 (2002): 1–19.

Cooper, Michael. "Overlooked No More: Sissieretta Jones, a Soprano Who Shattered Racial Barriers." *New York Times*, August 15, 2018. https://www.nytimes.com/2018/08/15/obituaries/sissieretta-jones-overlooked.html.

Cvetkovich, Ann. *An Archive of Feelings: Trauma, Sexuality, and Lesbian Public Cultures*. Durham, NC: Duke University Press, 2003.

———. *Depression: A Public Feeling*. Durham, NC: Duke University Press, 2012.

Davis, Angela Y. "Reflections on the Black Woman's Role in the Community of Slaves." *Massachusetts Review* 13, nos. 1– 2 (Winter–Spring 1972): 81–100.

Davis, Lennard J. "Constructing Normalcy: The Bell Curve, the Novel, and the Invention of the Disabled Body in the Nineteenth Century." In *The Disability Studies Reader*, 2nd ed., edited by Davis, 3–16. New York: Routledge, 2017.

Davis, Thadious. "Mapping the Son(g)'s Echo: *Song of the Shank* by Jefferey Renard Allen." *Obsidian* 40, nos. 1–2 (Spring 2015): 249–264.

Debo, Annette. "Ophelia Speaks: Resurrecting Still Lives in Natasha Trethewey's *Bellocq's Ophelia*." *African American Review* 42, no. 2 (2008): 201–214.

de Groot, Jerome. *Remaking History: The Past in Contemporary Historical Fictions*. New York: Routledge, 2016.

DeLillo, Don. "The Power of History." *New York Times Book Review*, September 7, 1997. https://archive.nytimes.com/www.nytimes.com/library/books/090797article3.html.

Derrida, Jacques. *Archive Fever: A Freudian Impression*. Translated by Eric Prenowitz. Chicago: University of Chicago Press, 1995.

DiAngelo, Robin. *White Fragility: Why It's So Hard for White People to Talk about Racism*. Boston: Beacon, 2018.

Dorgan, Tad. "Tad Shows How Johnson Kidded with Sparring Partners when Training for the Big Go." *Chicago American Sports*, July 8, 1910.

Drake, Philip, and Andy Miah. "The Cultural Politics of Celebrity." *Cultural Politics*, 6, no. 1 (2010): 49–64.

Dubey, Madhu. "Neo-Slave Narratives." In *A Companion to African American Literature*, edited by Gene Andrew Garrett, 332–346. Malden, MA: Wiley-Blackwell, 2010.

Du Bois, W. E. B. "The Prize Fighter." *Crisis* 8 (May 1914): 181.

———. *The Souls of Black Folk*. 1903. Reprint, New York: Barnes and Noble, 2003.

Dugar, Michael-Shawn. "NFL's New Anthem Policy Makes One Thing Clear: It Doesn't Care about Black People." *Athletic*, May 25, 2018.

https://theathletic.com/368148/2018/05/25/nfls-new-anthem-policy-makes-one-thing-clear-it-doesnt-care-about-black-people/.

Dunbar, Paul Laurence. "We Wear the Mask." In *The Norton Anthology of African American Literature*, 3rd ed., edited by Henry Louis Gates Jr. and Valerie A. Smith, vol. 1, 906. New York: Norton, 2014.

Dyer, Richard. *White: Essays on Race and Culture*. New York: Routledge, 1997.

Dyson, Michael Eric. "Famous Athletes Have Always Led the Way." *New York Times*, October 22, 2017. https://www.nytimes.com/2017/10/21/opinion/sunday/famous-athletes-have-always-led-the-way.html.

———. *Tears We Cannot Stop: A Sermon to White America*. New York: St. Martin's, 2017.

Early, Gerald. "The Black Intellectual and the Sport of Prizefighting." In *The Culture of Bruising: Essays on Prizefighting, Literature, and Modern American Culture*, 5–45. New York: Ecco, 1994.

Eckardt, Regine. *The Semantics of Free Indirect Discourse: How Texts Allow Us to Mind-Read and Eavesdrop*. Leiden: Brill, 2015.

Edmonds, Anthony O. "Joe Louis, Boxing, and American Culture." In *Out of the Shadows: A Biographical History of African American Athletes*, edited by David K. Wiggins, 133–146. Fayetteville: University of Arkansas Press, 2006.

Eligon, John, and Brandon K. Thorp. "Missed in Coverage about Jack Johnson, the Racism around Him." *New York Times*, May 24, 2018. https://www.nytimes.com/2018/05/24/sports/jack-johnson-racism.html.

Ellison, Ralph. "Change the Joke and Slip the Yoke." In *The Norton Anthology of African American Literature*, 3rd ed., edited by Henry Louis Gates Jr. and Valerie A. Smith, vol. 2, 279–287. New York: Norton, 2014.

Engel, Laura. *Women, Performance, and the Material Memory: The Archival Tourist, 1780–1915*. New York: Palgrave Macmillan, 2019.

Ferber, Abby L. "The Construction of Black Masculinity: White Supremacy Now and Then." *Journal of Sport and Social Issues* 31, no. 1 (2007): 11–24.

Fleetwood, Nicole. "Hip-Hop Fashion, Masculine Anxiety, and the Discourse of Americana." In *Black Cultural Traffic: Crosswords in Global Performance and Popular Culture*, edited by Harry J. Elam and Kennell Jackson, 326–345. Ann Arbor: University of Michigan Press, 2005.

———. *On Racial Icons: Blackness and the Public Imagination*. New Brunswick, NJ: Rutgers University Press, 2015.

———. *Troubling Vision: Performance, Visibility, and Blackness*. Chicago: University of Chicago Press, 2011.

Foner, Eric. *Forever Free: The Story of Emancipation and Reconstruction*. New York: Vintage, 2005.

Foucault, Michel. *The Archaeology of Knowledge and the Discourse on Language*. Translated by A. M. Sheridan Smith. New York: Pantheon Books, 1972. Originally published in French 1969.

Francis, Vievee. "Beyond Description: Ekphrasis and the Expanding Lens." *Callaloo* 34, no. 3 (2011): 708–710.

Frost, Linda. *Conjoined Twins in Black and White: The Lives of Millie-Christine McKoy and Daisy and Violent Hilton*. Madison: University of Wisconsin Press, 2008.

Fuentes, Marisa J. *Dispossessed Lives: Enslaved Women, Violence, and the Archive*. Philadelphia: University of Pennsylvania Press, 2016.

Galeano, Eduardo. "My Greatest Fear Is that We Are All Suffering from Amnesia." Interview by Gary Younge. *Guardian*, July 23, 2013. https://www.theguardian.com/books/2013/jul/23/eduardo-galeano-children-days-interview.

Gates, Henry Louis, Jr., and Cornel West. *The African American Century: How Black Americans Have Shaped Our Country*. New York: Free Press, 2000.

Gipson, L. Michael. "Interlude E: From Destiny's Child to Coachella: On Embracing Then Resisting Others' Respectability Politics." In *The Lemonade Reader*, edited Kinitra D. Brooks and Kameelah L. Martin, 144–154. New York: Routledge, 2019.

Glover, Donald (Childish Gambino). "This Is America." RCA, May 5, 2018, http://smarturl.it/TcIgA.

Griffen, Tom. "It's All in the Wind: A Review of *Olio* by Tyehimba Jess." *Tupelo Quarterly*, November 28, 2016. https://www.tupeloquarterly.com/its-all-in-the-wind-a-review-of-olio-by-tyehimba-jess/.

Griffin, Farah Jasmine. "At Last? Michelle Obama, Beyoncé, Race and History." *Daedalus* 140, no. 1 (2011): 131–141.

Haislop, Tadd. "What Is the NFL's National Anthem Protest Policy? Here Are the Rules for Kneeling in 2020." *Sporting News*, September 20, 2020. https://www.sportingnews.com/us/nfl/news/nfl-national-anthem-policy-2020-kneeling-protests/1o88fwivdxvqu1d8nnbiw5dw3z.

Hall, Perry A. "African-American Music: Dynamics of Appropriation and Innovation." In *Borrowed Power: Essays on Cultural Appropriation*, edited by Bruce Ziff and Pratima V. Rao, 31–51. New Brunswick, NJ: Rutgers University Press, 1997.

Hartman, Saidiya. "Intimate History, Radical Narrative." *Black Perspectives*, May 22, 2020. https://www.aaihs.org/intimate-history-radical-narrative/.

———. *Scenes of Subjection: Terror, Slavery, and Self-Making in Nineteenth-Century America*. 1997. Reprint, Oxford: Oxford University Press, 2007.

———. "Venus in Two Acts." *Small Axe* 26 (2008): 1–14.

———. *Wayward Lives, Beautiful Experiments: Intimate Histories of Social Upheaval.* New York: Norton, 2019.

Heaphy, Leslie. *The Negro Leagues, 1869–1960.* Jefferson, NC: McFarland, 2003.

Higginbotham, Evelyn Brooks. *Righteous Discontent: The Women's Movement in the Black Baptist Church, 1880–1920.* Cambridge, MA: Harvard University Press, 1994.

Higginbotham, Michael F. *Ghosts of Jim Crow: Ending Racism in Post-racial America.* New York: New York University Press, 2013.

Hill, Constance Valis. *Tap Dancing America: A Cultural History.* New York: Oxford University Press, 2010.

Hoberman, John. *Darwin's Athletes: How Sport Has Damaged Black America and Preserved the Myth of Race.* Boston: Houghton Mifflin, 1997.

Hoffman, Fred. "The Defining Years: Notes on Five Key Works." In *Basquiat*, edited by Marc Mayer, 129–161. London: Merrell, 2005.

hooks, bell. *Black Looks: Race and Representation.* Boston: South End, 1992.

———. *Reel to Real: Race, Sex, and Class at the Movies.* New York: Routledge, 1996.

Jackson, Mitchell S. "Command Performance." *New York Times*, June 19, 2014. https://www.nytimes.com/2014/06/22/books/review/song-of-the-shank-by-jeffery-renard-allen.html.

Jackson, Sarah J. *Black Celebrity, Racial Politics, and the Press: Framing Dissent.* New York: Routledge, 2014.

Jensen-Moulton, Stephanie. "Finding Autism in the Compositions of a 19th-Century Prodigy: Reconsidering 'Blind Tom' Wiggins." In *Sounding Off: Theorizing Disability in Music*, edited by Neil Lerner and Joseph Straus, 199–216. New York: Routledge, 2006.

Jess, Tyehimba. "Flames of History / Rivers of Song." Poetry Foundation, April 30, 2018. https://www.poetryfoundation.org/harriet/2018/04/flames-of-history-rivers-of-song.

———. *leadbelly.* Seattle: Wave Books, 2005.

———. *Olio.* Seattle: Wave Books, 2016.

———. "The Three-Dimensional World of Tyehimba Jess." Interview by E. Ethelbert Miller. *Writing Life*, Howard County Poetry and Literature Society, June 13, 2017. https://www.youtube.com/watch?v=phYE06UXHU8.

———. "Tyehimba Jess on Excavating Popular Music through Poetry." Interview by Adam Fitzgerald. *Lit Hub*, May 5, 2016. http://lithub.com/tyehimba-jess-on-excavating-popular-music-through-poetry/.

Johnson, Jack. *Jack Johnson—In the Ring—and Out.* 1927. Reprint, New York: Citadel, 1992.

Johnson, James Weldon. *Black Manhattan.* New York: Knopf, 1930.

Johnson, Stephen. "Introduction: The Persistence of Blackface and the Minstrel Tradition." In *Burnt Cork: Traditions and Legacies of Blackface Minstrelsy*, edited by Johnson, 1–17. Amherst: University of Massachusetts Press, 2012.

Judd, Bettina. "Sapphire as Praxis: Toward a Methodology of Anger." *Feminist Studies* 45, no. 1 (Spring 2019): 178–208.

Kai, Maiysha. "Interlude A: What Do We Want from Beyoncé?" In *The Lemonade Reader*, edited by Kinitra D. Brooks and Kameelah L. Martin, 5–8. New York: Routledge, 2019.

Keene, John. *Counternarratives*. New York: New Directions, 2015.

———. "Upending the Archive." Interview by Alex McElroy. *Guernica*, April 15, 2016. https://www.guernicamag.com/upending-the-archive/.

Kelly, Brian. "Jubilee and the Limits of African American Freedom after Emancipation." *Race & Class* 57, no. 3 (2016): 59–70.

Kimmel, Michael. "Masculinity as Homophobia: Fear, Shame, and Silence in the Construction of Gender Identity." In *Race, Class, and Gender in the United States*, 10th ed., edited by Paula S. Rothenberg with Soniya Munshi, 59–70. New York: Worth, 2013.

Kirlew, Shauna M. Morgan. "'For the Dark Star': Reading Womanism and Black Womanhood in the Novels of Caryl Phillips." *Ariel: A Review of International English Literature* 48, nos. 3–4 (2017): 49–76.

Krentz, Christopher. "'A Vacant Receptacle'?: Blind Tom, Cognitive Difference, and Pedagogy." *PMLA* 20, no. 2 (2005): 552–557.

Lamb, Chris. Introduction to *From Jack Johnson to LeBron James: Sports, Media, and the Color Line*, edited by Lamb, 1–18. Lincoln: University of Nebraska Press, 2016.

Ledbetter, Huddie (Leadbelly). "Titanic." In *The Leadbelly Songbook*, edited by Moses Asch and Alan Lomax. San Francisco: Oak, 1971.

Lee, Maureen D. *Sissieretta Jones: "The Greatest Singer of Her Race," 1868–1933*. Columbia: University of South Carolina Press, 2012.

Leight, Elias. "Lil Nas X's 'Old Town Road' Was a Country Hit. Then Country Changed Its Mind." *Rolling Stone*, March 26, 2019. https://www.rollingstone.com/music/music-features/lil-nas-x-old-town-road-810844/.

Leonard, David J. *Playing While White: Privilege and Power On and Off the Field*. Seattle: University of Washington Press, 2017.

Linton, Simi. *Claiming Disability: Knowledge and Identity*. New York: New York University Press, 1998.

Lornell, Kip. *From Jubilee to Hip Hop: Readings in African American Music*. New York: Prentice Hall, 2010.

Lott, Eric. *Love and Theft: Blackface Minstrelsy and the American Working Class*. 1993. Reprint, New York: Oxford University Press, 2013.

Lucas, Julian. "Beyond Genealogy: On the Wealth of Stories That Family Novels Leave Behind." *New York Times Book Review*, September 3, 2017, 18.

Manoff, Marlene. "Theories of the Archive from Across the Disciplines." *Libraries and the Academy* 4, no. 1 (2004): 9–25.

Martell, Joanne. *Millie-Christine: Fearfully and Wonderfully Made*. Winston-Salem, NC: John F. Blair, 2000.

Matejka, Adrian. "Adrian Matejka on *The Big Smoke*." Interview. *The Cloudy House: The Poetics of Building a Project Book*, September 15, 2014. http://www.thecloudyhouse.com/2014/09/15/adrian-matejka-on-the-big-smoke/.

———. *The Big Smoke*. New York: Penguin, 2013.

Mayer, Marc, ed. *Basquiat*. London: Merrell, 2005.

McCaskill, Barbara, and Caroline Gehard. Introduction to *Post-Bellum, Pre-Harlem: African American Literature and Culture, 1877–1919*, edited by McCaskill and Gehard, 1–16. New York: New York University Press, 2006.

McClaurin, Irma. "The Irma McClaurin Black Feminist Archive." University of Massachusetts, 2017, http://irmamcclaurin.com/works/black-feminist-archive/.

McDaniels, Pellom, III. *The Prince of Jockeys: The Life of Isaac Burns Murphy*. Lexington: University Press of Kentucky, 2013.

McKirdy, Euan. "Racial Slur Painted on LeBron's House: 'It's Tough Being Black in America.'" *CNN.com*, June 1, 2017. http://www.cnn.com/2017/05/31/sport/lebron-james-racist-graffiti-incident/index.html.

McLeod, Ken. "The Construction of Masculinity in African American Music and Sports." *American Music* 27, no. 2 (2009): 204–226.

———. *We Are the Champions: The Politics of Sports and Popular Music*. Burlington, VT: Ashgate, 2011.

McShane, Mike. "Three Questions about LeBron James' I Promise School." *Forbes*, August 6, 2018. https://www.forbes.com/sites/mikemcshane/2018/08/06/three-questions-about-lebron-james-i-promise-school/#121f91bab97a.

Miller, Patrick B. "Sport and the Paradoxes of Racial Reform." In *Race and Sport: The Struggle for Equality On and Off the Field*, edited by Charles K. Ross, 146–182. Jackson: University Press of Mississippi, 2004.

Mooney, Katherine. "How African-Americans Disappeared from the Race Track." *Smithsonian Magazine*, May 5, 2017. https://www.smithsonianmag.com/history/how-african-americans-disappeared-kentucky-derby-180963159/.

———. *Race Horse Men: How Slavery and Freedom Were Made at the Racetrack*. Cambridge, MA: Harvard University Press, 2014.

Moore, Louis A. *I Fight for a Living: Boxing and the Battle for Black Manhood, 1880–1915*. Urbana: University of Illinois Press, 2017.

Morgan, Jennifer L. "Accounting for 'The Most Excruciating Torment': Gender, Slavery, and Trans-Atlantic Passages." *History of the Present* 6, no. 2 (2016): 184–207.

Morris, Wesley. "African-American Art That's Shaping the 21st Century." *New York Times*, March 29, 2020.

———. "American Popular Music." *New York Times Magazine*, August 18, 2019.

Morrison, Toni. "The Site of Memory." In *The Norton Anthology of African American Literature*, 3rd ed., edited by Henry Louis Gates Jr. and Valerie A. Smith, vol. 2, 1071–1078. New York: Norton, 2014.

NFL. "Roger Goodell's Statement on National Anthem Policy." May 23, 2018. http://www.nfl.com/news/story/0ap3000000933962/article/roger-goodells-statement-on-national-anthem-policy.

Nowatzki, Robert. "'Blackin' Up Is Us Doin' White Folks Doin' Us': Blackface Minstrelsy and Racial Performance in Contemporary American Fiction and Film." *Literature Interpretation Theory* 18, no. 2 (2007): 115–136.

Nunn, Erich. *Sounding the Color Line: Music and Race in the Southern Imagination*. Athens: University of Georgia Press, 2015.

O'Connell, Deirdre. *The Ballad of Blind Tom, Slave Pianist*. New York: Overlook, 1993.

Painter, Nell Irvin. *The History of White People*. New York: Norton, 2010.

Perry, Imani. *Prophets of the Hood: Politics and Poetics in Hip Hop*. Durham, NC: Duke University Press, 2004.

Phillips, Caryl. *Dancing in the Dark*. New York: Vintage, 2005.

———. "*Dancing in the Dark*: Caryl Phillips in Conversation with John McLeod." In *Conversations with Caryl Phillips*, edited by Renée T. Schatteman, 143–150. Jackson: University Press of Mississippi, 2009.

Pickens, Therí A. "Blue Blackness, Black Blueness: Making Sense of Blackness and Disability." *African American Review* 50, no. 2 (Summer 2017): 93–103.

Pinto, Samantha. *Infamous Bodies: Early Black Women's Celebrity and the Afterlives of Rights*. Durham, NC: Duke University Press, 2020.

Porter, Horace A. "Inventing Truth: Facts, Fiction, and Slavery in *Song of the Shank*." *Obsidian* 40, nos. 1–2 (Spring 2015): 235–248.

Quashie, Kevin. *The Sovereignty of Quiet: Beyond Resistance in Black Culture*. New Brunswick, NJ: Rutgers University Press, 2012.

Rabaka, Reiland. *The Hip Hop Movement: From R&B and the Civil Rights Movement to Rap and the Hip Hop Generation*. Lanham, MD: Lexington Books, 2013.

Rambsy, Howard II. *Bad Men: Creative Touchstones of Black Writers*. Charlottesville: University of Virginia Press, 2020.

———. "Catching Holy Ghosts: The Diverse Manifestations of Black Persona Poetry." *African American Review* 42, nos. 3–4 (2008): 539–564.

———. "Persona Poems: A Major Trend in Black Poetry." *Cultural Front: A Notebook on Literary Art, Digital Humanities, and Emerging Ideas*, January 3, 2012. http://www.culturalfront.org/2012/01/persona-poems-major-trend-in-black.html.

Rancière, Jacques. *Dissensus: On Politics and Aesthetics.* Edited and translated by Steven Corcoran. London: Continuum, 2010.

———. *The Names of History: On the Poetics of Knowledge.* Translated by Hassan Melehy. Minneapolis: University of Minnesota Press, 1994. Originally published in French 1992.

———. *The Politics of Aesthetics: The Distribution of the Sensible.* Translated by Gabriel Rockhill. London: Bloomsbury, 2004.

———. *The Politics of Literature.* Translated by Julie Rose. Malden, MA: Polity, 2011. Originally published in French 2006.

Ratchford, Jamal L. "The LeBron James Decision in the Age of Obama." In *From Jack Johnson to LeBron James: Sports, Media, and the Color Line*, edited by Chris Lamb, 582–602. Lincoln: University of Nebraska Press, 2016.

Remnick, David. "The Racial Demagoguery of Trump's Assaults on Colin Kaepernick and Steph Curry." *New Yorker*, September 23, 2017. https://www.newyorker.com/news/daily-comment/the-racial-demagoguery-of-trumps-assaults-on-colin-kaepernick-and-steph-curry.

Rhoden, William C. *Forty Million Dollar Slaves: The Rise, Fall, and Redemption of the Black Athlete.* New York: Three Rivers, 2006.

Roach, Joseph. *Cities of the Dead: Circum-Atlantic Performance.* New York: Columbia University Press, 1996.

Robinson, Cedric J. *Forgeries of Memory and Meaning: Blacks and the Regimes of Race in American Theater and Film before World War II.* Chapel Hill: University of North Carolina Press, 2007.

Rosenberg, Michael. "Colin Kaepernick Can Be an Activist AND a Football Player." *Sports Illustrated*, August 15, 2017. https://www.si.com/nfl/2017/08/15/colin-kaepernick-national-anthem-protests-charlottesville.

Runstedtler, Theresa. *Jack Johnson, Rebel Sojourner: Boxing in the Shadow of the Global Color Line.* Berkeley: University of California Press, 2012.

Rushdy, Ashraf. *Neo-Slave Narratives: Studies in the Social Logic of a Literary Form.* New York: Oxford University Press, 1999.

Rutter, Emily Ruth. *The Blues Muse: Race, Gender, and Musical Celebrity in American Poetry.* Tuscaloosa: University of Alabama Press, 2018.

Sáma, Metta. "*Olio* by Tyehimba Jess (review)." *Prairie Schooner* 90, no. 3 (Fall 2016): 167–169.

Samuels, Ellen. "Examining Millie and Christine McKoy: Where Enslavement and Enfreakment Meet." *Signs* 37, no. 1 (2011): 53–81.

Sanderson, Jimmy. "Weighing In on the Coaching Decision: Discussing Sports and Race Online." In *From Jack Johnson to LeBron James: Sports, Media, and the Color Line*, edited by Chris Lamb, 555–581. Lincoln: University of Nebraska Press, 2016.

Schalk, Sami. "Interpreting Disability Metaphor and Race in Octavia Butler's *The Evening and the Morning and the Night*." *African American Review* 50, no. 2 (Summer 2017): 139–151.

Scheper, Jeanne. *Moving Performances: Divas, Iconicity, and Remembering the Modern Stage*. New Brunswick, NJ: Rutgers University Press, 2016.

Schilken, Chuck. "Colin Kaepernick Appears to Take a Shot at Jay-Z with Tweet." *Los Angeles Times*, August 19, 2019. https://www.latimes.com/sports/story/2019-08-19/colin-kaepernick-jay-z-eric-reid-protests.

Schultz, Kathy Lou. "To Save and Destroy: Melvin B. Tolson, Langston Hughes, and Theories of the Archive." *Contemporary Literature* 51, no. 1 (2011): 108–145.

Seraaj, Intisar, and Christina Zdanowicz. "From Jersey Burnings to Players Being Uninvited, Backlash to the #TakeAKnee Protest Grows." *CNN.com*, September 27, 2017. http://www.cnn.com/2017/09/25/us/anthem-protests-burning-nfl-jerseys-trnd/index.html.

Sharp, Ryan. "In the Shadow of the Archive: *The Big Smoke* and Black American Persona Poetry." *African American Review* 52, no. 4 (Winter 2019): 373–387.

Sharpe, Christina. *In the Wake: On Blackness and Being*. Durham, NC: Duke University Press, 2016.

Smallwood, Stephanie. "The Politics of the Archive and History's Accountability to the Enslaved." *History of the Present* 6, no. 2 (Fall 2016): 117–132.

Smethurst, James. *African American Roots of Modernism: Reconstruction to the Harlem Renaissance*. Chapel Hill: University of North Carolina Press, 2011.

Smith, Barbara. "Some Home Truths on the Contemporary Black Feminist Movement." In *Words of Fire: An Anthology of African-American Feminist Thought*, edited by Beverly Guy-Sheftall, 254–268. New York: New Press, 1995.

Smith, Patricia. "34." In *Blood Dazzler*, 50–57. Minneapolis: Coffee House, 2008.

Smith, Whitney Womack. "'Blind Tom' Abroad: Race, Disability, and Transatlantic Representations of Thomas Wiggins." *Journal of Transatlantic Studies* 14, no. 2 (2016): 164–175.

Sotiropoulos, Karen. *Staging Race: Black Performers in Turn of the Century America*. Cambridge, MA: Harvard University Press, 2006.

Stock, Mildred. "The Story of Blind Tom." Draft ms. Box 3, Mildred Stock Research Collection, sc MG 177, Schomburg Center for Research in Black Culture, Manuscripts, Archives and Rare Books Division, New York Public Library, New York.

Stoever, Jennifer. *The Sonic Color Line: Race and the Cultural Politics of Listening*. New York: New York University Press, 2016.

Strausbaugh, John. *Black like You: Blackface, Whiteface, Insult and Imitation in American Popular Culture*. New York: Penguin, 2006.

Sugrue, Thomas J. *Not Even Past: Barack Obama and the Burden of Race*. Princeton, NJ: Princeton University Press, 2010.

Sunderlin, Jacob. "'The Gut Meaning of Grace': Tyehimba Jess's *Olio*." *Kenyon Review*. Accessed January 20, 2020. https://kenyonreview.org/reviews/olio-by-tyehimba-jess-738439/.

Tate, Greg. Introduction to *Everything but the Burden: What White People Are Taking from Black Culture*, 1–14. New York: Broadway Books, 2003.

Taylor, Diana. *The Archive and the Repertoire: Performing Cultural Memory in the Americas*. Durham, NC: Duke University Press, 2003.

Taylor, Keenga-Yamahtta. *From #BlackLivesMatter to Black Liberation*. Chicago: Haymarket Books, 2016.

Taylor, Yuval, and Jake Austen. *Darkest America: Black Minstrelsy from Slavery to Hip-Hop*. New York: Norton, 2012.

Tobar, Hector. "Review: 'Song of the Shank' Gives Poetic Voice to a Unique American Musician." *Los Angeles Times*, July 11, 2014. https://www.latimes.com/books/jacketcopy/la-ca-jc-jeffery-renard-allen-20140713-story.html.

Tomlinson, Lisa. "The Ongoing Economic Exploitation of Black Music." *Huffington Post*, January 8, 2016. https://www.huffingtonpost.ca/dr-lisa-tomlinson/black-music-exploitation_b_8934870.html.

Trethewey, Natasha. "Disclosure." In *Bellocq's Ophelia*, 44. Minneapolis: Graywolf, 2002.

———. "Natasha Trethewey." Interview by Chard deNiord. In *I Would Lie to You If I Could: Interviews with American Poets*, 3–32. Pittsburgh: University of Pittsburgh Press, 2018.

Trouillot, Michel-Rolph. *Silencing the Past: Power and the Production of History*. Boston: Beacon, 1995.

von Hippel, Paul. "The Rise, Fall and Rise of Hispanic Jockeys in America." *Thoroughbred Racing Commentary*, September 4, 2017. https://www.thoroughbredracing.com/articles/rise-fall-and-rise-hispanic-jockeys-america/.

Walker, Frank X. "Conscious Narratives: Exploring Historical Poetry with Frank X Walker, by JoAnn LoVerde-Dropp." *Poetry Matters*, June 30, 2014. http://readwritepoetry.blogspot.com/2014/06/an-interview-with-frank-x-walker.html.

Walker, Frank X. *Isaac Murphy: I Dedicate This Ride.* Lexington, KY: Old Cove, 2010.

———. "Memory, Research, Imagination, and the Mining of Historical Poetry." In *Furious Flower: Seeding the Future of African American Poetry*, edited by Joanne V. Gabbin and Lauren K. Alleyne, 406–409. Evanston, IL: Northwestern University Press, 2020.

Wallace, Michele. *Dark Designs and Visual Culture.* Durham, NC: Duke University Press, 2004.

Walters, Wendy W. *Archives of the Black Atlantic: Reading between Literature and History.* New York: Routledge, 2013.

Ward, Abigail. "Performing Race in Caryl Phillips's *Dancing in the Dark.*" In *Postmodern Literature and Race*, edited by Len Platt and Sarah Upstone, 98–112. Cambridge: Cambridge University Press, 2015.

Ward, Geoffrey C. *Unforgivable Blackness: The Rise and Fall of Jack Johnson.* New York: Vintage, 2006.

Welter, Barbara. "The Cult of True Womanhood: 1820–1860." *American Quarterly* 18, no. 2 (1966): 151–174.

Wendell, Susan. *The Rejected Body: Feminist Philosophical Reflections on Disability.* New York: Routledge, 1996.

White, Miles. *From Jim Crow to Jay-Z: Race, Rap, and the Performance of Masculinity.* Urbana: University of Illinois Press, 2011.

Wiggins, David K. *Glory Bound: Black Athletes in White America.* Syracuse, NY: Syracuse University Press, 1997.

———, ed. *Out of the Shadows: A Biographical History of African American Athletes.* Fayetteville: University of Arkansas Press, 2006.

Wigginton, Russell T. *The Strange Career of the Black Athlete: African Americans and Sports.* Westport, CT: Praeger, 2006.

Williams, Andreá N. "Postbellum, Pre-Harlem Black Writing before the Renaissance." In *A Companion to the Harlem Renaissance*, edited by Cherene Sherrard-Johnson, 35–50. Malden, MA: Wiley-Blackwell, 2015.

Williams, Serena. "Serena Williams Sits Down with Common to Talk about Race and Identity." *Undefeated*, December 19, 2016. https://theundefeated.com/features/serena-williams-sits-down-with-common-to-talk-about-race-and-identity/.

Wolfe, Cameron. "Stills Criticizes Jay-Z: He's Never Been on a Knee." *ESPN.com*, August 19, 2019. https://www.espn.com/nfl/story/_/id/27421748/stills-criticizes-jay-z-never-knee.

Wortman, Stefanie. "What the Ghost Wants: Kevin Young's Ekphrasis." *Post45: Contemporaries* 211 (April 3, 2012). http://post45.org/2012/04/what-the-ghost-wants-kevin-youngs-ekphrasis/.

Yates, Clinton. "Childish Gambino's 'This Is America' Video Is a Beautiful Nightmare." *Undefeated*, May 8, 2018. https://theundefeated

.com/features/childish-gambinos-this-is-america-video-is-a-beautiful-nightmare/.

Yau, John. *The Passionate Spectator: Essays on Art and Poetry.* Ann Arbor: University of Michigan Press, 2006.

Young, Harvey. *Embodying Black Experience: Stillness, Critical Memory, and the Black Body.* Ann Arbor: University of Michigan Press, 2010.

Young, Kevin. *To Repel Ghosts: The Remix from the Original Masters.* New York: Knopf, 2005.

Zirin, Dave. "Kurt Busch, Ray Rice and How Sports Disseminates the Burdens of Racism." *Nation*, November 11, 2014. https://www.thenation.com/article/kurt-busch-ray-rice-and-how-sports-disseminates-burdens-racism/.

———. *What's My Name, Fool? Sports and Resistance in the United States.* Chicago: Haymarket Books, 2005.

INDEX

ABOUT THE AUTHOR

Emily Ruth Rutter is an associate professor of English and the assistant director of African American studies at Ball State University. She is the author of *Invisible Ball of Dreams: Literary Representations of Baseball behind the Color Line* (2018) and *The Blues Muse: Race, Gender, and Musical Celebrity in American Poetry* (2018). Along with Tiffany Austin, Sequoia Maner, and darlene anita scott, she coedited *Revisiting the Elegy in the Black Lives Matter Era* (2019). Her essays have appeared in *African American Review*, *MELUS*, *Aethlon*, *A Cambridge History of Twentieth-Century American Women's Poetry*, and *Some Other Blues: New Perspectives on Amiri Baraka*, among other journals and edited collections. Her current book project examines the white ally trope in contemporary Black television and film.